Global Warming and Food Security

GLOBAL WARMING AND FOOD SECURITY

Dr. S.K. Singh

PRASHANT PUBLISHING HOUSE
DELHI-110094

Published by :
Prashant Publishing House
C-34, 28 Foota Road, Gali No.-3,
West Karawal Nagar, Delhi-110094
Phone : 011-22963970, Mob. : 9810396373

Global Warming And Food Security

First Published 2012

ISBN 978-93-80565-21-7

PRINTED IN INDIA
Published by Mr. R.K. Jha M/s Prashant Publishing House and Published at H.S. Offset House Press, Delhi.

Preface

Climate change is a long-term change in the statistical distribution of weather patterns over periods of time that range from decades to millions of years. It may be a change in the average weather conditions or a change in the distribution of weather events with respect to an average, for example, greater or fewer extreme weather events. Climate change may be limited to a specific region, or may occur across the whole Earth. In recent usage, especially in the context of environmental policy, climate change usually refers to changes in modern climate. It may be qualified as anthropogenic climate change, more generally known as global warming or anthropogenic global warming (AGW).

The most general definition of *climate change* is a change in the statistical properties of the climate system when considered over periods of decades or longer, regardless of cause. Accordingly, fluctuations on periods shorter than a few decades, such as El Niño, do not represent climate change. The term sometimes is used to refer specifically to climate change caused by human activity; for example, the United Nations Framework Convention on Climate Change defines climate change as "a change of climate which is attributed directly or indirectly to human activity that alters the composition of the global atmosphere and which is in addition to natural climate variability observed over comparable time periods." In the latter sense climate change is synonymous with global warming.

Food security refers to the availability of food and one's access to it. A household is considered food-secure when its occupants do not live in hunger or fear of starvation. According to the World Resources Institute, global per capita food production has been increasing substantially for the past several decades. In 2006, MSNBC reported that globally, the number of people who are overweight has surpassed the number who are undernourished-the world had more than one billion people who were overweight, and an estimated 800 million who were undernourished. According to a 2004 article from the BBC, China, the world's most populous country, is suffering from an obesity epidemic. In India, the second-most populous country in the world, 30 million people have been added to the ranks of the hungry since the mid-1990s and 46% of children are underweight.

Worldwide around 852 million people are chronically hungry due to extreme poverty, while up to 2 billion people lack food security intermittently due to varying degrees of poverty. Six million children die of hunger every year-17,000 every day. As of late 2007, export restrictions and panic buying, US Dollar Depreciation, increased farming for use in biofuels, world oil prices at more than $100 a barrel, global population growth, climate change, loss of agricultural land to residential and industrial development, and growing consumer demand in China and India are claimed to have pushed up the price of grain. However, the role of some of these factors is under debate. Some argue the role of biofuel has been overplayed as grain prices have come down to the levels of 2006. Nonetheless, food riots have recently taken place in many countries across the world.

This book contains the fundamental and basic information of subject and the selection of contents makes it an appropriate book for the students, researcher and teacher.

—Editor

Contents

Preface (*vii*)

1. Introduction 1
2. Global Food Security under Climate Change 11
3. Food Security in the Changing Global Climate 78
4. Impact of Climate Change on Agriculture 120
5. Global Climate Change and Food Security in a Growing World 162
6. The Effects of Climate Change on Food Production 196
7. Climate Change and World Food Supply 255

Bibliography 285

Index 287

1

Introduction

The links between climate change and food security have, to date, largely been explored in relation to impacts on crop productivity and hence, food production.

For instance, Gregory *et al.* (1999) summarized experimental findings on wheat and rice that indicated decreased crop duration (and hence yield) of wheat as a consequence of warming and reductions in yields of rice of about 5% $°C^{-1}$ rise above 32 °C. These effects of temperature were considered sufficiently detrimental that they would largely offset any increase in yield as a consequence of increased atmospheric carbon dioxide (CO_2) concentration.

Several reviews have further assessed the potential consequences of changes in climate on the growth and yield of crop plants, concluding that the earlier-anticipated benefits of CO_2 fertilization would be largely offset by nutrient limitations, pollutants and further interactions with climatic factors. Similarly, simulations of maize production in Africa and Latin America using climate data from the HadCM2 model to generate characteristic daily weather data for 2055 predicted an overall reduction of 10%.

This, and other similar projections, uses a process-based crop production model to link climate to plant physiological processes. Yield can then be modelled for a uniform crop and upscaled to a larger area normally within some form of geographic information system (GIS). The aggregate result of Jones & Thornton (2003), though, hides considerable variability within and between countries, and, as they point out, also ignores the fact that maize is commonly used as fodder as well as food as part of a complex production system.

The spatial variation in effects of climate change was an explicit component of the study on potential yields of rainfed cereal crops undertaken by Fischer *et al.* (2001). In this analysis, climate predictions in 2080 were obtained from various global circulation models (GCMs) and assessments made based on current populations and socio-economic conditions. The output demonstrated that cereal producing regions of Canada, and northern Europe and Russia might be expected to increase production as a consequence of the climate changes predicted by GCMs, while many parts of the world would suffer losses including the western edge of the USA prairies, eastern Brazil and western Australia. Overall, the results of this and subsequent work that included assessments of future populations and alternative future socio-economic conditions, demonstrated that climate change would benefit the developed countries more than the developing countries even if cropping practices evolved to allow more than one rainfed crop per year. Moreover, the anticipated demographic growth and socio-economic development in these developing countries would result in substantial increases in food requirements thereby exacerbating the detrimental effects of climate change.

The spectre of climate change, together with other global environmental changes such as changes in water availability, and land cover, and altered nitrogen availability and cycling, has increased concerns about achieving food security especially for poor people. There is also concern that meeting the global demand for food resulting from higher population and changing dietary preferences will further degrade the environment both through additional destruction of native vegetation and increased intensification of cropped areas. This may, in turn, further undermine the food systems upon which food security is based.

While there has been considerable progress in understanding the sensitivities of crop yield to climate change, assessments of climate change effects on food security remain rather limited. Food security is concerned not only with food availability but also with access to and utilization of, food so that studies, which focus only on crop production provide only a partial assessment of food security–climate change relationships. This is of particular concern as many of the policy-based issues that are relevant to the international and sustainable development communities are posed in the context of food security prospects. Engagement of these policy communities requires a much broader and comprehensive research framework.

Recognition that food security depends on robust food systems that encompass issues of availability, access and utilization (not merely production alone), and consequently that the nature of key research issues changes as questions more related to food security are formulated, led the international global change research community to establish the joint project global environmental change and food systems (GECAFS) in 2001. GECAFS is an interdisciplinary research programme that aims to improve understanding of the relationship between food systems and the earth system to deliver science-based tools for analysing socio-economic and environmental consequences of strategies seeking to adapt to climate and other environmental changes. The purposes of this book are to: (i) outline the notion of food systems, their relation to food security, and links to climate change; (ii) explore the vulnerability of food systems to environmental change; (iii) examine some prospects for adaptation of food systems in response to climate change and (iv) highlight some of the environmental feedbacks resulting from modifications to food systems.

FOOD SECURITY, FOOD SYSTEMS AND THE LINK TO CLIMATE

There are several definitions of what constitutes food systems each formulated in relation to a specific range of issues. For GECAFSs purpose, food systems are defined as a set of dynamic interactions between and within the biogeophysical and human environments which result in the production, processing, distribution, preparation and consumption of food. They encompass components of: (i) food availability (with elements related to production, distribution and exchange); (ii) food access (with elements related to affordability, allocation and preference) and (iii) food utilization. Food systems, then, involve much broader considerations than productivity and production alone. They underpin food security, which is the state achieved when food systems operate such that 'all people, at all times, have physical and economic access to sufficient, safe and nutritious food to meet their dietary needs and food preferences for an active and healthy life' (FAO 1996). Food security is diminished when food systems are stressed. This can be caused by a range of factors in addition to climate and other environmental changes (e.g. conflict, changes in international trade agreements and policies, HIV/AIDS) and may be particularly severe when these factors act in combination. Access to culturally acceptable food by individuals and communities, or means for its procurement, is increasingly being elaborated into human rights legislation.

Food systems may be simple, as in the case of a subsistence farmer who produces, processes and consumes food on farm. However, there are comparatively few individuals or households in the world that are totally self-reliant for food throughout a year, and in almost all cases there is an element of bartering, exchange, or the cash economy to bring food into the household. In many places, the food system has changed radically in the last century and continues to become increasingly complex. The intensification of agricultural production, since the 1940s has been accompanied by profound changes in the organization of food systems around the world including changes in distribution, marketing, affordability and preferences for particular food items. These changes are especially obvious in the USA and Europe, where market globalization has occurred with global sourcing of products by retailers direct from producers in the case of fresh fruit and vegetables and from a few, large manufacturers for other food products. Such changes have also shifted economic and political power from farmers to retailers, from national legislative bodies to regional and global organizations, and from the state to multinational corporations. For example, in a study of selected OECD countries in Europe, Grievink (2003) determined that the food chain has some 160 million consumers of whom about 3.2 million are also farmers or food producers, but the link between these groups is increasingly determined by the small number of food processors/manufacturers (about 90 000) and the even smaller number of buyers (about 100) for the supermarket chains.

Food systems around the world are changing very rapidly as urbanization and globalization proceed apace. The urbanization of many predominantly rural countries in the last three decades has been accompanied by the rapid growth of supermarkets in many, often accompanied by foreign investment by global retail chains. However, even in poor countries such as Kenya, where per capita gross domestic product (GDP) was less than \$400 yr^{-1} in 2002, supermarkets have grown from a tiny niche market in 1997 to be greater than 20% of urban food retailing today. This growth has been a consequence of three major factors. First, rapid urbanization has seen the proportion of the population based in urban areas grow from 0.13 in 1975 to 0.36 in 2000 with an expectation of greater than 0.5 in 2013; second, trade and domestic market liberalization, since 1993 has seen the removal of import controls and the deregulation of prices and third, movement towards price-based competition between the indigenous chains. Success within Kenya is now spreading to other East African countries with important effects on the market conditions faced by farmers including the decline of traditional wholesalers (and the smallholder producers from whom they buy) and the increase in direct purchases from larger farms.

These marked changes in access and utilization of food around the world provide a context in which to evaluate the likely effects of climate and other environmental changes on crop production and food security. Not all food systems or parts of food systems are equally vulnerable to environmental changes because the capacity to cope with existing variability in bio-physical and socio-economic systems, and the ability of humans to perceive environmental changes and to adapt food systems, differs. Human vulnerability includes both the likelihood of exposure to stresses as well as the capacity to cope with such stresses (i.e. sensitivity). Vulnerability and poverty are often inter-related because both the likelihood of exposure to stresses is greater among the poor and because a large proportion of their resources are spent either purchasing or producing food, thereby reducing their capacity to cope with perturbations. Moreover, pursuit of food security frequently involves trade-offs with expenditure on health and education reducing still further the ability to improve longer-term living conditions or resilience to stress and shock (Boudreau 1998). Food insecurity is experienced at a range of spatial scales from individual households to regions, as well as a range of time-scales, and reductions of vulnerability at one scale do not automatically flow to the next scale. For example, regional policy decisions do not always convert to successful local implementation especially if distribution services are inadequate, or food preferences are ignored (Ellis 2003).

Climate variation is one of several interacting factors that affect food security. For example, in studies of household food security in southern Africa, climate/environment was only one of some 33 drivers mentioned as important by householders (Misselhorn 2005). The mix of drivers varied across the region but in all communities many interacting factors resulted in vulnerability to food shortages. Overall, however, climate/environment was one of the seven factors influencing food security that were frequently cited, because of its role both as an ongoing issue (57% of cases, where it was mentioned) and as a 'shock' (43%). The impacts of sudden shocks such as drought are felt, then, on top of ongoing long-term stresses, and the low ability to cope with such shocks and to mitigate long-term stresses means that the employment of coping strategies that might be available to others, is at a too high cost or, simply, unavailable. Typically, reliance on purchased food increases in drought years due to losses in food production leading to an increase in poverty due to the synergistic action of other drivers such as rising food prices and unemployment. Scholes & Biggs (2004) record that the food security crisis in southern Africa in 2002–2003 was not simply a result of drought alone and, indeed, climatic stress was not as severe as in previous crises. Maize production during the preceding growing season was only 5.5% less than the previous five year average so food stocks at the start of the climatic shock were not unusually low. It was concluded that the crisis was indicative of entrenched vulnerability resulting from a range of regional and global political and economic factors including high food prices, legacies of structural adjustment, government policies, conflict and war, policies on genetically modified foods, and poor responses to the HIV/AIDS pandemic. The key here was that conditions, which weakened food systems in the region were already in place. The moderate climatic shock intensified food insecurity and the long-term vulnerability of the region.

The seven most frequently cited drivers in 49 studies of household-level food insecurity in southern Africa. The numbers in the arrows indicate the number of citations, as a percentage of 555 citations of 33 possible drivers. The drivers shaded in grey were noted as being chronic, while those in white indicate drivers experienced mainly as 'shocks'. The shaded arrows indicate drivers that acted primarily via reductions in food production, while the white arrows indicate those which acted by restricting access to food.

VULNERABILITY OF FOOD SYSTEMS TO CLIMATE CHANGE

Much climatic change–agricultural research has been focused on assessing the sensitivity of various attributes of crop systems (e.g. land suitability, crop yields, pest regimes) to specified changes in climate. These partial assessments most often consider climate change in isolation, focus on bio-physical aspects of production, and provide little insight into the food accessibility and food utilization dimensions of food security. To better address the food security concerns that are central to economic and sustainable development agendas, it is desirable to develop a broader research framework, which integrates bio-physical and socio-economic aspects of food systems and thereby addresses key questions including: which aspects of food systems are most vulnerable to climate change? and Initial research in the Indo-Gangetic Plain (IGP) has used this more integrated approach to help define the vulnerability of the region's food systems. It has demonstrated that the conditions underpinning vulnerability are not uniform throughout the region. In the western IGP (a region of general surplus production), food systems are most vulnerable to issues related to the availability of water; excessive irrigation has lead to rising watertables and soil salinization in some areas while in others water shortage has resulted in falling watertables, rapidly increasing costs of pumping and shortage of drinking water. In the eastern IGP, resource poor farmers, who have very limited options to cope with and recover from external stresses, are most vulnerable to environmental changes such as rising sea-level, and climate change and climate variability leading to increased risk of flooding. Overall, this analysis suggests that food insecurity concerns cannot be effectively addressed by a single region-wide policy.

ADAPTATION: REDUCING THE VULNERABILITY OF FOOD SYSTEMS TO CLIMATE CHANGE

Development of human societies has involved a continuous process of adapting to changing stresses and opportunities. While climate change is seen as a relatively recent phenomenon, individuals and societies are used to adapting to a range of environmental and socio-economic stresses. In many parts of the world, and especially in semi-arid lands, there is an accumulated experience with phenomenon such as drought. As climate extremes are predicted to increase in frequency and intensity in future, it is important to understand and learn from relevant past adaptations and indigenous knowledge. However, changes in climate variability and mean values will bring additional complications to many, especially those dependent on food systems that are particularly vulnerable to these additional stresses.

Food systems fail to deliver food security when related determinants, and/or the links between them, are disrupted by climate change or other stresses. The food systems approach to research on food security allows for adaptation options aimed at reducing vulnerability to be considered in terms of any of these determinants and the stresses acting upon them. Adaptations may occur in relation to, for instance, agronomic or fisheries aspects regarding food production; or government-set prices and incomes concerning access to food; or changes in societal values concerning food utilization. The key issues for adapting food systems to reduce their vulnerability to climate change are to:

1. identify which related determinants are particularly sensitive to GEC;
2. enhance effective related determinants; and
3. restore disrupted related determinants.

To translate these theoretical considerations into practice requires research to:

1. identify and evaluate the possible adaptations mechanisms to reduce food system vulnerability to climate change;
2. identify, document and learn from past and current coping mechanisms employed by vulnerable groups in their day-to-day food supply systems;
3. analyse and strengthen the capability of communities and countries to adapt as much as possible; and
4. identify the most suitable level at which each adaptation strategy should be implemented (e.g. regional, national or local intervention).

Reducing food system vulnerability

Past increases in agricultural production have occurred as a result of both extensification (altering natural ecosystems to generate products) and intensification. In future, intensification will be the dominant means for increasing production although the cultivation of new land will be important in some regions (e.g. an estimated contribution of 47% from extensification in sub-Saharan Africa to cereal production by 2020; Alexandratos 1995). Increased yields per unit area, with a smaller contribution from an increased number of crops grown in a seasonal cycle, is expected to be the main way in which crop production will rise to meet demand. In the recent past, such increases have been achieved by a 'unique conjunction of three innovations', namely cheap nitrogenous fertilizers combined with semi-dwarf genotypes of cereals, effective weed control with herbicides, and the expansion of irrigation (Evans 1998). For the future, continued technological developments are anticipated to facilitate the adaptation of crops to changing environments.

Porter & Semenov (2005) has described some of the plant traits that may permit adaptation to climate change. An area in which progress may be possible is in improved selection of genotypes that utilize limited supplies of water stored in soils; less rainfall may be a consequence of climate change or increased climate variability in some regions. There are many plant characters and elements of crop management that contribute to the efficient use of water by crops (Gregory 2004), but relatively little attention has been paid to root characters that may allow more water to be exploited or used more efficiently, largely because root systems are very difficult to measure. However, genotypic differences are known to exist in many features of root systems (e.g. depth of rooting, rate of downward extension, diameter of roots, total length) which may be exploitable to improve crop yield in drier climates. Studies with existing genotypes in dry areas may inform the adaptation possible under conditions of changed climate.

For example, in the Mediterranean environment of northern Syria, crops are largely dependent on the use of growing season rainfall (very little water is stored from season to season). Studies of the root growth, water use and yield of the local landrace (Arabic abiad) at sites with typically less than 350 mm annual rainfall, showed that this genotype consistently had greater root lengths per unit soil volume at depths below 15 cm than other genotypes such as the variety Beecher, and that this was associated with greater water uptake in the 3–4 weeks before anthesis.

In this environment, faster rates of growth before anthesis were reflected in higher crop yields; senescence of the crop before the grains could fill ('haying off') was not observed. The development of DNA-based molecular markers has opened up opportunities for identifying the genetic factors (quantitative trait loci) underpinning various root traits. Again, this science is at an early stage of development for root traits, but significant progress has been made in studies of drought tolerance with rice. The distribution of root length with soil depth for the barley genotypes Arabic abiad (white bar) and Beecher (black bar). The distributions are the average for two sites in northern Syria with contrasting soils and rainfall (adapted from Gregory 1989).

Improving food distribution

Infrastructural and non-infrastructural controls on food distribution can be significant impediments to reducing food system vulnerability in a timely manner. This became strikingly apparent during the drought relief effort mounted in 1990/1991 in southern Africa in response to the estimated 86 million people at risk in the region (of whom some 20 millions were deemed at 'serious risk').

A massive international food aid programme was launched with food to be delivered via a number of rail 'corridors' from the region's major ports to the hinterland. Nearly, 8 million tonnes of food grains were imported by the relief programme for the 10 countries affected; this was almost four times the normal annual rate of imports for the region (Muchero 2003). This substantial increase in imports resulted in pressure on the region's distribution systems, leading to a number of problems which would not have been significant in 'normal' years. These are well illustrated by examples taken from the Maputo and Beira corridor. Infrastructural constraints included ongoing rehabilitation, physical impediments (steep gradients and tight curves at which points grain was stolen from the slow-moving wagons), a shortage of bags and tarpaulins, the need to tranship Malawi-bound cargo in Harare, and a shortage of rolling stock and locomotive power. In addition, a number of non-infrastructural constraints further complicated the situation. These included general security problems along the corridor, regulatory constraints for cargo destined for Zambia, conflict between humanitarian requirements and commercial concerns, poor labour management systems in ports (where there were no incentives to work more than necessary), and transit toll fees in Mozambique.

Food availability for the region was severely constrained due not to lack of food *per se* (there were ships queuing at anchor to unload), but by lack of investment in distribution systems and institutional constraints. This brief summary highlights several ways in which regional food insecurity could be reduced, and shows that adaptation options can include a range of issues including, among others, regional investment in port, rail and grain storage infrastructure and in region-wide political agreements to facilitate the flow of food in an emergency.

Increasing economic access to food

Improved economic access to food is an important development goal, but the means of achieving it and the consequences of strategies aimed at its achievement are the subject of much discussion. In the case of southern Africa, Arntzen *et al.* (2004) indicate that the discussion centres around varied means. First, price mechanisms and policies could be designed that serve the interest of producers (incentive to produce more food) and consumers (to facilitate access to food). Second, regional specialization in food production and regional trade would lower production costs and food prices and, therefore, improve access. This important adaptation is as yet hardly pursued, but should gain momentum with trade liberalization and policy shifts towards food security. Third, economic growth will lead to income and employment generation, both of which will facilitate access to food. Finally, stability and governance supported by an effective pool of human and institutional resources facilitate the establishment and maintenance of food systems. In south Asia, studies have examined how income growth has led to changes in diets away from traditional foods. This may have negative impacts on local farmers who grow traditional foods and are not well integrated into markets. The impact of trade liberalization on the poor is a topic of current study, but there is an emerging consensus that they should be protected from negative impacts through the implementation of safety nets.

FEEDBACKS FROM ADAPTATION OPTIONS TO THE GLOBAL ENVIRONMENT

In attempting to adapt food systems to cope with climate

and other environmental changes, it will be important to ensure that the changes proposed do not exacerbate climate change or other aspects of environmental degradation (i.e. that they contribute to sustainability). Past extensification (land cover change, especially the removal of trees) has made a large contribution to CO_2 emissions so that one means of mitigating further emissions is to intensify production on existing cleared areas and leave forests intact. Nelson & Maredia (1999) estimated that the introduction of high-yielding varieties as part of the 'green revolution' saved 170 Mha of forest from cropping in Africa, Asia and Latin America in the period 1970–1990. Assuming an average carbon stock of 100 Mg C ha^{-1}, this represents a saving of 17 Gt of carbon, equivalent to 2–3 years of total global carbon (C) emissions. Intensification can, then, contribute to reducing CO_2 emissions, although this saving is partially offset by the increased C costs of the new production system. Previous intensification via high-input technologies has resulted in detrimental environmental consequences such as reduced biodiversity and water pollution in some areas, resulting in substantial concerns about the environmental consequences of meeting projected demands for food by 2050. This has led to moves in many parts of the world towards intensive systems that are both high yielding and more environmentally benign. Such systems encourage the greater efficiency of use of inputs to minimize both on-and off-site environmental consequences but are yet to be widely adopted.

Gregory *et al.* (2002) suggested that regional changes in climate can be induced by both extensification (through effects on albedo and changes in latent/sensible heat balances) and intensification. Crop intensification has biogeophysical effects through changes in physical and physiological properties at the surface, in landscape heterogeneity, and in the production of dust, and biogeochemical effects through production of greenhouse gases and organic aerosols. For example, in the IGP, the increased adoption of the rice–wheat system during the last three decades has resulted in the heavy use of irrigation, fertilizers, electricity and diesel. These practices have had a direct impact on the emissions of greenhouse gases (especially CO_2, CH_4 and N_2O). Depending on the management practices used, emissions are estimated collectively to have a global warming potential equivalent to 3000–8000 kg C ha^{-1} yr^{-1}. This amounts to a significant quantity of C for the whole IGP. While increasing production in the future may further increase emissions if no changes in practice are wrought, alternative management strategies could effectively reduce emissions.

For example, surface seeding and/or zero-tillage, and the establishment of upland crops after rice gives similar yields to crops planted under normal conventional tillage over a diverse set of soil conditions, but reduces costs of production and allows earlier planting which offers higher yields. The practice also results in less weed growth and increases the efficiency of water and fertilizer use. Moreover, it reduces the use of natural resources such as steel for tractor parts and fuel because zero tillage saves 29.9 l of diesel per hectare compared to conventional tillage (equivalent to 21.2 kg C ha^{-1} a^{-1} reduction). In addition, resource-conserving technologies restrict the oxidation of soil carbon thus mitigating increases of CO_2 into the atmosphere.

The important contribution that agriculture makes to emissions of N_2O, a greenhouse gas that is about 200 times as radiatively active as CO_2. Much of this comes from applications of nitrogen (N) fertilizers which have increased substantially as crop intensification has proceeded estimated that of the 3.5 Tg N released annually from cultivated land as N_2O, about 1.5 Tg was directly attributable to synthetic N fertilizers, with an additional 0.5–5 Tg N emitted as NO.

Reducing the quantities of N_2O emitted from fertilizer applications may, though, be difficult. Adoption of the best available agronomic practices such as soil testing to match supply with demand and optimizing tillage and drainage, can reduce emissions but such practices would still be insufficient to offset the increases expected from the increased global use of N fertilizers. This poses a considerable challenge for the future sustainability of food systems.

A further environmental feedback that is an issue in some regions is the changes in groundwater availability as a consequence of water extraction for irrigation in intensive crop production systems. For example, in the Punjab province of

India, extraction has led to significantly lower watertables; these are expected to fall even further in the future. In addition to changes in aquifer and surface water dynamics *per se*, a significant consequence of this is the need to use ever increasing amounts of power (diesel and/or electric pumps) to access this dwindling.

The full range of environmental feedbacks that will result from adapting food systems are presently difficult to discern because there is no consensus yet as to how climate change impacts will manifest themselves at different scales. The possible environmental impacts of adaptations include: (i) changes in biodiversity due to extension of the agricultural frontier; (ii) water pollution associated with increased use of fertilizers and pesticides; (iii) waterlogging, salinization and water scarcity due to irrigation and (iv) land degradation due to use of less suitable land. However, there is no reason to suppose that the effects should be so uniformly negative if institutional support is given to more sustainable practices. The increasing concerns of human societies in Europe, North America and elsewhere to utilize land for food and other purposes (e.g. recreation, wildlife) suggests that greater emphasis will be placed on more efficient use of inputs than hitherto with consequent reductions in pollution and environmental degradation.

CLIMATE CHANGE

Climate change is a long-term change in the statistical distribution of weather patterns over periods of time that range from decades to millions of years. It may be a change in the average weather conditions or a change in the distribution of weather events with respect to an average, for example, greater or fewer extreme weather events. Climate change may be limited to a specific region, or may occur across the whole Earth.

In recent usage, especially in the context of environmental policy, climate change usually refers to changes in modern climate. It may be qualified as anthropogenic climate change, more generally known as global warming or anthropogenic global warming (AGW).

Terminology

The most general definition of *climate change* is a change in the statistical properties of the climate system when considered over periods of decades or longer, regardless of cause. Accordingly, fluctuations on periods shorter than a few decades, such as El Niño, do not represent climate change.

The term sometimes is used to refer specifically to climate change caused by human activity; for example, the United Nations Framework Convention on Climate Change defines climate change as "a change of climate which is attributed directly or indirectly to human activity that alters the composition of the global atmosphere and which is in addition to natural climate variability observed over comparable time periods." In the latter sense climate change is synonymous with global warming.

Causes

Factors that can shape climate are climate forcings. These include such processes as variations in solar radiation, deviations in the Earth's orbit, mountain-building and continental drift, and changes in greenhouse gas concentrations. There are a variety of climate change feedbacks that can either amplify or diminish the initial forcing. Some parts of the climate system, such as the oceans and ice caps, respond slowly in reaction to climate forcing because of their large mass. Therefore, the climate system can take centuries or longer to fully respond to new external forcings.

HUMAN INFLUENCES

In the context of climate variation, anthropogenic factors are human activities which affect the climate. The scientific consensus on climate change is, "that climate is changing and that these changes are in large part caused by human activities."

"Science has made enormous inroads in understanding climate change and its causes, and is beginning to help develop a strong understanding of current and potential impacts that will affect people today and in coming decades. This understanding is crucial because it allows decision makers to place climate change in the context of other large challenges facing the nation and the world. There are still some uncertainties, and there always will be in understanding a complex system like Earth's climate. Nevertheless, there is a strong, credible body of evidence, based on multiple lines of research, documenting that climate is changing and that these changes are in large part caused by human activities. While much remains to be learned, the core phenomenon, scientific questions, and hypotheses have been examined thoroughly and have stood firm in the face of serious scientific debate and careful evaluation of alternative explanations." — United States National Research Council, Advancing the Science of Climate Change.

Consequently, the debate is shifting onto ways to reduce further human impact and to find ways to adapt to change that has already occurred and is anticipated to occur in the future.

Of most concern in these anthropogenic factors is the increase in CO_2 levels due to emissions from fossil fuel combustion, followed by aerosols (particulate matter in the atmosphere) and cement manufacture. Other factors, including land use, ozone depletion, animal agriculture and deforestation, are also of concern in the roles they play-both separately and in conjunction with other factors-in affecting climate, microclimate, and measures of climate variables.

Plate tectonics

Over the course of millions of years, the motion of tectonic plates reconfigures global land and ocean areas and generates topography. This can affect both global and local patterns of climate and atmosphere-ocean circulation.

The position of the continents determines the geometry of the oceans and therefore influences patterns of ocean circulation. The locations of the seas are important in controlling the transfer of heat and moisture across the globe, and therefore, in determining global climate. A recent example of tectonic control on ocean circulation is the formation of the Isthmus of Panama about 5 million years ago, which shut off direct mixing between the Atlantic and Pacific Oceans. This strongly affected the ocean dynamics of what is now the Gulf Stream and may have led to Northern Hemisphere ice cover. During the Carboniferous period, about 300 to 360 million years ago, plate tectonics may have triggered large-scale storage of carbon and increased glaciation. Geologic evidence points to a "megamonsoonal" circulation pattern during the time of the supercontinent Pangaea, and climate modeling suggests that the existence of the supercontinent was conducive to the establishment of monsoons.

The size of continents is also important. Because of the stabilizing effect of the oceans on temperature, yearly temperature variations are generally lower in coastal areas than they are inland. A larger supercontinent will therefore have more area in which climate is strongly seasonal than will several smaller continents or islands.

Solar output

The sun is the predominant source for energy input to the Earth. Both long-and short-term variations in solar intensity are known to affect global climate.

Three to four billion years ago the sun emitted only 70% as much power as it does today. If the atmospheric composition had been the same as today, liquid water should not have existed on Earth. However, there is evidence for the presence of water on the early Earth, in the Hadean and Archean eons, leading to what is known as the faint young sun paradox. Hypothesized solutions to this paradox include a vastly different atmosphere, with much higher concentrations of greenhouse gases than currently exist Over the following approximately 4 billion years, the energy output of the sun increased and atmospheric composition changed, with the oxygenation of the atmosphere around 2.4 billion years ago being the most notable alteration. These changes in luminosity, and the sun's ultimate death as it becomes a red giant and then a white dwarf, will have large effects on climate, with the red giant phase possibly ending life on Earth.

Solar output also varies on shorter time scales, including the 11-year solar cycle and longer-term modulations. Solar intensity variations are considered to have been influential in triggering the Little Ice Age, and some of the warming observed from 1900 to 1950. The cyclical nature of the sun's energy output is not yet fully understood; it differs from the very slow change that is happening within the sun as it ages and evolves. While most research indicates solar variability has induced a small cooling effect from 1750 to the present, a few studies point toward solar radiation increases from cyclical sunspot activity affecting global warming.

Interestingly, a 2010 study *suggests*, "that the effects of solar variability on temperature throughout the atmosphere may be contrary to current expectations."

ORBITAL VARIATIONS

Slight variations in Earth's orbit lead to changes in the seasonal distribution of sunlight reaching the Earth's surface and how it is distributed across the globe. There is very little change to the area-averaged annually averaged sunshine; but there can be strong changes in the geographical and seasonal distribution. The three types of orbital variations are variations in Earth's eccentricity, changes in the tilt angle of Earth's axis of rotation, and precession of Earth's axis. Combined together, these produce Milankovitch cycles which have a large impact on climate and are notable for their correlation to glacial and interglacial periods, their correlation with the advance and retreat of the Sahara, and for their appearance in the stratigraphic record.

Volcanism

Volcanism is a process of conveying material from the crust and mantle of the Earth to its surface. Volcanic eruptions, geysers, and hot springs, are examples of volcanic processes which release gases and/or particulates into the atmosphere.

Eruptions large enough to affect climate occur on average several times per century, and cause cooling (by partially blocking the transmission of solar radiation to the Earth's surface) for a period of a few years. The eruption of Mount Pinatubo in 1991, the second largest terrestrial eruption of the 20th century (after the 1912 eruption of Novarupta) affected the climate substantially. Global temperatures decreased by about 0.5 °C (0.9 °F). The eruption of Mount Tambora in 1815 caused the Year Without a Summer. Much larger eruptions, known as large igneous provinces, occur only a few times every hundred million years, but may cause global warming and mass extinctions.

Volcanoes are also part of the extended carbon cycle. Over very long (geological) time periods, they release carbon dioxide from the Earth's crust and mantle, counteracting the uptake by sedimentary rocks and other geological carbon dioxide sinks. According to the US Geological Survey, however, estimates are that human activities generate 100-300 times the amount of carbon dioxide emitted by volcanoes.

Ocean Variability

The ocean is a fundamental part of the climate system. Short-term fluctuations (years to a few decades) such as the El Niño-Southern Oscillation, the Pacific decadal oscillation, the North Atlantic oscillation, and the Arctic oscillation, represent climate variability rather than climate change. On longer time scales, alterations to ocean processes such as thermohaline circulation play a key role in redistributing heat by carrying out a very slow and extremely deep movement of water, and the long-term redistribution of heat in the world's oceans.

PHYSICAL EVIDENCE FOR CLIMATIC CHANGE

Evidence for climatic change is taken from a variety of sources that can be used to reconstruct past climates. Reasonably complete global records of surface temperature are available beginning from the mid-late 19th century. For earlier periods, most of the evidence is indirect—climatic changes are inferred from changes in proxies, indicators that reflect climate, such as vegetation, ice cores, dendrochronology, sea level change, and glacial geology.

Historical and Archaeological Evidence

Climate change in the recent past may be detected by corresponding changes in settlement and agricultural patterns.

Archaeological evidence, oral history and historical documents can offer insights into past changes in the climate. Climate change effects have been linked to the collapse of various civilisations.

Glaciers

Glaciers are considered among the most sensitive indicators of climate change. Their size is determined by a mass balance between snow input and melt output. As temperatures warm, glaciers retreat unless snow precipitation increases to make up for the additional melt; the converse is also true.

Glaciers grow and shrink due both to natural variability and external forcings. Variability in temperature, precipitation, and englacial and subglacial hydrology can strongly determine the evolution of a glacier in a particular season. Therefore, one must average over a decadal or longer time-scale and/or over a many individual glaciers to smooth out the local short-term variability and obtain a glacier history that is related to climate.

A world glacier inventory has been compiled since the 1970s, initially based mainly on aerial photographs and maps but now relying more on satellites. This compilation tracks more than 100,000 glaciers covering a total area of approximately 240,000 km, and preliminary estimates indicate that the remaining ice cover is around 445,000 km^2. The World Glacier Monitoring Service collects data annually on glacier retreat and glacier mass balance From this data, glaciers worldwide have been found to be shrinking significantly, with strong glacier retreats in the 1940s, stable or growing conditions during the 1920s and 1970s, and again retreating from the mid 1980s to present.

The most significant climate processes since the middle to late Pliocene (approximately 3 million years ago) are the glacial and interglacial cycles. The present interglacial period (the Holocene) has lasted about 11,700 years. Shaped by orbital variations, responses such as the rise and fall of continental ice sheets and significant sea-level changes helped create the climate. Other changes, including Heinrich events, Dansgaard–Oeschger events and the Younger Dryas, however, illustrate how glacial variations may also influence climate without the orbital forcing.

Glaciers leave behind moraines that contain a wealth of material—including organic matter, quartz, and potassium that may be dated—recording the periods in which a glacier advanced and retreated. Similarly, by tephrochronological techniques, the lack of glacier cover can be identified by the presence of soil or volcanic tephra horizons whose date of deposit may also be ascertained.

Vegetation

A change in the type, distribution and coverage of vegetation may occur given a change in the climate; this much is obvious. In any given scenario, a mild change in climate may result in increased precipitation and warmth, resulting in improved plant growth and the subsequent sequestration of airborne CO_2. Larger, faster or more radical changes, however, may result in vegetation stress, rapid plant loss and desertification in certain circumstances.

Ice Cores

Analysis of ice in a core drilled from a ice sheet such as the Antarctic ice sheet, can be used to show a link between temperature and global sea level variations. The air trapped in bubbles in the ice can also reveal the CO_2 variations of the atmosphere from the distant past, well before modern environmental influences.

The study of these ice cores has been a significant indicator of the changes in CO_2 over many millennia, and continues to provide valuable information about the differences between ancient and modern atmospheric conditions.

Dendroclimatology

Dendroclimatology is the analysis of tree ring growth patterns to determine past climate variations. Wide and thick rings indicate a fertile, well-watered growing period, whilst thin, narrow rings indicate a time of lower rainfall and less-than-ideal growing conditions.

Pollen Analysis

Palynology is the study of contemporary and fossil palynomorphs, including pollen. Palynology is used to infer the geographical distribution of plant species, which vary under different climate conditions. Different groups of plants have pollen with distinctive shapes and surface textures, and since the outer surface of pollen is composed of a very resilient material, they resist decay. Changes in the type of pollen found in different layers of sediment in lakes, bogs, or river deltas indicate changes in plant communities. These changes are often a sign of a changing climate. As an example, palynological studies have been used to track changing vegetation patterns throughout the Quaternary glaciations and especially since the last glacial maximum.

Insects

Remains of beetles are common in freshwater and land sediments. Different species of beetles tend to be found under different climatic conditions. Given the extensive lineage of beetles whose genetic makeup has not altered significantly over the millennia, knowledge of the present climatic range of the different species, and the age of the sediments in which remains are found, past climatic conditions may be inferred.

Sea Level Change

Global sea level change for much of the last century has generally been estimated using tide gauge measurements collated over long periods of time to give a long-term average. More recently, altimeter measurements — in combination with accurately determined satellite orbits — have provided an improved measurement of global sea level change. To measure sea levels prior to instrumental measurements, scientists have dated coral reefs that grow near the surface of the ocean, coastal sediments, marine terraces, ooids in limestones, and nearshore archaeological remains. The predominant dating methods used are uranium series and radiocarbon, with cosmogenic radionuclides being sometimes used to date terraces that have experienced relative sea level fall.

FOOD SECURITY

Food security refers to the availability of food and one's access to it. A household is considered food-secure when its occupants do not live in hunger or fear of starvation. According to the World Resources Institute, global per capita food production has been increasing substantially for the past several decades. In 2006, MSNBC reported that globally, the number of people who are overweight has surpassed the number who are undernourished-the world had more than one billion people who were overweight, and an estimated 800 million who were undernourished. According to a 2004 article from the BBC, China, the world's most populous country, is suffering from an obesity epidemic. In India, the second-most populous country in the world, 30 million people have been added to the ranks of the hungry since the mid-1990s and 46% of children are underweight.

Worldwide around 852 million people are chronically hungry due to extreme poverty, while up to 2 billion people lack food security intermittently due to varying degrees of poverty. Six million children die of hunger every year-17,000 every day. As of late 2007, export restrictions and panic buying, US Dollar Depreciation, increased farming for use in biofuels, world oil prices at more than $100 a barrel, global population growth, climate change, loss of agricultural land to residential and industrial development, and growing consumer demand in China and India are claimed to have pushed up the price of grain. However, the role of some of these factors is under debate. Some argue the role of biofuel has been overplayed as grain prices have come down to the levels of 2006. Nonetheless, food riots have recently taken place in many countries across the world.

It is becoming increasingly difficult to maintain food security in a world beset by a confluence of "peak" phenomena, namely peak oil, peak water, peak phosphorus, peak grain and peak fish. Approximately 3.3 billion people, more than half of the planet's population, live in urban areas as of November 2007. Any disruption to farm supplies may precipitate a uniquely urban food crisis in a relatively short time. The ongoing global credit crisis has affected farm credits, despite a boom in commodity prices. Food security is a complex topic, standing at the intersection of many disciplines.

A new peer-reviewed journal of *Food Security: The Science, Sociology and Economics of Food Production and Access to Food* began publishing in 2009. In developing countries, often 70% or more of the population lives in rural areas. In that context, agricultural development among smallholder farmers and landless people provides a livelihood for people allowing them the opportunity to stay in their communities. In many areas of the world, land ownership is not available, thus, people who want or need to farm to make a living have little incentive to improve the land.

In the US, there are approximately 2,000,000 farmers, less than 1% of the population. A direct relationship exists between food consumption levels and poverty. Families with the financial resources to escape extreme poverty rarely suffer from chronic hunger, while poor families not only suffer the most from chronic hunger, but are also the segment of the population most at risk during food shortages and famines.

Two commonly used definitions of food security come from the UN's Food and Agriculture Organization (FAO) and the United States Department of Agriculture (USDA):

- Food security exists when all people, at all times, have physical, social and economic access to sufficient, safe and nutritious food to meet their dietary needs and food preferences for an active and healthy life.
- Food security for a household means access by all members at all times to enough food for an active, healthy life. Food security includes at a minimum (1) the ready availability of nutritionally adequate and safe foods, and (2) an assured ability to acquire acceptable foods in socially acceptable ways (that is, without resorting to emergency food supplies, scavenging, stealing, or other coping strategies). (USDA)

The stages of food insecurity range from food secure situations to full-scale famine. "Famine and hunger are both rooted in food insecurity. Food insecurity can be categorized as either chronic or transitory. Chronic food insecurity translates into a high degree of vulnerability to famine and hunger; ensuring food security presupposes elimination of that vulnerability. [Chronic] hunger is not famine. It is similar to undernourishment and is related to poverty, existing mainly in poor countries."

STUNTING AND CHRONIC NUTRITIONAL DEFICIENCIES

Many countries experience perpetual food shortages and distribution problems. These result in chronic and often widespread hunger amongst significant numbers of people. Human populations respond to chronic hunger and malnutrition by decreasing body size, known in medical terms as stunting or stunted growth. This process starts *in utero* if the mother is malnourished and continues through approximately the third year of life. It leads to higher infant and child mortality, but at rates far lower than during famines. Once stunting has occurred, improved nutritional intake later in life cannot reverse the damage. Stunting itself is viewed as a coping mechanism, designed to bring body size into alignment with the calories available during adulthood in the location where the child is born. Limiting body size as a way of adapting to low levels of energy (calories) adversely affects health in three ways:

- Premature failure of vital organs occurs during adulthood. For example, a 50-year-old individual might die of heart failure because his/her heart suffered structural defects during early development.
- Stunted individuals suffer a far higher rate of disease and illness than those who have not undergone stunting.
- Severe malnutrition in early childhood often leads to defects in cognitive development.

"The analysis... points to the misleading nature of the concept of subsistence as Malthus originally used it and as it is still widely used today. Subsistence in not located at the edge of a nutritional cliff, beyond which lies demographic disaster. Rather than one level of subsistence, there are numerous levels at which a population and a food supply can be in equilibrium in the sense that they can be indefinitely sustained. However, some levels will have smaller people and higher normal mortality than others."

GLOBAL WATER CRISIS

Water deficits, which are already spurring heavy grain imports in numerous smaller countries, may soon do the same in larger countries, such as China or India. The water tables are falling in scores of countries (including Northern China, the US, and India) due to widespread overpumping using powerful diesel and electric pumps. Other countries affected include Pakistan, Afghanistan, and Iran. This will eventually lead to water scarcity and cutbacks in grain harvest. Even with the overpumping of its aquifers, China is developing a grain deficit. When this happens, it will almost certainly drive grain prices upward. Most of the 3 billion people projected to be born worldwide by mid-century will be born in countries already experiencing water shortages. After China and India, there is a second tier of smaller countries with large water deficits—Afghanistan, Algeria, Egypt, Iran, Mexico, and Pakistan. Four of these already import a large share of their grain. Only Pakistan remains self-sufficient. But with a population expanding by 4 million a year, it will also likely soon turn to the world market for grain.

Multimillion dollar investments beginning in the 1990s by the World Bank have reclaimed desert and turned the Ica Valley in Peru, one of the driest places on earth, into the largest supplier of asparagus in the world. However, the constant irrigation has caused a rapid drop in the water table, in some places as much as eight meters per year, one of the fastest rates of aquifer depletion in the world. The wells of small farmers and local people are beginning to run dry and the water supply for the main city in the valley is under threat. As a cash crop, asparagus has provided jobs for local people, but most of the money goes to the buyers, mainly the British. A recent report concluded that the industry is not sustainable and accuses investors, including the World Bank, of failing to take proper responsibility for the impact of their decisions on the water resources of poorer countries. Diverting water from the headwaters of the Ica River to asparagus fields has also led to a water shortage in the mountain region of Huancavelica, where indigenous communities make a marginal living herding.

Land degradation

Intensive farming often leads to a vicious cycle of exhaustion of soil fertility and decline of agricultural yields. Approximately 40% of the world's agricultural land is seriously degraded. In Africa, if current trends of soil degradation continue; the continent might be able to feed just 25% of its population by 2025, according to UNU's Ghana-based Institute for Natural Resources in Africa.

Land deals

Rich governments and corporations are buying up the rights to millions of hectares of agricultural land in developing countries in an effort to secure their own long-term food supplies. The head of the Food and Agriculture Organisation (FAO), Jacques Diouf, has warned that the controversial rise in land deals could create a form of "neocolonialism", with poor states producing food for the rich at the expense of their own hungry people. The South Korean firm Daewoo Logistics has secured a large piece of farmland in Madagascar to grow maize and crops for biofuels. Libya has secured 250,000 hectares of Ukrainian farmland, and China has begun to explore land deals in Southeast Asia. Oil-rich Arab investors, including the sovereign wealth funds, are looking into Sudan, Ethiopia, Ukraine, Kazakhstan, Pakistan, Cambodia and Thailand.

Some countries are using the acquisition of land for agriculture in return for other gains. Egypt is seeking land acquisition in Ukraine in exchange for access to its natural gas. Qatar has plans to lease 40,000 hectares of agricultural land along Kenya's coast to grow fruit and vegetables, in return for building a £2.4 billion port close to the Indian Ocean tourist island of Lamu.

CLIMATE CHANGE AND AGRICULTURE

Approximately 2.4 billion people live in the drainage basin

of the Himalayan rivers. India, China, Pakistan, Afghanistan, Bangladesh, Nepal and Myanmar could experience floods followed by severe droughts in coming decades. In India alone, the Ganges provides water for drinking and farming for more than 500 million people. The west coast of North America, which gets much of its water from glaciers in mountain ranges such as the Rocky Mountains and Sierra Nevada, also would be affected. Glaciers aren't the only worry that the developing nations have, sea level is also reported to rise as climate change progresses, reducing the amount of land available for agriculture.

In other parts of the world, a big effect will be low yields of grain according to the World Food Trade Model, specifically in the low latitude regions where much of the developing world is located. From this the price of grain will rise, along with the developing nations trying to grow the grain. Due to this, every 2-2.5% price hike will increase the number of hungry people 1%. Low crop yields are just one of the problem facing farmers in the low latitudes and tropical regions. The timing and length of the growing seasons, when farmers plant their crops, are going to be changing dramatically, per the USDA, due to unknown changes in soil temperature and moisture conditions.

Children

On 2008-04-29, a UNICEF UK report found that the world's poorest and most vulnerable children are being hit the hardest by the impact of climate change. The report, "Our Climate, Our Children, Our Responsibility: The Implications of Climate Change for the World's Children," says access to clean water and food supplies will become more difficult, particularly in Africa and Asia.

Wheat stem rust

An epidemic of stem rust on wheat caused by race Ug99 is currently spreading across Africa and into Asia and is causing major concern. A virulent wheat disease could destroy most of the world's main wheat crops, leaving millions to starve. The fungus has spread from Africa to Iran, and may already be in Pakistan.

The genetic diversity of the crop wild relatives of wheat can be used to improve modern varieties to be more resistant to rust. In their centers of origin wild wheat plants are screened for resistance to rust, then their genetic information is analysed and finally wild plants and modern varieties are crossed through means of modern plant breeding in order to transfer the resistance genes from the wild plants to the modern varieties.

Dictatorship and kleptocracy

Nobel Prize-winning economist Amartya Sen has observed that "there is no such thing as an apolitical food problem." While drought and other naturally occurring events may trigger famine conditions, it is government action or inaction that determines its severity, and often even whether or not a famine will occur. The 20th century is full of examples of governments undermining the food security of their own nations–sometimes intentionally.

When governments come to power by force or rigged elections, and not by way of fair and open elections, their base of support is often narrow and built upon cronyism and patronage. Under such conditions "The distribution of food within a country is a political issue. Governments in most countries give priority to urban areas, since that is where the most influential and powerful families and enterprises are usually located. The government often neglects subsistence farmers and rural areas in general. The more remote and underdeveloped the area the less likely the government will be to effectively meet its needs. Many agrarian policies, especially the pricing of agricultural commodities, discriminate against rural areas. Governments often keep prices of basic grains at such artificially low levels that subsistence producers cannot accumulate enough capital to make investments to improve their production. Thus, they are effectively prevented from getting out of their precarious situation."

Further dictators and warlords have used food as a political weapon, rewarding their supporters while denying food supplies to areas that oppose their rule. Under such conditions food becomes a currency with which to buy support and famine becomes an effective weapon to be used against the opposition. Governments with strong tendencies towards kleptocracy can undermine food security even when harvests are good. When government monopolizes trade, farmers may find that they are free to grow cash crops for export, but under penalty of law only able to sell their crops to government buyers at prices far below the world market price. The government then is free to sell their crop on the world market at full price, pocketing the difference. This creates an artificial "poverty trap" from which even the most hard working and motivated farmers may not escape.

When the rule of law is absent, or private property is non-existent, farmers have little incentive to improve their productivity. If a farm becomes noticeably more productive than neighboring farms, it may become the target of individuals well connected to the government. Rather than risk being noticed and possibly losing their land, farmers may be content with the perceived safety of mediocrity.

As pointed out by William Bernstein in his book *The Birth of Plenty*: "Individuals without property are susceptible to starvation, and it is much easier to bend the fearful and hungry to the will of the state. If a [farmer's] property can be arbitrarily threatened by the state, that power will inevitably be employed to intimidate those with divergent political and religious opinions."

Economic approaches

There are many economic approaches advocated to improve food security in developing countries. Three typical approaches are listed below. The first is typical of what is advocated by most governments and international agencies. The other two are more common to non-governmental organizations (NGO's).

Westernized view

Conventional thinking in westernized countries is that maximizing the farmers profit is the surest way of maximizing agricultural production; the higher a farmer's profit, the greater the effort that will be forthcoming, and the greater the risk the farmer is willing to take.

Place into the hands of farmers the largest number and highest quality tools possible (tools is used here to refer to improved production techniques, improved seeds, secure land tenure, accurate weather forecasts, etc.) However, it is left to the individual farmer to pick and choose which tools to use, and how to use them, as farmers have intimate knowledge of their own land and local conditions.

As with other businesses, a percentage of the profits are normally reinvested into the business in the hopes of increasing production, and hence increase future profits. Normally higher profits translate into higher spending on technologies designed to boost production, such as drip irrigation systems, agriculture education, and greenhouses. An increased profit also increases the farmer's incentive to engage in double-cropping, soil improvement programs, and expanding usable area.

Food justice

An alternative view takes a collective approach to achieve food security. It notes that globally enough food is produced to feed the entire world population at a level adequate to ensure that everyone can be free of hunger and fear of starvation. That no one should live without enough food because of economic constraints or social inequalities is the basic goal.

This approach is often referred to as food justice and views food security as a basic human right. It advocates fairer distribution of food, particularly grain crops, as a means of ending chronic hunger and malnutrition. The core of the Food Justice movement is the belief that what is lacking is not food, but the political will to fairly distribute food regardless of the recipient's ability to pay.

Food sovereignty

A third approach is known as food sovereignty; though it overlaps with food justice on several points, the two are not identical. It views the business practices of multinational corporations as a form of neocolonialism. It contends that multinational corporations have the financial resources available to buy up the agricultural resources of impoverished nations, particularly in the tropics. They also have the political clout to convert these resources to the exclusive production of cash crops for sale to industrialized nations outside of the tropics, and in the process to squeeze the poor off of the more productive lands. Under this view subsistence farmers are left to cultivate only lands that are so marginal in terms of productivity as to be of no interest to the multinational corporations. Likewise, food sovereignty holds it to be true that communities should be able to define their own means of production and that food is a basic human right. With several multinational corporations now pushing agricultural technologies on developing countries, technologies that include improved seeds, chemical fertilizers, and pesticides, crop production has become an increasingly analysed and debated issue. Many communities calling for food sovereignty are protesting the imposition of Western technologies on to their indigenous systems and agency.

Those who hold a "food sovereignty" position advocate banning the production of most cash crops in developing nations, thereby leaving the local farmers to concentrate on subsistence agriculture. In addition, they oppose allowing low-cost subsidized food from industrialized nations into developing countries, what is referred to as "import dumping". Import dumping also happens by way of food aid distribution through programs like the USA's "Food for Peace" initiative.

WORLD FOOD SUMMIT

The World Food Summit was held in Rome in 1996, with the aim of renewing global commitment to the fight against hunger. The Food and Agriculture Organization of the United Nations (FAO) called the summit in response to widespread under-nutrition and growing concern about the capacity of agriculture to meet future food needs. The conference produced two key documents, the Rome Declaration on World Food Security and the World Food Summit Plan of Action. The Rome Declaration calls for the members of the United Nations to work to halve the number of chronically undernourished people on the Earth by the year 2015. The Plan of Action sets a number of targets for government and non-governmental organizations for achieving food security, at the individual, household, national, regional and global levels.

World Summit on Food Security

The World Summit on Food Security took place in Rome, Italy, between 16 and 18 November 2009. The decision to convene the summit was taken by the Council of FAO in June 2009, at the proposal of FAO Director-General Dr. Jacques Diouf. Heads of State and Government attended the summit, which took place at the FAO's headquarters.

Achieving food security

"The number of people without enough food to eat on a regular basis remains stubbornly high, at over 800 million, and is not falling significantly. Over 60% of the world's undernourished people live in Asia, and a quarter in Africa. The proportion of people who are hungry, however, is greater in Africa (33%) than Asia (16%). The latest FAO figures indicate that there are 22 countries, 16 of which are in Africa, in which the undernourishment prevalence rate is over 35%."

By way of comparison, in one of the largest food producing countries in the world, the United States, approximately one out of six people are "food insecure", including 17 million children, according to the U.S. Department of Agriculture. Food insecurity is measured in the United States by questions in the Census Bureau's Current Population Survey. The questions asked are about anxiety that the household budget is inadequate to buy enough food, inadequacy in the quantity or quality of food eaten by adults and children in the household, and instances of reduced food intake or consequences of reduced food intake for adults and for children. A National Academy of Sciences study commissioned by the USDA criticized this measurement and the relationship of "food security" to hunger, adding "it is not clear whether hunger is appropriately identified as the extreme end of the food security scale."

In its "The State of Food Insecurity in the World 2003", FAO states that: 'In general the countries that succeeded in reducing hunger were characterised by more rapid economic growth and specifically more rapid growth in their agricultural sectors. They also exhibited slower population growth, lower levels of HIV and higher ranking in the Human Development

Index'. As such, according to FAO, addressing agriculture and population growth is vital to achieving food security. Other organisations and people (e.g. Peter Singer) have come to this same conclusion, and advocate improvements in agriculture and population control.

USAID proposes several key steps to increasing agricultural productivity which is in turn key to increasing rural income and reducing food insecurity. They include:

- Boosting agricultural science and technology. Current agricultural yields are insufficient to feed the growing populations. Eventually, the rising agricultural productivity drives economic growth.
- Securing property rights and access to finance.
- Enhancing human capital through education and improved health.
- Conflict prevention and resolution mechanisms and democracy and governance based on principles of accountability and transparency in public institutions and the rule of law are basic to reducing vulnerable members of society.

The UN Millennium Development Goals are one of the initiatives aimed at achieving food security in the world. In its list of goals, the first Millennium Development Goal states that the UN "is to eradicate extreme hunger and poverty", and that "agricultural productivity is likely to play a key role in this if it is to be reached on time".

"Of the eight Millennium Development Goals, eradicating extreme hunger and poverty depends on agriculture the most. (MDG 1 calls for halving hunger and poverty by 2015 in relation to 1990.)

Notably, the gathering of wild food plants appears to be an efficient alternative method of subsistence in tropical countries, which may play a role in poverty alleviation.

The agriculture-hunger-poverty nexus

Eradicating hunger and poverty requires an understanding of the ways in which these two injustices interconnect. Hunger, and the malnourishment that accompanies it, prevents poor people from escaping poverty because it diminishes their ability to learn, work, and care for themselves and their family members. Food insecurity exists when people are undernourished as a result of the physical unavailability of food, their lack of social or economic access to adequate food, and/or inadequate food utilization. Food-insecure people are those individuals whose food intake falls below their minimum calorie (energy) requirements, as well as those who exhibit physical symptoms caused by energy and nutrient deficiencies resulting from an inadequate or unbalanced diet or from the body's inability to use food effectively because of infection or disease. An alternative view would define the concept of food insecurity as referring only to the consequence of inadequate consumption of nutritious food, considering the physiological utilization of food by the body as being within the domain of nutrition and health. Malnourishment also leads to poor health hence individuals fail to provide for their families. If left unaddressed, hunger sets in motion an array of outcomes that perpetuate malnutrition, reduce the ability of adults to work and to give birth to healthy children, and erode children's ability to learn and lead productive, healthy, and happy lives. This truncation of human development undermines a country's potential for economic development–for generations to come.

There are strong, direct relationships between agricultural productivity, hunger, and poverty. Three-quarters of the world's poor live in rural areas and make their living from agriculture. Hunger and child malnutrition are greater in these areas than in urban areas. Moreover, the higher the proportion of the rural population that obtains its income solely from subsistence farming (without the benefit of pro-poor technologies and access to markets), the higher the incidence of malnutrition. Therefore, improvements in agricultural productivity aimed at small-scale farmers will benefit the rural poor first.

Increased agricultural productivity enables farmers to grow more food, which translates into better diets and, under market conditions that offer a level playing field, into higher farm incomes. With more money, farmers are more likely to diversify production and grow higher-value crops, benefiting not only themselves but the economy as a whole."

Researchers suggest forming an alliance between the emergency food program and CSA Farms, as currently food stamps cannot be used at farmer's markets and places in which food is less processed and grown locally.

Biotechnology for smallholders in the (sub)tropics

The area sown to genetically engineered crops in developing countries is rapidly catching-up with the area sown in industrial nations. According to the International Service for the Acquisition of Agri-biotech Applications (ISAAA), genetically engineered (biotech, GM) crops were grown by approximately 8.5 million farmers in 21 countries in 2005, up from 8.25 million farmers in 17 countries in 2004. The largest increase in biotech crop area in any country in 2005 was in Brazil, provisionally estimated at 44,000 km^2 (94,000 km^2 in 2005 compared with 50,000 km^2 in 2004). India had by far the largest year-on-year proportional increase, with almost a threefold increase from 5,000 km^2 in 2004 to 13,000 km^2 in 2005. However, it should be noted that the ISAAA is funded by organisations including prominent agricultural biotechnology corporations, such as Monsanto and Bayer, and there have been several challenges made to the accuracy of ISAAA's global figures.

Current high regulatory costs imposed on varieties created by the more modern methods are a significant hurdle for development of genetically engineered crops well suited to developing country farmers by modern genetic methods. Once a new variety is developed, however, seed provides a good vehicle for distribution of improvements in a package that is familiar to the farmer.

Currently there are some institutes and research groups that have projects in which biotechnology is shared with contact people in less-developed countries on a non-profit basis. These institutes make use of biotechnological methods that do not involve high research and registration costs, such as conservation and multiplication of germplasm and phytosanitation.

Apart from genetic engineering, other forms of biotechnology also hold promise for enhancing food security. For instance, perennial rice is being developed in China, which could dramatically reduce the risk of soil erosion on upland smallholder farms.

RISKS TO FOOD SECURITY

While agricultural output increased as a result of the Green Revolution, the energy input into the process (that is, the energy that must be expended to produce a crop) has also increased at a greater rate, so that the ratio of crops produced to energy input has decreased over time. Green Revolution techniques also heavily rely on chemical fertilizers, pesticides and herbicides, some of which must be developed from fossil fuels, making agriculture increasingly reliant on petroleum products.

Between 1950 and 1984, as the Green Revolution transformed agriculture around the globe, world grain production increased by 250%. The energy for the Green Revolution was provided by fossil fuels in the form of fertilizers (natural gas), pesticides (oil), and hydrocarbon fuelled irrigation.

David Pimentel, professor of ecology and agriculture at Cornell University, and Mario Giampietro, senior researcher at the National Research Institute on Food and Nutrition (INRAN), place in their study *Food, Land, Population and the U.S. Economy* the maximum U.S. population for a sustainable economy at 200 million. To achieve a sustainable economy and avert disaster, the United States must reduce its population by at least one-third, and world population will have to be reduced by two-thirds, says the study.

The authors of this study believe that the mentioned agricultural crisis will only begin to impact us after 2020, and will not become critical until 2050. The oncoming peaking of global oil production (and subsequent decline of production), along with the peak of North American natural gas production will very likely precipitate this agricultural crisis much sooner than expected. Geologist Dale Allen Pfeiffer claims that coming decades could see spiraling food prices without relief and massive starvation on a global level such as never experienced before. However, one should take note that, (numbers taken from the CIA World Factbook), the country of Bangladesh achieved food self-sufficiency in 2002 with both a far higher population density than the USA (~1000 inhabitants per square kilometre in comparison to just 30/km for the USA-so this is more than 30 times as many), and at only a tiny fraction of the USA's usage of oil, gas, and electricity. Also, pre-industrial Chinese mini-farmers/gardeners developed techniques to feed a population of more than 1000 people per square kilometre. Hence, the dominant problem is not energy availability but the need to stop and revert soil degradation.

Hybridization, genetic engineering and loss of biodiversity

In agriculture and animal husbandry, the Green Revolution popularized the use of conventional hybridization to increase yield by creating "high-yielding varieties". Often the handful of hybridized breeds originated in developed countries and were further hybridized with local varieties in the rest of the developing world to create high yield strains resistant to local climate and diseases. Local governments and industry have been pushing hybridization which has resulted in several of the indigenous breeds becoming extinct or threatened. Disuse because of unprofitability and uncontrolled intentional and unintentional cross-pollination and crossbreeding (genetic pollution), formerly huge gene pools of various wild and indigenous breeds have collapsed causing widespread genetic erosion and genetic pollution. This has resulted in loss of genetic diversity and biodiversity as a whole. A genetically modified organism (GMO) is an organism whose genetic material has been altered using the genetic engineering techniques generally known as recombinant DNA technology. Genetically Modified (GM) crops today have become a common source for genetic pollution, not only of wild varieties but also of other domesticated varieties derived from relatively natural hybridization.

Genetic erosion coupled with genetic pollution may be destroying unique genotypes, thereby creating a hidden crisis which could result in a severe threat to our food security.

Diverse genetic material could cease to exist which would impact our ability to further hybridize food crops and livestock against more resistant diseases and climatic changes.

Livestock Biodiversity

Genetic erosion in agricultural and livestock biodiversity is the loss of genetic diversity, including the loss of individual genes, and the loss of particular combinants of genes (or gene complexes) such as those manifested in locally adapted landraces of domesticated animals or plants adapted to the natural environment in which they originated. The term genetic erosion is sometimes used in a narrow sense, such as for the loss of alleles or genes, as well as more broadly, referring to the loss of varieties or even species. The major driving forces behind genetic erosion in crops are: variety replacement, land clearing, overexploitation of species, population pressure, environmental degradation, overgrazing, policy and changing agricultural systems. The main factor, however, is the replacement of local varieties of domestic plants and animals by high yielding or exotic varieties or species. A large number of varieties can also often be dramatically reduced when commercial varieties (including GMOs) are introduced into traditional farming systems. Many researchers believe that the main problem related to agro-ecosystem management is the general tendency towards genetic and ecological uniformity imposed by the development of modern agriculture.

Intellectual Property Rights

There is much debate on whether IPRs hurt or harm independent development in terms or agriculture and food production. Hartmut Meyer and Annette von Lossau describe both sides of the issue, while saying “Among scholars, the thesis that the impetus to self-determined development and the protection of intellectual property go hand in hand is disputed-to put it mildly. Many studies have concluded that there is virtually no positive correlation between establishing self-sustained economic growth and ensuring protection of intellectual property rights.

2

Global Food Security under Climate Change

The Food and Agriculture Organization (FAO) defines food security as a "situation that exists when all people, at all times, have physical, social, and economic access to sufficient, safe, and nutritious food that meets their dietary needs and food preferences for an active and healthy life".

This definition comprises four key dimensions of food supplies: availability, stability, access, and utilization. The first dimension relates to the availability of sufficient food, i.e., to the overall ability of the agricultural system to meet food demand.

Its subdimensions include the agro-climatic fundamentals of crop and pasture production and the entire range of socio-economic and cultural factors that determine where and how farmers perform in response to markets. The second dimension, stability, relates to individuals who are at high risk of temporarily or permanently losing their access to the resources needed to consume adequate food, either because these individuals cannot ensure *ex ante* against income shocks or they lack enough "reserves" to smooth consumption *ex post* or both.

An important cause of unstable access is climate variability, e.g., landless agricultural laborers, who almost wholly depend on agricultural wages in a region of erratic rainfall and have few savings, would be at high risk of losing their access to food.

However, there can be individuals with unstable access to food even in agricultural communities where there is no climate variability, e.g., landless agricultural laborers who fall sick and cannot earn their daily wages would lack stable access to food if, for example, they cannot take out insurance against illness. The third dimension, access, covers access by individuals to adequate resources (entitlements) to acquire appropriate foods for a nutritious diet. Entitlements are defined as the set of all those commodity bundles over which a person can establish command given the legal, political, economic, and social arrangements of the community of which he or she is a member. Thus a key element is the purchasing power of consumers and the evolution of real incomes and food prices. However, these resources need not be exclusively monetary but may also include traditional rights, e.g., to a share of common resources. Finally, utilization encompasses all food safety and quality aspects of nutrition; its subdimensions are therefore related to health, including the sanitary conditions across the entire food chain. It is not enough that someone is getting what appears to be an adequate quantity of food if that person is unable to make use of the food because he or she is always falling sick.

Agriculture is not only a source of the commodity food but, equally importantly, also a source of income. In a world where trade is possible at reasonably low cost, the crucial issue for food security is not whether food is "available," but whether the monetary and nonmonetary resources at the disposal of the population are sufficient to allow everyone access to adequate quantities of food. An important corollary to this is that national self-sufficiency is neither necessary nor sufficient to guarantee food security at the individual level. Note that Hong Kong and Singapore are not self-sufficient (agriculture is nonexistent) but their populations are food-secure, whereas India is self-sufficient but a large part of its population is not food-secure.

Numerous measures are used to quantify the overall status and the regional distribution of global hunger. None of these measures covers all dimensions and facets of food insecurity described above. This also holds for the FAO indicator of undernourishment (1), the measure that was used in essentially all studies reviewed in this article. The FAO measure, however, has a number of advantages. First, it covers two dimensions of food security, availability and access; second, the underlying methodology is straightforward and transparent; and third, the parameters and data needed for the FAO indicator are readily available for past estimates and can be derived without major difficulties for the future.

This article reviews recent studies that have quantified the impacts of climate change on global food security. It starts with an overview of the principal aspects of climate change and their impacts on the four dimensions of food security. It then reviews model-based results and discusses the main findings that have arisen from these assessments. Finally, limitations of the current modeling systems are discussed; this final section includes a discussion of potential surprises and some suggestions to improve future assessments to enhance their overall robustness and their relevance for policy makers.

CLIMATE CHANGE AND FOOD SECURITY

Climate change affects agriculture and food production in complex ways. It affects food production directly through changes in agro-ecological conditions and indirectly by affecting growth and distribution of incomes, and thus demand for agricultural produce. Impacts have been quantified in numerous studies and under various sets of assumptions. A selection of these results is presented in *Quantifying the Impacts on Food Security*. Here it is useful to summarize the main alterations in the agro-ecological environment that are associated with climate change.

Changes in temperature and precipitation associated with continued emissions of greenhouse gases will bring changes in land suitability and crop yields. In particular, the Intergovernmental Panel on Climate Change (IPCC) considers four families of socio-economic development and associated emission scenarios, known as Special Report on Emissions Scenarios (SRES) A2, B2, A1, and B1. Of relevance to this review, of the SRES scenarios, A1, the "business-as-usual scenario," corresponds to the highest emissions, and B1 corresponds to the lowest. The other scenarios are intermediate between these two. Importantly for agriculture and world food supply, SRES A2 assumes the highest projected population growth of the four (United Nations high projection) and is thus associated to the highest food demand. Depending on the SRES emission scenario and climate models considered, global mean surface temperature is projected to rise in a range from 1.8°C (with a range from 1.1°C to 2.9°C for SRES B1) to 4.0°C (with a range from 2.4°C to 6.4°C for A1) by 2100. In temperate latitudes, higher temperatures are expected to bring predominantly benefits to agriculture: the areas potentially suitable for cropping will expand, the length of the growing period will increase, and crop yields may rise. A moderate incremental warming in some humid and temperate grasslands may increase pasture productivity and reduce the need for housing and for compound feed. These gains have to be set against an increased frequency of extreme events, for instance, heat waves and droughts in the Mediterranean region or increased heavy precipitation events and flooding in temperate regions, including the possibility of increased coastal storms ; they also have to be set against the fact that semiarid and arid pastures are likely to see reduced livestock productivity and increased livestock mortality. In drier areas, climate models predict increased evapotranspiration and lower soil moisture levels. As a result, some cultivated areas may become unsuitable for cropping and some tropical grassland may become increasingly arid. Temperature rise will also expand the range of many agricultural pests and increase the ability of pest populations to survive the winter and attack spring crops.

Another important change for agriculture is the increase in atmospheric carbon dioxide (CO_2) concentrations. Depending on the SRES emission scenario, the atmospheric CO_2 concentration is projected to increase from H”379 ppm today to >550 ppm by 2100 in SRES B1 to >800 ppm in SRES A1FI. Higher CO_2 concentrations will have a positive effect on many crops, enhancing biomass accumulation and final yield. However, the magnitude of this effect is less clear, with important differences depending on management type (e.g., irrigation and fertilization regimes) and crop type. Experimental yield response to elevated CO_2 show that under optimal growth conditions, crop yields increase at 550 ppm CO_2 in the range of 10% to 20% for C_3 crops (such as wheat, rice, and soybean), and only 0–10% for C_4 crops such as maize and sorghum. Yet the nutritional quality of agricultural produce may not increase in line with higher yields. Some cereal and forage crops, for example, show lower protein concentrations under elevated CO_2 conditions.

Finally, a number of recent studies have estimated the likely changes in land suitability, potential yields, and agricultural production on the current suite of crops and cultivars available today. Therefore, these estimates implicitly include adaptation using available management techniques and crops, but excluding new cultivars from breeding or biotechnology. These studies are in essence based on the FAO/ International Institute for Applied Systems Analysis (IIASA) agro-ecological zone (AEZ) methodology. The suggested that total land and total prime land would remain virtually unchanged at the current levels of 2,600 million and 2,000 million hectares (ha), respectively. The same study also showed, however, more pronounced regional shifts, with a considerable increase in suitable cropland at higher latitudes (developed countries +160 million ha) and a corresponding decline of potential cropland at lower latitudes (developing countries "110 million ha). An even more pronounced shift within the quality of cropland is predicted in developing countries. The net decline of 110 million ha is the result of a massive decline in agricultural prime land of H"135 million ha, which is offset by an increase in moderately suitable land of >20 million ha. This quality shift is also reflected in the shift in land suitable for multiple cropping. In sub-Saharan Africa alone, land for double cropping would decline by between 10 million and 20 million ha, and land suitable for triple copping would decline by 5 million to 10 million ha. At a regional level, similar approaches indicate that under climate change, the biggest losses in suitable cropland are likely to be in Africa, whereas the largest expansion of suitable cropland is in the Russian Federation and Central Asia.

Impacts on the Stability of Food Supplies

Global and regional weather conditions are also expected to become more variable than at present, with increases in the frequency and severity of extreme events such as cyclones, floods, hailstorms, and droughts. By bringing greater fluctuations in crop yields and local food supplies and higher risks of landslides and erosion damage, they can adversely affect the stability of food supplies and thus food security.

Neither climate change nor short-term climate variability and associated adaptation are new phenomena in agriculture, of course. As shown, for instance, in ref. 9, some important agricultural areas of the world like the Midwest of the United States, the northeast of Argentina, southern Africa, or southeast Australia have traditionally experienced higher climate variability than other regions such as central Africa or Europe. They also show that the extent of short-term fluctuations has changed over longer periods of time. In developed countries, for instance, short-term climate variability increased from 1931 to 1960 as compared with 1901 to 1930, but decreased strongly in the period from 1961 to 1990. What is new, however, is the fact that the areas subject to high climate variability are likely to expand, whereas the extent of short-term climate variability is likely to increase across all regions. Furthermore, the rates and levels of projected warming may exceed in some regions the historical experience.

If climate fluctuations become more pronounced and more widespread, droughts and floods, the dominant causes of short-term fluctuations in food production in semiarid and subhumid areas, will become more severe and more frequent. In semiarid areas, droughts can dramatically reduce crop yields and livestock numbers and productivity. Again, most of this land is in sub-Saharan Africa and parts of South Asia, meaning that the poorest regions with the highest level of chronic undernourishment will also be exposed to the highest degree of instability in food production. How strongly these impacts will be felt will crucially depend on whether such fluctuations can be countered by investments in irrigation, better storage facilities, or higher food imports. In addition, a policy environment that fosters freer trade and promotes investments in transportation, communications, and irrigation infrastructure can help address these challenges early on.

Impacts of Climate Change on Food Utilization

Climate change will also affect the ability of individuals to use food effectively by altering the conditions for food safety and changing the disease pressure from vector, water, and food-borne diseases. It examines how the various forms of diseases, including vector-borne diseases such as malaria, are likely to spread or recede with climate change. This article focuses on a narrow selection of diseases that affect food safety directly, i.e., food and water-borne diseases.

The main concern about climate change and food security is that changing climatic conditions can initiate a vicious circle where infectious disease causes or compounds hunger, which, in turn, makes the affected populations more susceptible to infectious disease. The result can be a substantial decline in labor productivity and an increase in poverty and even mortality. Essentially all manifestations of climate change, be they drought, higher temperatures, or heavy rainfalls have an impact on the disease pressure, and there is growing evidence that these changes affect food safety and food security.

The recent IPCC report also emphasizes that increases in daily temperatures will increase the frequency of food poisoning, particularly in temperate regions. Warmer seas may contribute to increased cases of human shellfish and reef-fish poisoning (ciguatera) in tropical regions and a poleward expansion of the disease. However, there is little new evidence that climate change significantly alters the prevalence of these diseases. Several studies have confirmed and quantified the effects of temperature on common forms of food poisoning, such as salmonellosis. These studies show an approximately linear increase in reported cases for each degree increase in weekly temperature. Moreover, there is evidence that temperature variability affects the incidence of diarrhoeal disease. A number of studies found that rising temperatures were strongly associated with increased episodes of diarrhoeal disease in adults and children. These findings have been corroborated by analyses based on monthly temperature observations. Several studies report a strong correlation between monthly temperature and diarrhoeal episodes on the Pacific Islands, Australia, and Israel. Extreme rainfall events can increase the risk of outbreaks of water-borne diseases particularly where traditional water management systems are insufficient to handle the new extremes. Likewise, the impacts of flooding will be felt most strongly in environmentally degraded areas, and where basic public infrastructure, including sanitation and hygiene, is lacking. This will raise the number of people exposed to water-borne diseases (e.g., cholera) and thus lower their capacity to effectively use food.

Impacts of Climate Change on Access to Food

Access to food refers to the ability of individuals, communities, and countries to purchase sufficient quantities and qualities of food. Over the last 30 years, falling real prices for food and rising real incomes have led to substantial improvements in access to food in many developing countries. Increased purchasing power has allowed a growing number of people to purchase not only more food but also more nutritious food with more protein, micronutrients, and vitamins. East Asia and to a lesser extent the Near-East/North African region have particularly benefited from a combination of lower real food prices and robust income growth. From 1970 to 2001, the prevalence of hunger in these regions, as measured by FAO's indicator of undernourishment, has declined from 24% to 10.1% and 44% to 10.2% respectively. In East Asia, it was endogenous income growth that provided the basis for the boost in demand for food, which was largely produced in the region; in the Near-East North African region demand was spurred by exogenous revenues from oil and gas exports, and additional food supply came largely from imports. But in both regions, improvements in access to food have been crucial in reducing hunger and malnutrition.

FAO's longer-term outlook to 2050 suggests that the importance of improved demand side conditions will even become more important over the next 50 years. The regions that will see the strongest reductions in the prevalence of undernourishment are those that are expected to see the highest rates of income growth. South Asia stands to benefit the most. Spurred by high income growth the region is expected to reduce the prevalence of undernourishment from >22% currently to 12% by 2015 and just 4% by 2050. Progress is also expected for sub-Saharan Africa, but improvements will be less pronounced and are expected to set in later. Over the next 15 years, for instance, the prevalence of undernourishment will decline less than in other regions, from H"33% to a still worrisome 21%, as significant constraints (soil nutrients, water, infrastructure, etc.) will limit the ability to further increase food production locally, while continuing low levels of income rule out the option of importing food. In the long run, however, sub-Saharan Africa is expected to see a more substantial decline in hunger; by 2050, <6% of its total population are expected to suffer from chronic hunger. It is important to note that these FAO projections do not take into account the effects of climate change.

By coupling agro-ecologic and economic models, others have gauged the impact of climate change on agricultural gross domestic product (GDP) and prices. At the global level, the impacts of climate change are likely to be very small; under a range of SRES and associated climate-change scenarios, the estimates range from a decline of "1.5% to an increase of +2.6% by 2080. At the regional level, the importance of agriculture as a source of income can be much more important. In these regions, the economic output from agriculture itself (over and above subsistence food production) will be an important contributor to food security. The strongest impact of climate change on the economic output of agriculture is expected for sub-Saharan Africa, which means that the poorest and already most food-insecure region is also expected to suffer the largest contraction of agricultural incomes. For the region, the losses in agricultural GDP, compared with no climate change, range from 2% to 8% for the Hadley Centre Coupled Model, version 3 and 7–9% for the Commonwealth Scientific and Industrial Research Organisation projections.

Impacts on Food Prices

Essentially all SRES development paths describe a world of robust economic growth and rapidly shrinking importance of agriculture in the long run and thus a continuation of a trend that has been underway for decades in many developing regions. SRES scenarios describe a world where income growth will allow the largest part of the world's population to address possible local production shortfalls through imports and, at the same time, find ways to cope with safety and stability issues of food supplies. It is also a world where real incomes rise more rapidly than real food prices, which suggests that the share of income spent on food should decline and that even high food prices are unlikely to create a major dent in the food expenditures of the poor. However, not all parts of the world perform equally well in the various development paths and not all development paths are equally benign for growth. Where income levels are low and shares of food expenditures are high, higher prices for food may still create or exacerbate a possible food security problem.

The share of agriculture in total GDP in many developing countries has rapidly declined over the last decades; it is worth noting that in the high-income Organization for Economic Cooperation and Development countries today, the share of agriculture in GDP is <2%.

There are a number of studies that have ventured to measure the likely impacts of climate change on food prices. The basic messages that emerge from these studies are: first, on average, prices for food are expected to rise moderately in line with moderate increases of temperature (until 2050); some studies even foresee a mild decline in real prices until 2050. Second, after 2050 and with further increases in temperatures, prices are expected to increase more substantially. In some studies and for some commodities (rice and sugar) prices are forecast to increase by as much as 80% above their reference levels without climate change. Third, price changes expected from the effects of global warming are, on average, much smaller than price changes from socio-economic development paths. For instance, the SRES A2 scenario would imply a price increase in real cereal prices by H"170%. The (additional) price increase caused by climate change (in the Hadley Centre Coupled Model, version 3, climate change case) would only be 14.4%. Overall, this appears to be the sharpest price increase reported and it is not surprising that this scenario would imply a stubbornly high number of undernourished people until 2080. However, it is also needless to say that a constant absolute number of undernourished people would still imply a sharp decline in the prevalence of hunger, and, given the high population assumptions in the SRES A2 world (>13.6 billion people globally and >11.6 billion in the developing world) this would imply a particularly sharp drop in the prevalence from currently 17% to H"7% by 2080.

QUANTIFYING THE IMPACTS ON FOOD SECURITY

A number of studies have recently quantified the impacts of climate change on food security. In terms of quantifying agronomic yield change projections, these studies are either based on the AEZ tools developed by the IIASA analysis or the Decision Support System for Agrotechnology Transfer suite of crop models; all use the IIASA-Basic Linked System (BLS) economic model for assessing economic impacts. These tools, with some modifications relating to how crop yield changes are simulated, have also been used by others to undertake similar assessments and provide sensitivity analyses across a range of SRES and general circulation model (GCM) projections. Many other simulations have also examined the effects of climate change with and without adaptation (induced technological progress, domestic policy change, international trade liberalization, etc.), with and without mitigation (e.g., CO_2 stabilization, variants for temperature, rainfall change and distribution) or provide impact assessments for different speeds of climate change. This section focuses on the quantitative results for food security, trying to illuminate some of the differences and extract the main messages that emerge from the various studies. Unless indicated, all simulation results discussed below include the combined effects of climate change and elevated CO_2 on crops. The key messages can be summarized as follows:

First, it is very likely that climate change is likely to increase the number of people at risk of hunger compared with reference scenarios with no climate change; the exact impacts will, however, strongly depend on the projected socio-economic developments. For instance, it is estimated that climate change would increase the number of undernourished in 2080 by 5–26%, compared with no climate change or by between 5 million and 10 million (B1 SRES) and 120 million to 170 million people (A2 SRES), with within-SRES ranges depending on GCM climate projections. Using only one GCM scenario, others projected small reductions by 2080, i.e., " 5%, or "10 million (B1) to "30 million (A2) people, and slight increases of +13%–26%, or H"10 million (B2) to 30 million (A1) people.

Second, it is likely that the magnitude of these climate impacts will be small compared with the impact of socio-economic development. The limitations of socio-economic forecasts, these studies suggest that robust economic growth and a decline in population growth projected for the 21st century will, in all but one scenario (SRES A2), significantly reduce the number of people at risk of hunger in 2080. At any rate, the prevalence of undernourishment will decline as all scenarios assume that world population will continue to grow to 2080, albeit at lower rates.

Compared with FAO estimates of 820 million undernourished in developing countries today, several studies estimate reductions of >75% by 2080, or H"560 million to 700 million people, projecting 100 million to 240 million undernourished by 2080 (A1, B1, and B2). As mentioned, the only exception is scenario A2, where the number of the hungry is forecast to decrease only slightly by 2080; but the higher population growth rates in A2 compared with other scenarios mean that the prevalence of undernourishment will decline drastically. However, these analyses also confirm that the progress will be unevenly distributed over the developing world, and more importantly progress will be slow during the first decades of the outlook. With or without climate change, the millennium development goal of halving the prevalence of hunger by 2015 is unlikely to be realized before 2020–2030.

In addition to socio-economic pressures considered within the IPCC SRES scenarios, food production may increasingly compete with bio-energy in coming decades; studies addressing possible consequences for world food supply have only started to surface, providing both positive and negative views. Importantly, none of the major world food models discussed herein have yet considered such competition.

Third, sub-Saharan Africa is likely to surpass Asia as the most food-insecure region. However, this is largely independent of climate change and is mostly the result of the socio-economic development paths assumed for the different developing regions in the SRES scenarios. Throughout most SRES and climate-change scenarios sub-Saharan Africa accounts for 40–50% of global hunger by 2080, compared with H"24% today ; in some simulations sub-Saharan Africa even accounts for 70–75% of global undernourishment by 2080. These high estimates have emerged from slower growth variants of the A2 and B2 scenarios ; also an A2 variant with slower population growth yields a sharper concentration of hunger in sub-Saharan Africa. For regions other than sub-Saharan Africa, results largely depend on GCM scenarios and therefore are highly uncertain.

Fourth, although there is significant uncertainty on the effects of elevated CO_2 on crop yields, this uncertainty is carried to a much lesser extent on food security. This result emerges from a comparison of climate change simulations with and without CO_2 fertilization effects on crop yields. The higher CO_2 fertilization would not greatly affect global projections of hunger. In view of the fact that essentially all SRES worlds are characterized by much higher real incomes, much improved transportation and communication options, and still sufficient global food production, the somewhat smaller supplies will not be able to make a dent in global food security outcomes. Many studies find that climate change without CO_2 fertilization would reduce the number of undernourished people by 2080 only by some 20 million to 140 million (120 million to 380 million for SRES A1, B1, and B2 without, compared with 100 million to 240 million with CO_2 fertilization effect). The exception again in these studies is SRES A2, under which the assumption of no CO_2 fertilization results in a projected range of 950 million to 1,300 million people undernourished in 2080, compared with 740 million to 850 million projected under climate change, but with CO_2 effects on crops.

Finally, recent research suggests large positive effects of climate stabilization for the agricultural sector. However, as the stabilizing effects of mitigation measures can take several decades to be realized from the moment of implementation, the benefits for crop production may be realized only in the second half of this century. Importantly, even in the presence of robust global long-term benefits, regional and temporal patterns of winners and losers that can be projected with current tools are highly uncertain and depend critically on the underlying GCM projections.

UNCERTAINTIES AND LIMITATIONS

The finding that socio-economic development paths have an important bearing on future food security and that they are likely to top the effects of climate change should not, or at least not only, be interpreted as a probability-based forecast. This is because SRES scenarios offer a range of possible outcomes "without any sense of likelihood". Yet SRES scenarios, like all scenarios, do not overcome the inability to accurately project future changes in economic activity, emissions, and climate.

Second, the existing global assessments of climate change and food security have only been able to focus on the impacts on food availability and access to food, without quantification of the likely important climate change effects on food safety and vulnerability (stability). This means that these assessments neither include potential problems arising from additional impacts due to extreme events such as drought and floods nor do they quantify the potential impacts of changes in the prevalence of food-borne diseases (positive as well as negative) or the interaction of nutrition and health effects through changes in the proliferation of vector-borne diseases such as malaria. On the food availability side, they also exclude the impacts of a possible sea-level rise for agricultural production or those that are associated with possible reductions of marine or freshwater fish production. Third, it is important to note that even in terms of food availability, all current assessments of world food supply have focused only on the impacts of mean climate change, i.e., they have not considered the possibility of significant shifts in the frequency of extreme events on regional production potential, nor have they considered scenarios of abrupt climate or socio-economic change; any of these scenario variants is likely to increase the already negative projected impacts of climate change on world food supply. Models that take into account the specific biophysical, technological, and market responses necessary to simulate realistic adaptation to such events are not yet available.

Fourth, this review finds that recent global assessments of climate change and food security rest essentially on a single modeling framework, the IIASA system, which combines the FAO/IIASA AEZ model with various GCM models and the IIASA BLS system, or on close variants of the IIASA system. This has important implications for uncertainty, given that the robustness of all these assessments strongly depends on the performance of the underlying models. There is, therefore, a clear need for continued and enhanced validation efforts of both the agro-climatological and food trade tools developed at IIASA and widely used in the literature.

Finally, we note that assessments that do not only provide scenarios, but also attach probabilities for particular outcomes to come true could provide an important element for improved or at least better-informed policy decisions. A number of possibilities are offered to address the related modeling challenges.

One option would be to produce such estimates with probability-based estimates of the (key) model parameters. Alternatively, the various scenarios could be constructed so that they reflect expert judgements on a particular issue. It would be desirable to attach probabilities to existing scenarios. Information on how likely the suggested outcomes are would contribute greatly to their usefulness for policy makers and help justify (or otherwise) policy measures to adapt to or mitigate the impacts of climate change on food security.

Climate change will affect all four dimensions of food security, namely food availability (i.e., production and trade), access to food, stability of food supplies, and food utilization. The importance of the various dimensions and the overall impact of climate change on food security will differ across regions and over time and, most importantly, will depend on the overall socio-economic status that a country has accomplished as the effects of climate change set in. Essentially all quantitative assessments show that climate change will adversely affect food security. Climate change will increase the dependency of developing countries on imports and accentuate existing focus of food insecurity on sub-Saharan Africa and to a lesser extent on South Asia. Within the developing world, the adverse impacts of climate change will fall disproportionately on the poor. Many quantitative assessments also show that the socio-economic environment in which climate change is likely to evolve is more important than the impacts that can be expected from the biophysical changes of climate change.

Less is known about the role of climate change for food stability and utilization, at least in quantitative terms. However, it is likely that differences in socio-economic development paths will also be the crucial determinant for food utilization in the long run and that they will be decisive for the ability to cope with problems of food instability, be they climate-related or caused by other factors.

Finally, all quantitative assessments we reviewed show that the first decades of the 21st century are expected to see low impacts of climate change, but also lower overall incomes and still a higher dependence on agriculture. During these first decades, the biophysical changes as such will be less pronounced but climate change will affect those particularly adversely that are still more dependent on agriculture and have lower overall incomes to cope with the impacts of climate change. By contrast, the second half of the century is expected to bring more severe biophysical impacts but also a greater ability to cope with them. The underlying assumption is that the general transition in the income formation away from agriculture toward nonagriculture will be successful.

How strong the impacts of climate change will be felt over all decades will crucially depend on the future policy environment for the poor. Freer trade can help to improve access to international supplies; investments in transportation and communication infrastructure will help provide secure and timely local deliveries; irrigation, a promotion of sustainable agricultural practices, and continued technological progress can play a crucial role in providing steady local and international supplies under climate change.

INTEGRATING PESTS AND PATHOGENS INTO THE CLIMATE CHANGE

The last 10 50 years have seen major changes to agricultural systems worldwide that have contributed to, and interacted with, new food systems. Von Braun (2007) highlighted the transforming role of the interacting driving forces of population increase, income growth, urbanization, and globalization on food production, markets, and consumption. To these forces can be added the twin elements of climate variability and climate change which have direct effects on both food production and food security. It is well known that the sensitivity of agricultural systems to climate differs between systems depending on whether they are temperature-or water-limited, and whether they are operating near their optimum or not. Fuhrer (2006) concluded that there was ample evidence to demonstrate the sensitivity of agricultural systems to climate change, and that the range of effects on potential productivity was from extremely negative in areas that were already water-limited to positive in areas that were temperature-limited. Similarly, the effects of climate variability and change on food security are also location-specific and, more importantly, societally-specific with countries and groups with low income and limited adaptive capacity facing significant threats to food security. In particular, food insecurity in Sub-Saharan Africa will be increased by climate change although the size of the effect is affected more by socio-economic factors than by climate change *per se*.

Although many studies have detailed considerable progress in understanding the sensitivities of plants and of crop yield to climate variables and change, a major challenge for the agricultural research community is to relate these findings to the broader societal concern with food security. Food security (defined as when all people, at all times, have physical and economic access to sufficient, safe, and nutritious food to meet their dietary needs and food preferences for an active and healthy life, FAO) is concerned not only with food availability (production, distribution, and exchange) but also with access to, and utilization of, food so that studies which focus only on agricultural production only provide a partial assessment of food security/climate change relationships.

Gregory *et al.* (2005) demonstrated that climate variation is only one of several interacting factors that affect food security. In studies of household food security in southern Africa, Misselhorn (2005) found that climate/environment was only one of some 33 drivers mentioned in surveys as important by householders, so that in all communities many interacting factors resulted in vulnerability to food shortages. However, climate/environment was one of the seven most frequently cited factors influencing food security, because of its role both as an ongoing issue (57% of cases where it was mentioned) and as a 'shock' (43%; Scholes and Biggs, 2004). The effects of sudden shocks such as drought are felt, then, on top of other ongoing, long-term stresses. The result is that the long-term stresses deplete household resilience so that the employment of coping strategies that might be available to other better-prepared communities to deal with sudden shocks, is at too high a cost or, simply, unavailable. For example, reliance on purchased food typically increases in drought years due to losses in food production leading to an increase in poverty due to the synergistic action of other drivers such as rising food prices and unemployment. Scholes and Biggs (2004) noted that the food security crisis in southern Africa in 2002–2003 was not simply a result of drought alone and, indeed, climatic stress was not as severe as in many previous years. Maize production during the preceding growing season was only 5.5% less than the previous 5-year average so food stocks at the start of the climatic shock were not unusually low. However, a range of regional and global political and economic factors including high food prices, legacies of structural adjustment, government policies, conflict, and war, policies on genetically-modified foods, and poor responses to the HIV/AIDS pandemic reduced the resilience of the communities to cope with the shock of drought. The moderate climatic shock intensified food insecurity and the long-term vulnerability of the region.

While many agricultural systems are a mix of crop, pasture, tree, and animal production, this book focuses on crops. Ingram *et al.* (2008) outlined three major challenges for agronomic research in the climate/food security debate: (i) to understand better how climate change will affect cropping systems (as opposed to crop productivity); (ii) to assess technical and policy options for reducing the deleterious impacts of climate change on cropping systems while minimizing further environmental degradation; and (iii) to understand how best to address the information needs of policy-makers and report and communicate agronomic research results in a manner that will assist the development of food systems adapted to climate change. In addition, to contribute effectively to the food security/climate change debate, the agricultural research community should think more about the issues of scale and how to translate findings at plot-scale over a few seasons to larger spatial and temporal scales and to the issues of food security.

Many assessments of climate change effects on crops have focused on potential yields, but factors such as pests and pathogens have major effects in determining actual yields. This book reviews the direct effects of climate on crop growth and yield and the evidence that existing change or variation has affected production. The effects of climate on plant pests and pathogens and the interactions that may occur between crops, pests, and pathogens under changed climate are also reviewed. Finally, the contribution that better understanding of the roles of pests and diseases in crop production systems might make to enhanced food security in changed climates is considered.

CLIMATE, CROP GROWTH, AND YIELD

Current research suggests that while many crops may

respond positively to increased atmospheric CO_2 concentrations in the absence of climate changes, the associated effects of higher temperatures and altered patterns of precipitation will probably combine to reduce yields. Estimates of the CO_2 fertilization effect vary depending on which experimental approach is used, but current estimates for increases in crop yield are 10–20% for C_3 crops and 0–10% for C_4 crops. However, it is widely recognized that these figures are likely to represent an overestimate in actual field and farm level responses because they are derived from experiments and crop models that do not necessarily take limiting factors such as pests and pathogens, competition, nutrient competition, and soil water fully into account.

Because of the fundamental effects of radiation, temperature, and water on the growth of plants, it is unsurprising that there has been considerable research to understand the effects of climate and climate change on crop production. Gregory *et al.* (1999) summarized experimental findings on wheat and rice crops that indicated decreased crop duration (and hence yield) of wheat as a consequence of warming, and reductions in yields of rice of about 5% per °C rise above 32 °C. Similarly, simulations of maize production in Africa and Latin America using climate data from the Hadley Climate Model 2 to generate characteristic daily weather data for 2055 predicted an overall reduction of 10%, although there was considerable variability within and between countries with some areas benefitting from changed climate. The likelihood of some regions benefitting from changed climate while others suffer has been highlighted by a number of modelling exercises that combine biophysically based crop models with global simulations of climate. For example, Fischer *et al.* (2001) modelled the global variation in effects of climate change anticipated in 2050 on potential yields of rainfed cereal crops and demonstrated that cereal-producing regions of Canada, and northern Europe and Russia might be expected to increase production, while many parts of the world would suffer losses, including the western edge of the USA prairies, eastern Brazil, Western Australia, and many, though not all, parts of Africa. Overall, the results of this and subsequent work demonstrated that climate change would benefit the cereal production of developed countries more than the developing countries, even if cropping practices evolved to allow more than one rainfed crop per year. They concluded that production losses in some 40 poor, developing countries (mainly in Sub-Saharan Africa) with a combined population of 2 billion, including 450 million undernourished people, may drastically increase the number of those undernourished.

While model predictions of crop responses to projected climate changes are numerous, relatively few assessments have been made of the effects of the measured changes in climate that have already occurred in the last 50 years or so, a period in which the global mean air temperature has increased by 0.13 °C per decade (IPCC, 2007). Gregory and Ingram (2008) show that the majority of such assessments have been made on temperate cereals grown in northern mid-latitudes with very little information available for crops in the tropics. Although the results were variable, there were some common features including (i) a measured increase in mean temperature at many locations across the globe of about 1.0–1.4 °C over the last 30–40 years often with a larger change in minimum than maximum temperatures but with no detected trend in precipitation; (ii) warmer temperatures have resulted in phenological change and there is some evidence for changes to disease incidence and to farming practices; (iii) the effects of changed temperatures (not all were warmer) on crops is complex because different species have different base and optimum temperatures for development, some processes are daytime only (e.g. photosynthesis) while others occur throughout the day (e.g. respiration), and many processes are non-linearly related to temperature; (iv) typically, the climate effects were small relative to the increased yields resulting from technological improvements, but they can be regionally significant; and (v) use of crop models combined with climatic data suggests that, for vegetative crops grown in areas where higher temperatures permit earlier sowing and hence increased duration of green leaf area, crop yields may have increased. No such effects were found for crops such as wheat which forms a distinct reproductive structure because while warming may advance flowering, it reduces the period of grain filling and thereby does not benefit yield.

CLIMATE AND CROP PESTS

Few studies addressing the impacts of climate change on crop yield have incorporated the effects of crop pests. For example, when reviewing how elevated [CO_2] might affect crop yields, Ziska and Bunce (2007) listed only two papers that considered how insect pests might modify the predictions. This is despite the wealth of studies that address the impacts of climate change variables on insect pests using growth chambers, open-top chambers and free air carbon dioxide enrichment (FACE) approaches. Most studies continue to address the responses of crop pests to separate variables (usually elevated [CO_2] or temperature), but some studies have illustrated the importance of combining climatic variables for more realistic climate change scenarios. For example, Newman (2004) presented a model for cereal aphid (*Rhopalosiphum padi*) dynamics under elevated CO_2 concentrations and warmer temperatures, and demonstrated that, while under optimal conditions elevated CO_2 was likely to promote aphid populations, this effect was negated by predicted increases in temperature. However, even though *R. padi* did not become more prevalent under simultaneously elevated CO_2 and temperature, Newman (2004) pointed out that the 10% earlier timing of population peaks and the 10% increase in winged forms could result in greater spread and incidence of barley yellow dwarf virus for which this aphid is a vector.

While crop biomass is predicted to increase in response to elevated CO_2 concentrations under many circumstances, it is also recognized that crops and soils may subsequently become nutrient limited, especially in terms of nitrogen availability. The increased use of legumes within arable rotations has therefore been of considerable interest since legumes can increase N_2 fixation in response to elevated CO_2. However, soil-dwelling *Sitona* spp. weevil larvae are known to target legume root nodules (which house the N_2-fixing bacteria) which potentially reduces N_2 fixation in the plant. Recent findings suggest that elevated CO_2 promotes *Sitona* spp. larvae. In this example, root nodules of white clover (*Trifolium repens*) became both more numerous and larger in size, which was accompanied by larger populations of *Sitona lepidus* larvae that developed at a much faster rate. More root nodules were damaged as a consequence and nitrogen concentrations in the roots declined. Any accompanying increase in such pests could therefore compromise the perceived benefits of legumes in arable rotations under future climate scenarios.

Temperature effects

In addition to empirical studies and models of effects of climate change variables on crop pests, extrapolations based on responses of crop pests to recent changes in climate have also been attempted (Scherm, 2004). One of the most detailed examples of this approach is the use of historical flight phenology records of aphids in the UK. These have shown reduced overwintering mortality of some aphids due to increasing temperatures, resulting in flight phenologies occurring as much as a month earlier. Like the models presented by Newman (2004), these fingerprint studies suggest that climate change is likely to increase the spread of plant pathogens spread by aphid vectors in a number of crops which could ultimately reduce yields. Again in the UK, warmer winters have already resulted in aphids being detected in suction traps in Scotland several weeks earlier than previously, and the aphid populations themselves, previously of a few clonal genotypes, are becoming much more variable. The current Scottish Seed Potato industry is dependent on the virus-free status of its crops which has historically been sustained through the absence of the aphid vectors early in the season; this status is increasingly under threat.

Rainfall

Rainfall can have substantial effects on insect populations. For example, Staley *et al.* (2007) investigated the impacts of enhanced summer rainfall and drought conditions on soil-dwelling *Agriotes lineatus* (wireworms) in grassland plots. Wireworms are damaging pests of crops such as potatoes, especially when planted on land taken out of grass and there is speculation that they are likely to become more of a problem as a result of climate change. Staley *et al.* (2007) found that there was a rapid increase in the population of wireworms in the upper soil as a consequence of enhanced summer rainfall events compared to ambient and drought conditions. In Sub-Saharan Africa, there is already increasing evidence that changes in rainfall patterns are driving migratory patterns of the desert locust (*Schistocerca gregaria*), which devastates crops in Africa, the Middle East, and Asia. Hulme *et al.* (2001) suggest that precipitation patterns in Southern Africa are likely to decrease in December–February, but increase in June–August when this will most benefit *S. gregaria* and lead to further problems.

Crop–pest interactions

While many observations of insect responses to elevated CO_2 and temperature have been made in natural ecosystems, a feature of insect herbivores in agro-ecosystems is that crops that they graze have usually been selected for pest resistance and therefore have specific traits that reduce pest damage (Russell, 1978). This may involve traits that directly deter or inhibit herbivory, or traits that result in the production of compounds that recruit antagonists of the pest. There are now several examples of climate change compromising such crop resistance to pests. In soyabean, elevated CO_2 caused a down-regulation of genes that produce cysteine proteinase inhibitors, which are specific deterrents to coleopteran herbivores. This resulted in increased crop susceptibility to western corn rootworm (*Diabrotica virgifera virgifera*) and Japanese beetle (*Popilla japonica*), both of which have significant impacts on yields. Indirect resistance (e.g. recruitment of pest antagonists) can also be affected by climate change. For example, elevated CO_2 altered the production of volatile defence compounds in white cabbage (*Brassica oleracea*) responsible for recruiting natural enemies (*Cotesia plutellae*) of the diamond back moth (*Plutella xylostella*), resulting in lower searching efficacy of *C. plutellae* (Vuorinen *et al.*, 2004).

Elevated CO_2 and temperature can affect the production of plant secondary compounds with pharmacological impacts on crop–pest interactions. For example, Ziska *et al.* (2008*a*) found that elevated CO_2 increased concentrations of nicotine in tobacco and scopolamine in jimson weed (*Datura stramonium* L.), but had no effect on atropine concentration in tobacco. Because growth was enhanced in both plant species, the amount of all three secondary compounds was increased on a per plant basis. Likewise elevated CO_2 increased production per plant of morphine, codeine, papaverine, and noscapine in wild poppy (*Papaver setigerum*; Ziska *et al.*, 2008*b*). The consequences for herbivory were not determined.

CLIMATE AND CROP PATHOGENS

There are several reports of changes in disease incidence or severity in response to components of climate change, although their usefulness is limited because the experiments normally involved only single parameters and thus do not fully capture the possible change scenarios. Furthermore, most environmental variables will affect both host and pathogen, and affect them in different ways through different mechanisms. Also, in crop stands, there are further complex interactions that are not captured in controlled environment chambers. Consequently, most studies to date only provide some indicative trends which mainly serve to highlight where more resilience needs to be built into the system. Nevertheless, there are reports of some diseases occurring earlier in the growing season as a consequence of warming. For example, the number of days after planting when the first outbreak of late blight occurs in Finland, decreased progressively over a decade in the 1990s.

CO_2 effects

While elevated CO_2 has direct effects on plant growth, it can also result in indirect effects such as reduced expression of induced resistance. Elevated levels of both ozone and CO_2 can also affect expression of resistance more directly. There can also be direct effects on pathogen growth, for example, the enhanced growth of *Colletotrichum gloeosporioides* infecting *Stylosanthes scabra* at high CO_2. Pathogen-specific effects are common, and different stages of infection can be affected differentially with the cumulative effects resulting in the observed disease. However, perhaps as important as both the direct and indirect effects of CO_2 on pathogen growth and subsequent disease is the effect on pathogen fecundity, which has been shown to increase under elevated CO_2 levels leading to enhanced rates of pathogen evolution. Elevated ozone can have a similar range of effects (such as a 3–5-fold increase in rust infection on poplar), but this response is reduced by elevated CO_2.

Overall, the effects of elevated CO_2 concentration on plant disease can be positive or negative, although in a majority of the examples reviewed by Chakraborty *et al.* (2000), disease severity increased. Similarly, the effects of ozone and other abiotic stresses can be in either direction and the effects of many stresses are interactive, so it is not possible to generalize.

Temperature and drought effects

Disease resistance can be differentially affected by temperature. For example, cultivars of wheat on the UK Recommended List were routinely tested against isolates of brown rust (leaf rust) (*Puccinia recondita*) at 10 °C and 25 °C for 20 years. Generally about half showed differential resistance expression, either effective at 10 °C and not at 25 °C or vice versa (Jones, 2003). Browder and Eversmeyer (1986) also reported similar differential temperature responses in the same host–pathogen system, and both groups also demonstrated that the effect was not necessarily attributable simply to resistance gene expression as isolates showed differential responses too. Similar temperature sensitivities have been reported previously to the same rust, to *Puccinia striiformis*, and to *Puccinia tritici* in oats. Expression of resistance to broomrape in sunflower, black shank resistance in tobacco and rice resistance to *Xanthomonas oryzae* pv. *oryzae* provide other examples of temperature sensitivity.

Under drought stress, pathogens can have reduced impact or symptoms, but resistance expression can also be reduced. Resistance genes can also show temporary loss of expression due to stress or stress relief. For example, the sudden relief of drought stress resulted in a loss of effectiveness of the *mlo* resistance gene against powdery mildew in barley. This was probably not specific to the *mlo* gene but rather to the speed of resistance gene response which is critical for the efficacy of *mlo* gene expression. A possible mechanism for the changed levels of resistance is that enhanced levels of free radicals were found under drought-stressed conditions in the barley genotype which expressed most loss of resistance, whereas other genotypes did not differ significantly. Stress-related and defence-related gene expression were shown to be compromised in stress-relieved barley plants compared with non-stressed plants with the differences in accumulation of defence gene transcripts correlated with levels of resistance breakdown in different barley genotypes. The same breakdown problem occurred in response to sudden relief of cold stress but not salt stress. Together, these findings suggest that the efficacy of current resistance genes may be compromised under more extreme and variable climatic conditions.

Crop–pathogen interactions

Many pathogens exhibit so much capacity for generating, recombining, and selecting fit combinations of variants in key pathogenicity, fitness, and aggressiveness traits that there is little doubt that any new opportunities which result from crop responses to climate change will be exploited by them. However, there is also evidence that, under stressed conditions, some organisms enhance their ability to generate variants. For example, stress can stimulate the activity of retrotransposons thereby enhancing the generation of variability in pathogens such as *Fusarium oxysporum*. Similarly, in the Dutch elm disease fungi, *Ophiostoma ulmi* and *Ophiostoma nono-ulmi*, the mobility of its transposons is activated by stress. Organisms have genes which regulate such transposon activity in response to particular stress factors.

There is evidence for adaptive mutation and amplification as routes for inducible genetic instability which allow more rapid evolution under stress and an escape from growth inhibition. Enhanced mutation rate is specifically related to an increased background of reactive oxygen species characteristically produced in stress responses. Fungal pathogens such as *Phaeosphera nodorum* and *Phytophthora infestans* have been observed to generate very high levels of variability and Newton (1988) suggested that the mechanisms described facilitated mutant instability as a means of generating enhanced levels of variation for adaptation without disadvantageous mutation load. In higher plants, alternate splicing of mRNA is another mechanism which can give different gene products in response to stress, and stresses such as pathogen infection can induce this. Alternative intron processing has also been reported in the pathogens themselves, such as in the Oomycetes *Phytophthora* species and true fungi such as *Ustilago maydis*. Clearly these and other post-translational regulatory mechanisms may contribute to adaptive response to climate. In these ways enhanced genome plasticity can be achieved for response to environmental changes affecting gene expression levels and achieving ectopic recombination—changes which can later become fixed through conventional mutation and recombination.

Most models used to investigate the probable changes in pathogen prevalence are relatively simple and frequently employ climate-matching approaches. Others improve predictions by combining climate change models with other models such as a weather-based disease forecasting models. This approach, used to simulate the effects of climate change on *Phoma* stem canker on oilseed rape, has been modelled with respect to both its severity and spread over the next 10–20 years. The results clearly indicate not only increased severity across its existing range, but also rapid progress into more northern areas where the crop is largely disease-free at present. Another example of this type of model is the increased range of stem rust, and, in particular, the race known as Ug99 which has virulence towards the *Sr31* resistance gene (1B/1R translocation) which is used extensively in wheat varieties across the world. Barley is generally susceptible to Ug99 but hitherto not generally exposed to suitable climatic conditions. About 30 wild barley accessions have already been identified in a screen for effective resistance (B Steffenson, personal communication). There are several other examples where the distribution ranges of pathogens have been shown to change in response to climatic variables such as, for example, *Puccinia striiformis* f.sp. *tritici* in response to rainfall patterns in South Africa. Similarly, the northward extension of the range of needle blight (*Dothistroma septosporum*) is attributed to climate warming.

While such models are useful indicators of potential new diseases in hitherto disease-free areas, the effects of covariates and the details of complex interactions at other trophic levels are usually absent. For example, although populations of aphids may increase on cotton, the response of predators, such as wasps, is unknown. Similarly, while a combination of heat and drought may reduce the population of cereal aphids in southern Britain, if aphid predators are affected to an even greater degree, then the predicted reduction in aphids may be negated. Changes in crop rotations in response to climate change may also influence the future importance of specific pathogens. For example, if warming of northern latitudes enables forage maize to be grown in the rotation then this will leave residues in which pathogens such as Fusarium Head Blight (FHB) could build up high levels of inoculum for subsequent wheat and barley crops. Changes in land use will have many such implications for climate change (Dale, 1997). Effective deployment of crop diversity across all scales, from individual plant interactions to regions, results in the reduced progress of crop epidemics, improved resource utilization, and the enhanced stability of yield and quality. These, in turn, combine to enhance crop resilience to the effects of climatic stress, and stresses in general, thereby improving crop performance.

EXTREME EVENTS AND CROP PESTS AND PATHOGENS

Extreme events may become more frequent in the future, increasing the risks to crop yields. However, this is not always so and the consequence for yield is often dependent on the particular scenario that is considered (Porter and Semenov, 2005). Two main types of extreme events can be characterized either as (i) exceeding normal maxima or minima parameter ranges by a rare magnitude, or (ii) maintaining a normal maxima or minima for an unusually long duration. Events which do not normally occur in a region such as violent storms or floods can be included in these categories. Extreme parameters can include temperature (including lack of, or occurrence of, unseasonal frosts), precipitation (including snow, hail or extreme intensity), wind, light (e.g. lack of intensity due to cloud or dust), humidity, or any unusual sequences of such extremes or even unusual combinations, none of which is extreme on its own. The effect of extremes is illustrated by events in the summer of 2003 in parts of Europe, where temperatures were 6 °C warmer than long-term means and precipitation deficits of up to 300 mm were recorded. As a consequence, parts of the EU such as the Po valley in Italy, reported record reductions in maize yield of 36%. For the EU as a whole, uninsured losses were estimated at 13 billion Euros for 2003. In many respects, rapid changes in the climate caused by extreme events are likely to be more devastating for crop production if they lead to sudden pest outbreaks and disease epidemics because control measures are difficult to apply quickly enough or on a sufficiently large scale to contain the problem.

When addressing how climate change will affect pests, experimentalists have conventionally focused on long-term climate changes such as elevated global CO_2 concentration and air temperatures (reviewed above) but there are several examples of extreme events having impacts on pest incidence in the shorter term. Historically, there are also many examples of invertebrate food webs responding to short-term changes in climatic conditions. For example, conditions in the UK in 1975 and 1976 were particularly beneficial for aphids in terms of early development and reduced overwintering mortality, leading to large increases in aphid populations, including the cereal aphids *Sitobion avenae* and *Metopolophium dirhodum* (Jones, 1979). This caused an explosion in populations of predatory ladybirds (*Adalia* spp.) which fed on the abundant prey in early spring and developed to adult stage rapidly. Indeed, populations became so abundant that there were widespread reports of ladybirds biting humans when they had exhausted supplies of their aphid prey.

Extreme events can also have indirect or secondary consequences as illustrated by outbreaks of potato late-blight in Canada. The epidemics in 1994 to 1996 were due to genotypes of *Phytophthora infestans* from distant regions which were associated with the unusual tropical storm tracks moving up the eastern seaboard of the USA. In the UK, the unusually wet season of 2007, coinciding with the prevalence of epidemiologically-fit new pathotypes of *P. infestans*, resulted in an unprecedented number of outbreaks of late-blight. This was also reflected in the number of isolates and their genotypes.

The frequency of different genotypes of *Phytophthora infestans,* indicated by the different shaded sections of the bars, over five successive sampling years in the UK. Note the increased sample number together with increased frequency of a new fit genotype (black bar) in the unusually wet summer of 2007, when an unprecedented number of outbreaks of potato late-blight were reported.

CROPS, PESTS AND DISEASES IN THE CONTEXT OF FOOD SECURITY

The impacts of pests and diseases on yield in current conditions are well known, but the consequences of climate change on pests and diseases are complex and, as the preceding descriptions attest, are still only imperfectly understood. Scherm *et al.* (2000) highlighted the importance of pests and diseases both as important yield-reducing components and as early indicators of environmental changes because of their short generation times, high reproductive rates, and efficient dispersal mechanisms. Attempts have been made to model the effects of changing climate on the distribution of pests and pathogens particularly using climatic mapping to delineate potential distributions based on the concept of the fundamental niche. While such approaches are open to criticism because climate alone does not determine distribution and species interactions are ignored, climatic mapping provides a pragmatic means of investigating the potential for exotic pests and pathogens to establish in new areas and a basis for implementing phytosanitary controls to restrict the entry, for example, of karnal bunt (*Tilletia indica*) into Europe. Changing climate has already affected the geographical distribution of some crop pests and pathogens and advanced the appearance in the growing season of others. Some pests which are already present, but only occur in small areas or at low densities, may be able to exploit the changing conditions by spreading more widely and reaching damaging population densities. Aphids, for instance, key pests of agriculture, horticulture, and forestry throughout the world, are expected to be particularly responsive to climate change because of their low developmental threshold temperature, short generation time, and considerable dispersal abilities. Together, the effects of changing climate and more variable weather suggest that pest and pathogen attacks are likely to be more unpredictable and the amplitude larger. The consequences for other elements of agro-ecosystems and crop yields are still uncertain and greater effort is required to integrate this science into estimates of actual crop productivity.

The ability to include realistic impacts of pests and diseases in future climates has a direct link to considerations of food security. Ingram *et al.* (2008) point out that more mechanistic inclusion of pests and disease effects on crops would lead to more realistic predictions of crop production on a regional scale and thereby assist in the development of more robust regional food security policies. As described in the introduction, economic and social issues are often dominant determinants of household food security, but changed pest and disease incidence under climate change is an essential influence on future food security. The currently limited ability to model crop and pest and pathogen interactions, coupled with increased unpredictability of future pest and pathogen attacks means that systematic monitoring, increased research on the biology of the organisms, breeding of durable resistance in crops, and improved modelling of the many interacting processes, would be an essential underpinning investment for future food security.

FOOD SECURITY, CLIMATE CHANGE AND HEATH PROMOTION

The world's climate is clearly changing. Effects include heat waves, storms, flooding, droughts, sea level rise and air pollution. Each can harm health directly through, for example, heat stress, injuries, drowning, respiratory illnesses, as well as vector, food and water-borne diseases. However, the indirect effects of ecosystem change can be even more disastrous; likely impacts include food and water shortages, malnutrition, mass population movement, international conflict and consequential mental health disorders.

There is no cause for complacency as the Intergovernmental Panel on Climate Change demonstrated in their fourth assessment report (IPCC, 2007). 'There is high agreement and much evidence that with current climate change mitigation policies and related sustainable development practices, global green house gas emissions will continue to grow over the next few decades'. The health impacts of the IPCC projections include:

- In Africa by 2020, reduced yields from rain-fed agriculture by up to 50%, which would further adversely affect food security and exacerbate malnutrition.
- In Asia, increased endemic morbidity and mortality due to diarrhoeal disease primarily associated with floods and droughts.
- In Australasia by 2030, decreased production from agriculture and forestry over much of southern and eastern Australia and eastern New Zealand, due to increased drought and fire.
- In southern Europe, reduced water availability, hydropower potential and crop productivity due to higher temperatures and drought.
- In Latin America, decreased productivity of some important crops and livestock, with adverse consequences for food security and increased number of people at risk of hunger.
- In North America, decreased snow pack, more winter flooding and reduced summer flows, exacerbating competition for over-allocated water resources.
- In small islands, increased inundation, storm surge, erosion and other coastal hazards due to sea level rise, thus threatening vital infrastructure, settlements and facilities that support island communities.

Governments, arguably prompted by community concern and media commentary, are now responding across the globe, but sadly not all with the level of energy or sincerity required. International organizations are also reviewing their contributions.

For example, the World Bank has indicated a significant new direction through its forthcoming *Strategic Framework for Climate Change and Development.* The Framework will, among other things, provide direction on how adaptation—in agriculture and other impacted areas, such as flood-prone coasts—can be integrated into country, sectoral and regional development strategies.

In addition to economic, environmental and agricultural responses, there is also a pressing need for the health sector to prepare for and prevent potential health risks.

There have been calls for health services action by the IPCC and the World Health Organization as well as by numerous national bodies, for example the Australian Medical Association and Australian Conservation Foundation in a joint statement. The response of the health sector to date has been variable but encouragingly there appears to be increasing engagement. For example, in Australia a major conference on climate change and human health was held in October 2007 in Victoria to raise awareness of the public health challenges (DHS, 2007).

In the US, the Centers for Disease Control and Prevention have also taken a lead and identified the following priority health actions for climate change (CDC, 2008a):

1. Serve as a credible source of information on the health consequences of climate change for the United States and global populations.
2. Track data on environmental conditions, disease risks and disease occurrence related to climate change.
3. Expand capacity for modelling and forecasting health effects that may be climate-related.
4. Enhance the science base to understand better the relationship between climate change and health outcomes.
5. Identify locations and population groups at greatest risk for specific health threats, such as heat waves.

6. Communicate the health-related aspects of climate change, including risks and ways to reduce them, to the public, decision makers and healthcare providers.
7. Develop partnerships with other government agencies, the private sector, non-governmental organizations, universities and international organizations to address more effectively the US and global health aspects associated with climate change.
8. Provide leadership domestically and internationally to the private and public sectors including state and local governments, community leaders, healthcare professionals, non-governmental organizations and faith-based communities regarding health protection from climate change effects.
9. Develop and implement preparedness and response plans for health threats such as heat waves, severe weather events and infectious diseases.
10. Provide technical advice and support to state and local health departments, the private sector and others in implementing national and global preparedness measures related to the health effects of climate change.
11. Promote workforce development by helping to ensure the training of a new generation of competent, experienced public health staff to respond to the health threats posed by climate change.

Such public health responses, although necessary and urgent, tend to focus on managing the health consequences of climate change. In a parallel, there is also a compelling need to mobilize the capacity of the health sector in developing broader mitigation strategies and adaptive measures that concentrate more on the causes and determinants. This is the sort of ground well-trodden by health promoters but progress on the climate change agenda has been slow. This journal, for example, has received few articles on the subject.

In April 2008, however, an important breakthrough occurred with the publication of a guidance document by the UK Department of Health in collaboration with the Faculty of

Public Health, UK Public Health Association and the Chartered Institute of Environmental Health (DH, 2008). Developed by the South East Regional Public Heath Group, it contains advice for public health professionals on what can be done to mitigate and adapt to climate change and promote sustainable communities. One useful health promotion contribution is the development of a *Reducing Our Carbon Footprint Code* for the health sector, hospitals and communities, which is presented under the following headings:

1. Take a lead in addressing carbon emissions
2. Undertake a carbon audit
3. Place energy at the heart of the organization—save money, increase efficiency
4. Reduce water consumption and flooding
5. Make sustainable transport policies
6. Ensure sustainable catering and food procurement policies
7. Influence sustainable housing and the built environment
8. Develop a carbon neutral waste management policy
9. Promote local employment and skills

A core commitment of health promotion should now be to address the growing health impact of climate change. There are many opportunities that those working in the field can take which will complement and reinforce their own specific responsibilities and directions.

For example, all of us can adopt simple changes in our own lifestyle, e.g. *eat differently, travel differently, go green at home and work and be prepared* (CDC, 2008b). We can also advocate in our every day contacts about the health improvements and financial savings from producing less carbon and for the benefits of sustainable development.

In our diverse professional work, we should engage with and help individuals and communities understand the health consequences of climate change and encourage sustainable living. Health promotion practitioners should integrate climate change mitigation strategies into health program delivery and should strengthen partnerships with environmental and recreational groups, and those responsible for managing the built and natural environments.

To maximize the effectiveness of policy and legislation that target climate change, health policy makers should work cooperatively with decision makers in the economic, environment and energy sectors. Care must be taken, however, that new policy measures such as carbon taxes and carbon-trading schemes do not bear unfavourably on disadvantaged people with the least capacity to pay. This will result in diminished personal well-being and a further-reduced ability to comply with strategies designed to reduce greenhouse gas emissions (Nicholson, 2007).

Health Board Directors should secure organizational commitment, identify a 'Carbon Champion' and institute energy audits particularly focusing on reducing unnecessary travel. Managers of health facilities should improve electrical efficiency, building insulation and reduce water usage, and monitor progress against targets. They should assess preparedness for heatwaves and flooding.

3

Food Security in the Changing Global Climate

Food security is defined by FAO as the physical and economic access to food for all people at all times. Swaminathan (1983) has pleaded for enlarging this concept into one of Nutritional Security, since only access to balanced nutrition and safe drinking water can ensure that every child has an opportunity for the full expression of its innate genetic potential for physical and mental development. Today, there are marketable surpluses of food grains in most developed and in some developing countries like China and India. The widespread hunger prevailing in many nations of the world is not due to the non-availability of food in the market but is due to the lack of adequate purchasing power among the rural and urban poor. Inadequate purchasing power in its turn is due to insufficient opportunities for gainful employment. The famines of jobs and of purchasing power are becoming the primary causes for the famines of food in the households of the poor.

In most developing countries, land-and-water-based occupations consisting of crop husbandry, animal husbandry, fisheries and forestry are the major sources of employment and income in rural areas. In this context, agriculture assumes a more significant role in the development of national and global food and nutrition security systems than just being the source of food. Therefore, in predominantly agricultural countries, importing food would have the additional consequence of enhancing rural unemployment, when this is done to compensate for inadequate national attention to agricultural development. Thus food security has to be viewed in the contexts of food production, job creation and income generation. An additional issue of overriding importance, if we are to ensure that today's progress is not at the expense of tomorrow's prospects, is that of conservation of the ecological base for sustained agricultural production. The various issues relating to the sustainable production of food for the growing population have been dealt with by the Panel on Food Security and Environment, of the World Commission on Environment and Development (WECD, 1987). Although the problems we face today to promote sustainable nutrition security are staggering, we will have to be prepared to face the challenges of the future, particularly in relation to probable changes in climate. These include changes in precipitation and temperature, induced by increasing concentrations of CO2 and other industrial gases in the atmosphere. Also, with damage to the ozone layer, the incidence of UV radiation is likely to increase. We do not know the potential impact of higher levels of UV radiation on the yield of crops. These changes will have a visible impact in about 25 years from now. Whatever the magnitude of the changes may be, it will be prudent to make the scientific investment necessary to face different climate scenarios.

We should maximize the advantages of favourable weather and minimize the adverse impact of unfavourable weather on human, animal and plant populations. Since the oceans and inland waters may not be able to provide more than 5% of the total food needs, soil-based cultivation has to be the mainstay of our food and nutrition security system. But land is a shrinking resource for agriculture and we have to produce more and more food from less and less land and water in the decades ahead.

In this paper, some of the major problems and possibilities associated with food security and the projected changes in climate are discussed. The paper deals mainly with implications for the production of cereals since these are relevant to food security. Since climate effects on agricultural production and food security are important, we have considered the relevant issues under two scenarios as follows:

FOOD SECURITY IN THE CURRENT CLIMATE REGIME

The important consideration for food security is whether the food production would remain higher than the population growth rate. Between 1970 and 1982, the world population grew at a rate of 1.8% per annum but cereal production, which constitutes 94% of the total grain production, grew at a rate of 2.3% per annum. Thus food production outstripped population growth by 0.5% on a global scale. In 1986, 1942 million tonnes of food grains were produced for a population of 4915 million. Globally, this corresponds to about 395 kg of food grains per capita. But there were regional disparities to the extent that near-famine conditions occurred in many parts of the world. Thus, hunger existed amongst plenty and food production did not provide food security to everyone.

A United Nations study has projected the population size and growth rates for the periods between 1985 and 2000 and 2000 and 2025. The growth rate is likely to decline to 1.6 and 1.2% between 1985 and 2000 and 2000 and 2025, respectively. The projected world population is 6.1 billion in 2000 and 8.2 billion in 2025. Sanderson (1984) estimated per capita grain consumption in A.D. 2000 based on the expected per capita consumption in the recent past. Assuming that no significant changes in per capita grain consumption occur, the food grain requirements in various regions of the world were estimated. The global requirement of food grains in 2025 is about 3050 million tonnes, including food, feed and industrial use.

It has been pointed out in the WCED (1987) report, Food 2000, that food imports are not the answer for the increasing populations in developing countries—because importing leads to growing crops with export potential. Importing food also results in unemployment in predominantly agricultural countries. Coupled with this is the poor price of exported farm commodities in developed countries. This has resulted in the increasing indebtedness of developing countries, with several undesirable ecological and political consequences.

Assuming no significant change in food consumption patterns, the projected additional demand of food grains in 2025 over that in 1986, would be 330 Mt in Africa, 130 Mt in

South America, 582 Mt in Asia, 73 Mt in Europe and 16 MT in USSR. If individual regions are to be self-sufficient in food grains, the above projections lead to the following questions.

i) What changes in productivity and cultivated areas will be needed to grow the additional food grains?

ii) Will the regions requiring additional food grains be able to produce them?

Increase in Area and Productivity

Food production in different regions must increase substantially if each region has to meet its requirements. For example, production in Africa would have to increase almost fivefold and in Latin America threefold to meet the projected demand. In Asia, the required increase would be 1.75 fold whereas in USSR and Europe increases of the order of 1.25 and 1.82 fold would be needed.

In Asia and Europe, 83 and 88%, respectively, of the potentially arable land is already being cultivated. Therefore, yield increases would be the major or almost the exclusive means of realizing the projected food grain demands of these regions. In Africa and South America, since they have only 22 and 11% of the potentially arable land under cultivation, an increase in area could be a major means of additional food grain production. The USSR will have to combine both increases in yield and increases in the area under cultivation to meet the situation.

In regions where land is available, an appropriate strategy that balances the increases in productivity with that in land area needs to be developed. The relative emphasis on each of the two components for increasing production will differ in each region. One feasible combination of area and productivity. The rates of growth of area and productivity required to attain these levels of production.

Globally, the estimated arable land is 3190 million hectares, of which 1406 Mha is cultivated. Cereals account for 721 Mha, or nearly 50% of the total cultivated land. The remaining cultivated land is used for other crops. Assuming no change in this pattern, 2102 Mha would need to be cultivated by 2025, accounting for 65.8% of the arable land compared with the present 44%.

Factors Limiting Agricultural Production

Agricultural production operations include preparation of land, use of the appropriate crop and its cultivars, application of fertilizers and pesticides, and water management. All these operations require energy. Historically, draft animals provided a major source of energy (Pimental and Pimental, 1979). With mechanization providing a more efficient means of farm operations, draft energy was gradually replaced by fossil fuels. This has lead to a gradual decrease in farm families. As a result, today in developed countries less than 5% of the total population is engaged in agriculture. However, in developing countries agriculture continues to be the major occupation of a majority of the population (FAO, 1987).

In developed countries, the main agricultural operations and inputs have remained the same up to the early 1960s. Since then there has been a qualitative change after high yielding, short-stature cultivars replaced the conventional locally adapted cultivars. The new cultivars of wheat and rice required more fertilizer and better pest management. Since the productivity of these cultivars was higher, it made mechanization imperative. This in effect led to a situation where the commercial energy input became about equal to the equivalent energy output of edible grains (Slesser, 1986). If the energy input to the whole agricultural system was estimated, from land preparation to canned provisions in Supermarkets, then the commercial energy expended was greater than the solar energy harvested by the crops. Thus it would be virtually true to say that ultimately fossil fuels serve as food in developed countries.

In developing countries, agricultural production ranges from traditional to transitional and modern. The traditional agriculture is based on the use of local cultivars, almost no inputs of fertilizer and pesticides, poor water management, and draft energy. The transitional agriculture includes improved seeds, fertilizer, pesticides, water management, but mostly draft and human energy. The modern agriculture is mostly a replica of the Western agriculture with the exception that many practices, such as weeding and harvesting, are still manual. Therefore, in developing countries, more than 50% of the population continues to work on farms.

Thus, while projecting the need to produce food grains to meet the additional requirements in each region, it is important to consider the technological level of agriculture and the source of energy. Agricultural production systems are getting transformed in Asia and Africa. Many countries are moving from a traditional to a transitional form of agriculture. However, in all these instances draft energy continues to be the mainstay of agricultural production. Both in Africa and South America, the required additional land cannot possibly be brought under cultivation with draft energy alone. Consequently, there would be a need to introduce commercial energy into agricultural production. Sinha (1986) estimated the oil requirement for producing 2412 Mt of grain to meet the world demand in AD 2000, based on U.S. commercial energy-intensive and Indian transitional agricultural production. For each tonne of grain (wheat, rice and coarse grains) the U.S. technology uses 0.110 tons of oil whereas the Indian technology uses 0.038 tons of oil. The implications of this to food security has to be viewed in the context of the availability of fossil fuels. If the countries with food-grain deficits have to import grains from the United States or any other country, their cost would rise, whereas the indigenous resources of these nations may not be adequate to produce the required food grains.

Decreasing Fertilizer Response

Fertilizers and chemical control agents form an important component of farm inputs. FAO attributed the 55% increase in yield in developing countries between 1965 and 1976 to fertilizers. This implies that fertilizer consumption in developing countries in Africa, Asia and South America would have to rise substantially in the future. However, it is likely that the fertilizer response ratio would decrease with increasing fertilizer use in the way it has happened in the past five decades.

Limitations on the Genetic Improvement of Crops

A breakthrough in the improvement of rice and wheat was responsible for the worldwide increase in agricultural production, and for the green revolution in developing countries. Therefore, scientists, administrators, planners, politicians and the public have great faith in the possibility of developing new cultivars with greater yield potentials. However, it may appear surprising, though true, that the maximum yields of rice (Paddy) and wheat in experimental trials were reached in the late sixties at the International Rice Research Institute and CYMMIT. The rice yield was 10,130 and 7476 kg ha[-1] in the dry and wet seasons, respectively, in 1966-67. In 1986 the best variety gave 8200 kg ha[-1] in the dry season but only 4100 kg ha[-1] in the wet season. The maximum yields of bread and durum wheats at CYMMIT in 1968-69 were 9313 and 8458 kg ha[-1], respectively. In 1984, their corresponding maximum yields were 8403 and 8382 kg ha[-1]. The situation for other cereals is no different. A major change in rice productivity is that the yield of some recently developed cultivars is higher on a daily basis. Nonetheless, it is reasonably clear that we may have to wait for another scientific breakthrough for a major advance in the yield potentials of various cereal crops.

Degradation of the Resource Base

The urgent need to meet the food demands of the growing population and of industries has led to the degradation of the agricultural resource base on almost every continent. Often the poor are held responsible for environmental degradation, including the agricultural resources. The following statements at the public hearings of the World Commission on Environment and Development (WCED) sum up the situation beautifully.

Geoffrey Bruce of the Canadian International Development Agency said "Small farmers are held responsible for environmental destruction as if they had a choice of resources to depend on for their livelihood, when they really don't. In the context of basic survival, today's needs tend to overshadow consideration for the environmental future. It is poverty that is responsible for the destruction of natural resources, not the poor". Adolfo Mascarenhas of the International Union for Conservation of Nature and Natural Resources (IUCN) highlighted the African situation succinctly. "There are many contradictions in agricultural development. The blind imitation of models developed under different circumstances will have to give way to the realities and conditions existing in Africa. Large areas of virgin land have been opened up for export crops whose prices keep declining. This is not in the interest of developing countries."

"There are so many problems to be overcome that we forget that every problem is an opportunity to do something positive. This is an opportunity for us to think of conservation and environment in a broad educational context. In doing so, we will be able to capture the next generation and demonstrate the wonder and the benefits of the world around them".

The need for opening new land for cultivation, timber and fuelwood has caused extensive deforestation in different parts of the world. This, particularly in mountainous regions, has adversely influenced water conservation and led to soil erosion, silting and floods. Many river basins in India experience the impacts of deforestation. There is no conclusive evidence linking afforestation with precipitation but the loss of animal and plant genetic resources is clearly evident in many parts of the world.

Measures to be Adopted

Narrowing the gap between the maximum and the average national yields of crops would be the main objective of future research and development. Consequently, it would be important to analyse the contribution of different industrial inputs and environmental factors to assess the realizable potential of the genetically superior cultivars. The actual realization of this potential will be governed by the technologies adopted with respect to three factors:

a) land and water management

b) crop management

c) post-harvest management

These aspects have been discussed in sufficient detail in "Food 2000" (WECD, 1987).

CLIMATE CHANGE AND FOOD SECURITY

Food production in any given year is affected most directly by the values of the critical climate elements (temperature, radiation, precipitation, etc.) during the year. The stability of available food supplies is governed by the interannual variability of these elements. Access to food supplies in different regions of the world is determined by their share of the food production, the role of cereals in the diet of the people, and the various political and market forces that act upon the global food security system. The climate anomalies that occurred during the 1970s caused fairly small fluctuations in the world cereal supply. But they occurred at a time of an increasing use of cereal as livestock feed. The food shortages were particularly severe in the Soviet Union and its large grain purchases led to dramatic fluctuations in world cereal prices. The disastrous effects these had on the world food security system are now well documented (Garcia, 1981). Climate fluctuations of the kind witnessed in the 1970s lie within the variability of the present climate. They could have been anticipated by prudent societies if an eye had been kept on the climatic record. In addition to the normal variability of the climate, there is increasing evidence for a change in atmospheric optical properties as a result of the buildup of CO2 and other "greenhouse gases". It is also clear that their buildup will continue. It is expected that in the long term this will result in "climate change".

Mathematical models of the potential climatic impact of such a change have been developed by various groups. Such models attempt to predict the changes in critical climate elements for a doubling of the CO2 concentration. Although there is little agreement between various models about the specific magnitudes of the regional changes during the next 50 to 100 years, and details needed for regional planning, there is considerable agreement on the global changes, which may be summarized as follows:

1. The lower atmosphere will warm and the stratosphere will cool.
2. The annual average global warming will be 1.5 to 4deg.C. This is much greater than any natural climate change.

The rise in temperature is, in general, greater in the Northern Hemisphere than in the Southern Hemisphere and increases (by a factor of 2 to 3) polewards.

3. The temperature rise will be greater (by about 50%) in winter than in summer. Consequently, we may expect the production of winter season crops to be more affected than that of summer crops.
4. Freeze-free periods will lengthen in higher latitudes so that larger areas may be brought under cultivation, if soil conditions are suitable. The increase in the freeze-free period will depend on the current length of this period, e.g., a 1deg.C rise in temperature will lengthen an 80-day freeze-free period by about 20 days but a 120- to 130-day period by only 6 days.
5. General warming will be accompanied by a weakening of temperature differences between the equator and the poles, which will affect the atmosphere's general circulation. This could lead to longer dry periods.
6. The global average annual precipitation will increase by about 7 to 11%, but its regional and temporal variations are uncertain.
7. Relationship between precipitation and evaporation is not likely to change in the lower latitudes. Evaporation will increase more than precipitation in the mid-to higher latitudes.
8. Soil moisture conditions will be "wetter" in some regions of the world (35deg.N-35deg.S), but "drier" in others, compared with present conditions.
9. A sea-level rise is foreseen but its magnitude and time-scale are uncertain. The effects on agriculture in coastal regions could be disastrous.
10. Agroclimatic zones will shift poleward (about 100 km per degree of warming).
11. The variability of temperature and precipitation may decrease because of the weaker circulation. The regional variations are uncertain.

12. Only changes in mean climate conditions are specified by the models. Sizeable uncertainties remain about the timing, intensity and direction of specific effects.

However, it may be noted that climate is a complex, non-linear multiple feedback system with dominant positive feedbacks. From a cybernetic systems viewpoint, a fairly rapid forced change in such a system, such as a change in the CO_2 concentration, is likely to destabilize the system. The magnitude of the destabilization tends to be proportional to the rate of change of the forcing function.

Because the rate of change of CO_2 concentration is expected to be greatest between 2000 and 2060, these decades may experience chronic and severe weather variability (Markley and Hurley, 1983). One aspect of the climate change, even at the present level of CO_2 increase, is provided by a simulation study of Rowntree and Bolton (1983). They showed that, as a result of positive feedback, a hot, dry spell occurring in midsummer in central Europe, when coupled with a weak atmospheric circulation pattern, could persist for as long as 50 days and expand into Scandinavia, Spain and North Africa. Even under conditions of moist airflow, initial hot, dry conditions maintained themselves for up to 20 days.

Thus, even though mean changes in the global climate resulting from a doubling of CO_2 concentration can be anticipated, the specific changes in the annual variability of climate are uncertain during the period when the doubling is occurring. But, keeping with the complex, non-linear and multiple feedback characteristics of the climate system, it is likely that the next 50 to 100 years will experience chronic and severe climate variability.

What are the implications of climate change for the world food security system? To answer this it is necessary to examine the effects of climate change on both the regional food production as a result of changes in mean climate, as well as the variability of the food production resulting from increased climate variability. In the ultimate analysis, the annual variability of total food production as well as the regional share of production are the determinants of food security.

EFFECTS OF CLIMATE CHANGE ON FOOD PRODUCTION

The climate changes envisaged in the next century are mostly attributed to the increasing concentration of CO_2 and other "greenhouse gases". Since CO_2 is an essential reactant in photosynthesis to produce organic matter, it was postulated that farmers could look forward to better harvests (Wittwer, 1986). Often these postulates were based on short-term experiments in controlled environments or glasshouses with adequate supplies of water and plant protection measures. Rosenberg (1987) made an analysis of gas exchange and concluded that climate change, at least as far as CO_2 concentration effects are concerned, may prove advantageous. However, Gifford (1987) made a more cautious assessment of CO_2 effects by including temperature change as an additional component. The following observations are relevant for assessing the effects of climate change, including CO_2 concentration, on crop yields:

1. The highest yields in C3 crops are obtained around a mean daily temperature of 15deg.C and in C4 crops around 30deg.C.
2. The temperature optima for vegetative growth and the reproductive phases are often different. An increase of temperature beyond a mean of 22deg.C causes sterility in rice resulting in reduced grain yield, though it has no effect on photosynthesis. In wheat, an increase in mean temperature above 16deg.C results in a decrease in grain weight and a poor yield. A higher temperature significantly reduces tillering, which is essential to building shoot population.
3. The crops having a high growth rate in the preflowering phase usually deplete soil moisture, which is necessary to normally complete the grain development phase. Consequently, high initial growth, in the absence of irrigation, results in a poor grain yield despite high dry matter accumulation.

Gifford (1987) estimated the rise in temperature that would cancel out the advantageous effects of CO_2 fertilization. At locations ranging from 50deg.N in Canada to 37deg.S in Australia a rise of 1.5deg. to 2.4deg.C is required to cancel the advantageous effects of CO_2 on grain yield, presumably under irrigated conditions. In the absence of irrigation, crop yields may in fact be reduced.

The optimistic predictions for agricultural production made by several people in the recent past based on CO_2 fertilization effects should not lead to complacency about the question of food security. These projections have been based on a study of the individual effects of only one or two factors. It should be recognized that agricultural production is a complex process. The available evidence on CO_2 fertilization effects, when two or more factors are simultaneously considered is, at best, inconclusive.

Effect of Changes in Mean Temperature and Precipitation

Crop production is directly influenced by temperature and precipitation. Both are critical elements for determining the agroclimatic zones. Temperature determines the duration of a crop's growing season and controls its phenological development and water requirements. Precipitation provides the critical input for crop growth, water. The distribution of these variables during the period of crop growth is also critical. But, information on intraseasonal variations in temperature and precipitation in the 2 x CO_2 climate is not available. This discussion is, therefore, limited to anticipated changes in seasonal/annual values of the variables. The direct effects of CO_2 on crop yields are excluded since the available information is inconclusive.

In general, an increase in the average annual temperature will result in shorter freeze periods than now. As a result, larger areas can be brought under cultivation at the climatic margins. But, in the existing crop belts, the growing season duration will be reduced and productivity (crop yield) losses will result. Some crops may also be forced out of cultivation to be replaced by others. To what extent the losses in crop yield can be compensated by the increases in crop area is uncertain and will be governed to a significant extent by technology. An increase in precipitation will have beneficial effects on both productivity and crop area.

Wheat, rice and maize are the three major crops of the world accounting for about 80% of its total cereal production in 1985. The impacts of changed climate conditions on their production, when considered independently and assuming current levels of technology. The climate scenario considered here is based on temperature changes predicted by the GFDL model for various regions (latitude limits) for the summer and winter seasons. This model predicts the maximum increases compared with those of other commonly used models, GISS and NCAR (Rosenberg, 1987). Precipitation scenarios are considered indirectly by using the results presented by Kellogg and Schware(1981). The impacts on production are indicated as increases (+) or decreases (-) over current crop yields or areas. The results are presented for the countries/regions that accounted for significant shares of each crop's production in 1985.

The following observations may be made:

1. In mid-to higher latitudes (developed countries) significant increases in area, accompanied by reductions in crop yield are expected. In the lower latitudes, because of increasing temperature, significant areas become unavailable for wheat and yields will also decline. An increase in water requirements may be anticipated in all regions in these latitudes, and irrigation management will acquire a greater significance. A net reduction in wheat production is anticipated, with the balance of production shifting further in favour of developed countries.
2. About 94% of the rice is grown in developing countries mostly during the summer monsoon. However, better yields are obtained in the dry season when temperatures are lower and pest problems are fewer. An increase in precipitation would help increase the area of this crop and its yield, but an increase in temperature promotes sterility and yields would be reduced. Almost one third of the rice is grown under upland unirrigated conditions

that may benefit from increased precipitation. On a balance it would appear that developing countries will continue to be major growers of rice, and this crop will continue to be a major diet of the people in these regions.

3. The mid-latitudes account for more than 50% of the maize production. Increased precipitation may increase the share of the developing countries in the world's maize production.

Overall, the declines in the production levels of wheat are expected whereas the production of rice may remain unaffected and maize may increase, under a doubled-CO2 climate. The existing wheat production imbalances in favour of the developed countries may be further accentuated. Similarly, the share of developing countries in rice production may also rise. Maize production may become more uniform across developed and developing countries.

The above analysis excluded the possibility of replacing one crop by another more suitable for the changed climate conditions. But this is expected to happen. For example, wheat belts may be replaced by barley, barley by maize, maize by sorghum and so on. Rice may be substituted if adequate irrigation facilities are available. But these substitutions are likely to take place only gradually since there will be problems of adaptation.

The current advantage, with respect to food security, remains with the developed countries primarily because of the rapid progress of technology or the absence of population pressure or both. Based on currently available information it is clear that these two factors will continue to be the significant determinants of food security, whether a climate change occurs or not.

Effects of Climate Change on Pests and Diseases

Currently about 25% of food is lost as a result of pest damage. Today the high productivity of various crops in temperate regions could be attributed not only to improved technology, but also to the limited number of diseases and pests, better soil health including microflora and better response to fertilizers. The generally warmer and moist conditions in the changed climate coupled with a low general circulation and longer freeze-free periods are highly conducive to crop pests. By far, the most predictable effect of climate change is that it will cause significant increases in the pest populations. Thus, some of the advantages of existing temperate regions may be canceled by increased temperature and uncertain precipitation.

Climate Change and Variability of Food Production

Under the current climate, the coefficient of variation (CV) of the global total cereal production for the trend in the 1970s was about 3% (Anderson et al., 1987), but is higher in some individual countries. The variability is greatest in semi-arid areas and least in humid areas. The regions of high variability also have low average crop yields. CV also tends to be less in larger countries because risk pooling is spread across regions and crops.

For individual crops at the global level, the CVs of maize, sorghum, wheat and rice around the trend are about 4, 6, 5 and 4%, respectively, but are higher in individual countries. For example, in India, the CVs of wheat, rice and sorghum are 11, 8 and 16%, respectively. In the United States, the values for maize, winter wheat and sorghum are 10, 10 and 11% respectively (Hazell, 1984). Some of the sources of inter-annual variability in national agricultural production are:

i) Variability of weather

ii) Variability of areas sown under different crops

iii) Variability of yield correlations between regions and crops

iv) Production expansion into riskier regions

v) Increased sensitivities of new technologies to weather and disease

vi) Variations in agricultural prices, policy and levels of rural infrastructure

The relative contribution of these factors to the overall variability of food production is different in different regions. It also depends on the current level of production variability in the region. For example, the variability in cereal production in India was shown to be (Hazell, 1984) a consequence of the increased adoption of high yield technology and the variability of weather, crop yields, areas cropped and prices. On the other hand, the predominant sources of production variability in the United States were crop yields and yield correlations between states.

In this context the question relevant to food security under future CO2-induced changes of climate is whether such climate changes will lead to an increased or decreased variability of food production. Even when anticipated changes in mean climate conditions only are considered, it is clear (from the previous section) that an increased variability of production would result from sources (ii) to (v) listed above. When an increased variability of weather (i) resulting from climate change is also included, significant increases in the variability of food supplies are foreseen.

This leads to many concerns that need to be addressed by the international community. Prominent among these are: perceptions of increased risk that may discourage the adoption of new technologies and retard agricultural growth; increased instability of national and international food supplies; increased frequencies of droughts and floods over larger areas; increased destabilizing effects of agricultural prices on food production and consumption; and risk pooling across regions and crops by diversification of the crop production systems.

CLIMATE IMPACT ASSESSMENT

Climate fluctuations influence the lives of millions of people around the world. There are now several studies on the interaction of climate and society. Whether climate change induced effects could be discerned as a warning or as an attempt to mitigate adverse effects are important questions. Parry et al. (1987) have developed a methodology based on climate impact assessment in marginal areas. This is useful when the objective of such studies is to evaluate the sensitivity of ecosystems to climate changes However, food security is concerned more with stabilizing the available food supplies. Both national and global food security are dependent more on the stable and productive areas than on the marginal areas. For example, in India, seven out of 35 meteorological divisions are important determinants of food security (Sinha, 1987). This is clear from the impact of droughts of nearly equal magnitude on national food production in the two years, 1979-80 and 1982-83. There was a 17% shortfall in grain production in 1979-80 compared with the previous year's 131.4 Mt.

However, in 1982-83, food grain production declined by only 3.7% relative to the previous year's 133.3 Mt. This was because, in this year, the highly productive divisions were not affected (Sinha, 1987). Therefore, for the assessment of food security, it is necessary that thc impact of climate fluctuations on productive areas be studied as well. For studying global food security, it may be prudent to perform such studies on a selected group of nations.

Conclusions

1. The projected population growth rates and the ensuing food demands, even in the current global climate, would make it difficult to provide for human sustenance and food security in the twenty-first century.
2. Africa and South America are the most vulnerable regions in regard to food security. The food demands of these regions can be met by increasing the cultivated area. Asia is next in order of vulnerability. Significant increases in crop productivity are required in this region since it is difficult to bring additional areas under cultivation. Appropriate strategies for increasing agricultural production that balance an increase in cultivated area with an increase in crop productivity need to be designed for various regions of the world.
3. There is a near-consensus that the rising concentrations of CO2 and other greenhouse gases in the atmosphere will lead to a climate change. This will directly affect agricultural production and food security.
4. Some recent reports on the favourable impact of climate change on agricultural production should not lead to complacency. The available evidence in support of this

is inconclusive and is not based on the complex dynamics of interactions between agricultural production processes and the environment.

5. Two aspects of the effects of the changing climate on agricultural production and food security need to be considered:
   i) Changes in the mean values of the critical variables that will affect the trends of global agricultural production and the regional shares of production.
   ii) Increased instability of climate that will result in greater instabilities in food supplies.
6. In the 2 x CO2 climate, an overall decline in production of wheat may be expected as a consequence of an increase in temperature in mid-latitudes. The production of rice may be unaffected whereas that of maize may increase as a result of the increased area and wetness in lower latitudes. Food supplies in smaller nations are likely to be affected more by the climate change compared with those in larger nations. This is because of the advantage of risk pooling across regions and crops in large nations.
7. Even in the changed climate, the current balance of food supplies in favour of the developed nations will continue. In the future also, even more than now, technology and resource management will continue to determine this balance. The availability of energy, the decreasing marginal response of crops to fertilizers relative to that in the 1960s and 1970s, the leveling off of the production potential of major cereals and the eroding natural resource base will be the major limiting factors on the agricultural technology of the future.

Implications for Research and Policy

Measures to improve food security by maintaining adequate food reserves and developing efficient transportation and distribution networks require huge capital resources. The planners in many small nations are reluctant to commit the financial resources required to establish such networks. But in a changing climate, the smaller nations will also be the most vulnerable in regard to food security. Such nations may be encouraged to group and pool the resources required for stepping up food security measures. This will also provide the advantage of risk-pooling across regions and crops, and the group of nations as a whole will be less susceptible to climate effects. In the long term, the adoption of food security measures will come to be viewed in the broader context of regional development. Specific studies need to be initiated on the criteria to be adopted for forming the nation groups, the crops and production technologies required, the appropriate balance between increasing crop area and productivity, and the related aspects of infrastructural development such as transportation, distribution and marketing networks.

In the future, particularly in the changing climate conditions, to ensure food security will require a greater emphasis than now on land and water management, crop management and post-harvest management. The availability of energy will be a significant factor affecting production. Developments in the use of non-polluting, renewable resources of energy will play a significant role in conserving the resource base of agricultural production. Any major breakthrough in this sector, should be globally shared without reservations about political, social or economic considerations. Such a breakthrough, in addition to supporting agricultural production, would help control the "greenhouse effect" itself and will be to the benefit of mankind. Considerable additional research is required on the annual, seasonal and intraseasonal variabilities of climate in individual regions. Linkages between the results of this research and agricultural production need to be established. The predictive power of GCMs has to be extended considerably before this can be done.

An important issue of research, in the context of food security, relates to the methodology of climate impact assessment. Current methodologies, developed for impact assessment in marginal areas, are not directly applicable. Such methodologies are useful as long as the goal of research is to analyse and demonstrate the sensitivities of agroecological and social systems to climate change. In this case, the marginal areas provided the analytical advantage required for isolating the effects of climate variables. However, to provide food security, the major source of food is agricultural production in regions with a high potential for production. In these regions, it is difficult to isolate the climate effects from other factors. Thus, on the question of food security in a changing climate, methodological issues relating to climate impact assessment need to be critically addressed.

Specific research is required on the costs of not considering the effects of climate change when planning and designing agricultural production and food security systems with lifetimes of several decades. Examples are irrigation systems and agricultural expansion in coastal areas.

The instability of food supplies results from various sources. These include, in addition to climate variability, the uncertainties in agricultural policy. Whereas the effects of climate variability are difficult to anticipate and control, the resulting instabilities may be minimized through appropriate food policy.

This requires from individual nations explicit statements about their food policy objectives (efficient growth of agriculture and related sectors, income distribution through employment, subsidies, insurance, etc.), and their specific programs and policies, not just projects.

Many projects in tropical Africa achieved only a limited success because a framework for monetary, fiscal and trade policy did not exist. In recent times, considerable progress has been made in drawing the attention of policy-makers to the issues related to climate change. But much more persuasion is needed before their interest gets translated into public policy and action. This requires developing the capabilities for obtaining and analysing information, developing policy alternatives and presenting them to development planners to initiate action. Simultaneously, it must be recognized that the political will to initiate action is driven by public opinion. Informed public opinion must be mobilized through the systematic communication of available research information.

IMPACT OF CLIMATE CHANGE ON SMALLHOLDER AND SUBSISTENCE AGRICULTURE

Although both are widely used terms, there are surprisingly few published definitions of either "subsistence agriculture" or "smallholder agriculture." Subsistence farming has been defined by Barnett *et al.* as "farming and associated activities which together form a livelihood strategy where the main output is consumed directly, where there are few if any purchased inputs and where only a minor proportion of output is marketed." However, the term is also sometimes used to denote the activity of self-provisioning with agricultural produce or a relative move toward such activity, as in developments in Eastern Europe following the end of the planned economies. It is also frequently used in a nontechnical sense to describe the rural poor of developing countries. Such a usage diverts attention from the fact that market relations have entered deeply into agriculture in virtually all parts of the world, and that many of these farmers' most important problems stem from the terms of their inclusion in the market.

"Smallholder agriculture" is used more generally to describe rural producers, predominantly in developing countries, who farm using mainly family labor and for whom the farm provides the principal source of income. Definition of "peasants," for example as given by Ellis, are similar but give more emphasis to inclusion in wider economic systems and imperfect markets. "Smallholder and subsistence farmers" is used here to denote these farmers, who can be found on a continuum between subsistence production and concentration on crop production for the market. Definitions by scale are relative to national contexts, and "smallholders" in transitional or developed countries may have farms (and incomes) many times larger than those in developing countries.

Pastoralists, who almost all depend on the sale of livestock and livestock products to buy staple foods and other necessities and people dependent on artisanal fisheries and aquaculture enterprises are also included in this category. All suffer, in varying degrees, similar problems associated with isolation and low levels of technology, but also unpredictable exposure to world markets. These systems have been characterized as "complex, diverse and risk-prone".

Farms are generally small, often held under traditional or informal tenure, and are in marginal or risk-prone environments. Soil-related constraints to productivity are widespread, severe, and increasing, although diversity of soils and farmer soil management strategies is also important. Production systems are complex and diverse in the combinations of plant and animal species exploited, the types of integration between them, the production objectives and the institutional arrangements for managing natural resources. Risks are also various—drought and flood, crop and animal disease, and market shocks—and may be felt by individual households or entire communities. Smallholder and subsistence farmers and pastoralists often practice hunting/gathering of wild resources as well as crop and livestock production to fulfil energy, clothing, health, and cash income needs as well as direct food requirements. They also widely participate in off-farm and/or nonfarm employment. Beyond these points, smallholder agriculture is subject to what has been called "the centrality of the social:" its grounding in social relations within households (particularly gender relations) and between households, profoundly affecting the negotiation of production decisions, management of knowledge, and marketing.

Given the lack of clear and standardized definitions of these categories, there are few informed estimates of world or regional population of smallholder or subsistence farmers. The United Nations Food and Agriculture Organization (FAO), for example, does not publish data disaggregated to these categories. Although not all smallholders, even in developing countries, are poor, data published by international agencies concerned with rural poverty give some idea of the scale of these livelihood systems. According to The International Fund for Agricultural Development (IFAD), 75% of the world's 1.2 billion poor (defined as consuming less than one purchasing-power adjusted dollar per day) live and work in rural areas. The developing-country rural population were smallholders (farming 3 ha or less of crop land), and H"25% were landless, which may have included some agricultural laborers, nonpastoralist livestock keepers, and poor people not engaged in agriculture. The proportion of smallholders in sub-Saharan Africa was higher at 73%. Smallholders are responsible for cultivating a hugely variable proportion of land across developing countries. They are responsible in many countries for very high proportions of food and cash crop production, for example, 90% of rice, wheat, other food crops, cocoa, and cotton in Nigeria.

The complex interaction of such stressors in increasing vulnerability can be illustrated with reference to pastoralists of the Horn of Africa and elsewhere. There are debates on whether environmental degradation in such tropical dryland areas is widespread, irreversible or appropriately referred to as "desertification", but there are, at the least, important processes of localized environmental degradation around small towns that are driven by the sedentarization of destitute pastoralists but also further weaken their livelihoods. Enclosure of land for farming by outsiders and by pastoralists themselves and demarcation of rangelands as Protected Areas has also been an issue: at the basis of all of these is a lack of government recognition of communal ownership of rangelands and traditional natural resource management.

Human population increase, long neglected in pastoral studies, has been given new prominence by Sandford, who argues that its recognition, alongside other stressors, necessitates a major shift in views on pastoral development, with greater emphasis on diversification away from pastoralism and out-migration from the rangelands. Pastoralists are also subject to market-related stressors: the rapid withdrawal of government and parastatals from direct involvement in livestock purchasing and meat processing in Kenya in the 1980s is still lamented by Kenyan pastoralists. Although Horn of Africa pastoralists do not trade directly with Europe or North America, they are heavily involved in trade with Middle Eastern countries, in which they have been highly vulnerable to abrupt import bans on meat and livestock on veterinary grounds, in some cases with disputed scientific justification, but also seen as an indicator of a general trend to greater concern of Arab markets with meat quality and safety. Although there is a serious lack of information, but some concern, about the impact of HIV/AIDS on these pastoral populations, the impacts of armed conflicts, from international wars to quasitraditional raiding, on pastoralists throughout the region are now well known. All these, and other stressors, are seen as contributing to an increased vulnerability to drought, which in turn feeds back in to environmental degradation, conflict and underdevelopment of markets.

However, all of the populations grouped as smallholder and subsistence farmers, including pastoralists and artisanal fisherfolk, also possess certain important resilience factors: efficiencies associated with the use of family labor, livelihood diversity allowing spreading of risks, and indigenous knowledge allowing exploitation of risky environmental niches and coping with crises.

The combinations of stressors and resilience factors give rise to complex positive and negative livelihood trends, envisaged differently by different authors, and depending largely on policy environments. Rural–urban migration will continue to be important; urban population growth in many large developing country cities is >4% per annum, and rural migrants account for between 35% and 60% of recorded urban population growth. Within rural areas, there will be continued diversification away from agriculture: nonfarm activities already account for 30–50% of rural income in developing countries.

Although Vorley, Hazell, Lipton, and Toulmin and Gueye see the possibility, given appropriate policies, of pro-poor growth based on the efficiency and employment generation associated with family farms, it is overall likely that smallholder and subsistence households will decline in numbers, as they are pulled or pushed into other livelihoods, with those that remain suffering increased vulnerability and increased poverty. The decline in numbers and qualitative changes in livelihoods mean that global and regional projections made for the category of smallholder and subsistence farmers will be progressively less meaningful over the medium-and long-term time scales associated with research and modeling on climate change.

Coping and Adaptation

Smallholder, subsistence, and pastoral systems, especially those located in marginal environments, areas of high variability of rainfall or high risks of natural hazards, are often characterized by livelihood strategies that that have been evolved (*i*) to reduce overall vulnerability to climate shocks ("adaptive strategies"), and (*ii*) to manage their impacts *ex-post* ("coping strategies"). The distinction between these two categories is however frequently blurred : what start as coping strategies in exceptional years can become adaptations for households or whole communities.

Many defining features of dryland livelihoods in Africa and elsewhere can be regarded as adaptive strategies to climate variability. For example, Mortimore and Adams for Northern Nigeria mention five major elements of adaptation:

- Allocating farm labor across the season in ways that follow unpredictable intra-season rainfall variations: "negotiating the rain."
- Making use of biodiversity in cultivated crops and wild plants.
- Increasing integration of livestock into farming systems (at a cost of increased labor demands).
- Working land harder, in terms of labor input per hectare, without increasing external non-labor inputs.
- Diversifying livelihoods.

Other authors have mentioned on-farm storage of food and feed, strategic use of fallow, and late planting of legume crops when cereals fail as drought responses—examples from rain-fed areas of Morocco.

African pastoralism has evolved in adaptation to harsh environments with very high spatial and temporal variability of rainfall. Several recent studies on Northern Kenya and Southern Ethiopia reviewed by Morton have focused on the coping strategies used by pastoralists during recent droughts and the longer-term adaptations that underlie them

- *Mobility* remains the most important pastoralist adaptation to spatial and temporal variations in rainfall, and in drought years many communities make use of fall-back grazing areas unused in "normal" dry seasons because of distance, land tenure constraints, animal disease problems, or conflict. However, encroachment on and individuation of communal grazing lands and the desire to settle to access human services and food aid have severely limited pastoral mobility.

- Pastoralists engage in *herd accumulation*, and most evidence now suggests that this is a rational form of insurance against drought. There is considerable debate on the extent to which pastoralists cope by systematically selling livestock during drought or drought-onset, and why they might not do this, but some evidence that they would sell more stock if markets were more efficient.
- Pastoralists classically keep multispecies herds to take advantage of different ecological niches and the labor of men, women, and children. Shifts in the balance of species can occur as responses to climate variability and changes in the environment, market conditions, and availability of labor.
- A small proportion of pastoralists now hold some wealth in bank accounts, and others use informal savings and credit mechanisms through shopkeepers.
- Pastoralists also use *supplementary feed* for livestock, purchased or lopped from trees, as a coping strategy, they intensify *animal disease management* through indigenous and scientific techniques, and they increasingly *pay for water* from powered boreholes.
- *Livelihood diversification* away from pastoralism in this region predominantly takes the form of shifts into low-income or environmentally unsustainable occupations such as charcoal production, rather than an adaptive strategy to reduce *ex-ante* vulnerability.
- There are a number of *intracommunity mechanisms*, to distribute both livestock products and the use of live animals to the destitute, but these appear to be breaking down due to high levels of covariate risk within communities.

Shifting to irrigated farming is sometimes seen as a coping strategy in the face of climate variability across the developing world. Eakin describes this for Mexico, but notes that the interaction of market uncertainty with climatic risk may in fact increase the vulnerability of households making this shift. In South Asia, agricultural strategies such as increasing livestock production relative to crops, and selection of crop varieties, are responses to both drought and floods, but several case studies show the importance of livelihood diversification, in the villages and in towns, and both responsively to disaster and proactively. These and other studies also show the importance of information and networks or social capital in coping with climate change and variability.

Complexity and Location Specificity

Impacts on these systems should be considered in terms of hard to predict compound impacts highly specific to location and livelihood systems in different ecosystems and regions of the world. These livelihood systems are typically complex; they involve a number of crop and livestock species, between which there are interactions—for example, intercropping practices or the use of draught animal power for cultivation, and potential substitutions such as alternative crops. Many smallholder livelihoods will also include use of wild resources, and nonagricultural strategies, such as use of remittances. Coping strategies for extreme climatic events such as drought typically involve changes in the relative importance of crops, livestock species and nonagricultural activities, and in interactions between them. Positive and negative impacts on different crops may occur in the same farming system. Agrawala *et al.* suggest that impacts on maize, the main food crop, will be strongly negative for the Tanzanian smallholder, whereas impacts on coffee and cotton, significant cash crops, may be positive.

Nonclimate Stressors and Vulnerability

The intrinsic vulnerability of smallholder and subsistence farmers has been discussed above, as have the diverse powerful nonclimate stressors to which they are currently and increasingly subject. All these contribute to a very specific context of high vulnerability and limited adaptive capacity. Management of nonclimate stressors, such as poor market access, by governments and development donors, would itself constitute a powerful strategy for assisting adaptation, but some stressors, particularly various forms of environmental degradation, will themselves be influenced by climate change. Approaches to mapping the combined vulnerability of rural populations to climate change and nonclimate stressors, have been explored for globalization by O'Brien and Leichenko and for HIV/AIDS by Gommes *et al.*

Biological Processes at Organism and Field Level

Easterling *et al.* and relevant articles in this volume show the growing understanding of the direct impacts of changes in temperature, CO_2, and precipitation on yields of specific food and cash crops and productivity and health of livestock. In particular:

- New syntheses of the growing number of regional and global simulation studies of changes in crop yields against temperature suggest that in the tropics, even moderate temperature increases (1–2°C) are likely to have negative impacts on yields of rice, maize, and wheat (the three major cereals worldwide and among smallholder and subsistence farmers). Higher levels of warming will have serious negative impacts on yields of maize and wheat, and less so on rice. Where simulations have included the effects of agronomic adaptation strategies, trends still represent declining yields at all levels of warming.
- Increases in temperature may increase irrigation water requirements of major crops, increasing water stress, particularly in Southeast Asia.
- The conclusion of the Third Assessment Report of the IPCC of likely significant negative impacts on semiarid rangelands is confirmed, although there are still very few impact studies for tropical grasslands or rangelands. There is also new knowledge on the direct negative effects of thermal stress on productivity, conception rates and health of livestock, that may be relevant to

exotic (*Bos taurus*) cattle kept for small-scale dairy production in the tropics.

- There is evidence of increased risk of crop pests and diseases of crops under climate change, although knowledge of likely impacts in the tropics and on smallholder systems is much less developed. Modeling responses of both pathogens and (where relevant) insect vectors to rising temperatures and changing precipitation is complex, but there is cause for concern over possible spread of major diseases that attack smallholder crops in Africa: e.g., Maize Streak Virus and Cassava Mosaic Virus in areas where rainfall increases, and sorghum head smut (a fungal disease) in areas where rainfall decreases (which would be compounded by farmers switching adaptively to sorghum in areas where maize becomes marginal). For diseases of livestock, modeling studies suggest overall slight declines in habitat suitable for tsetse-transmitted trypanosomiasis and East Coast Fever, although effects will be localized. Increased frequency of floods may increase outbreaks of epizootic diseases such as Rift Valley Fever and African Horse Sickness.

A general principle that crosscuts these projections of impacts on crops and livestock species is the increased understanding of the importance of extreme events. Increases in frequency of extreme events may go beyond the impacts of mean climate change in lowering long-term yields by damaging crops at particular developmental stages, making the timing of agricultural operations more difficult, and reducing incentives to cultivate. Increased frequency of heat waves and heavy precipitation events is regarded as very likely by IPCC Working Group 1 and increased drought regarded as likely. Burke *et al.* demonstrate the risk of widespread drought in many regions including Africa. Focus on extreme events in much of the literature on developing countries implicitly recognizes that their impacts are likely to be felt more strongly than the impacts of changing means in the medium-term (to 2025), a point made explicitly by Corbera *et al.*.

Environmental and Physical Processes

Another class of impacts is felt at the level of communities, landscapes, and watersheds, and has been less considered in literature on climate change and agriculture, although there is some overlap with consideration given to extreme events. One such impact is the effects of decreasing snowcap on major irrigation systems involving hundreds of millions of smallholders, particularly in the Indo-Gangetic plain. As a result of warming, less precipitation falling as snow, and earlier spring melting, there will be a shift in peak water supply to winter and early spring and away from the summer months when irrigation is most needed, with likely severe effects in areas where storage capacity cannot be expanded. Combined with increased water demand, and preexisting vulnerability of many poorer irrigated farmers, such an impact could be catastrophic.

Also to be included here are effects of climate change on soil fertility and water-holding properties. Global warming and accompanying hydrological changes are likely to affect all soil processes in complex ways, including by accelerated decomposition of organic matter and depression of nitrogen-fixing activity. Kundzewicz *et al.* note the projected increased erosivity of rainfall, and several factors likely to increase the erodibility of soils worldwide.

Other examples of such environmental or larger-scale impacts are the effects of sea level-rise on coastal areas, increased intensity of landfall tropical storms, and other forms of environmental impact still being identified, such as increased forest fire risk for the Mount Kilimanjaro ecosystem and remobilization of dunes for semiarid Southern Africa.

Nonagricultural Climate Change Impacts

The above impacts on agriculture will be combined with impacts on human health and ability to provide labor for agriculture, such as increased malaria risk, and on important secondary nonfarm livelihood strategies for many rural people in developing countries. One such strategy involves activities connected to tourism, and some negative impacts of climate change on tourism in developing countries have already been projected.

The above framework shows how complex and location-specific the projection of climate change impacts on smallholder and subsistence agriculture will be. A further complexity is given by the problem of distinguishing impact and adaptation. These systems are already characterized by constant adaptation to climate variability, which is forming the basis of adaptation to climate change: there will be profound methodological problems in observing or predicting impacts that do not also involve adaptation.

In general, however, the location of a large body of smallholder and subsistence farming households in the dryland tropics gives rise to especial concern over temperature-induced decline in crop yields, and increasing frequency and severity of drought. These lead to the following generalizations:

- increased likelihood of crop failure;
- increased diseases and mortality of livestock and/or forced sales of livestock at disadvantageous prices ;
- livelihood impacts including sale of other assets, indebtedness, out-migration and dependency on food relief.;
- possible feedbacks through unsustainable adaptation strategies into environmental degradation including loss of biodiversity ; and
- eventual impacts on human development indicators such as health and education.

IMPLICATIONS FOR FUTURE RESEARCH NEEDS

Understanding the interactions between the different forms of climate change impact will require further research on a variety of topics, and with a variety of approaches. One need is for modeling work based on a thorough understanding of the complexities of specific real-world smallholder systems. The multiagent modeling of Bharwani *et al.* is one possible approach here. Also important will be increased empirical research on the circumstances under which current strategies to cope with extreme events foster or constrain longer-term adaptation.

Knowledge of crop responses to climate change also needs to be extended to more crops, livestock, and wild species of interest to smallholders and subsistence farmers, such as tropical rootcrops, sorghum and millet, beverage crops, backyard poultry and pigs, and acacia-based browse systems. A further need is for research on the impacts of climate change on the storage and marketing of smallholder crops: including losses to insect pests and pathogens of crops stored on-farm or by small traders, damage in transport, and indirect costs of being less able to store on farm and more vulnerable to seasonal price swings.

Beyond these needs for research into impacts are needs for research into adaptation. Many of the potential agronomic adaptations identified, including improved soil and water conservation, are highly relevant to smallholder and subsistence systems, but require careful interdisciplinary and participatory research. The use of seasonal climate forecasting by smallholders needs to be carefully researched, with due emphases on farmers' ability to access, trust, and respond to forecasts.

FOOD SECURITY AND THE RISKS OF A CHANGING CLIMATE

Many facets of food security depend directly on environmental conditions including weather and climate; among them are food production and efficient distribution systems. The growth in agriculture this century is unprecedented due to the development of new technologies to increase crop yields. However, climate variability causes considerable fluctuations in crop yields and productivity. On top of that, day-to-day variations in weather which manifest themselves in the form of hurricanes and typhoons, floods and dry spells often lead to mass displacement of populations and cause damage to food production systems, resulting in food shortages and famine.

Beyond regional, seasonal and year-to-year climate variability, global warming is predicted to strongly affect agricultural production in some areas, especially in the tropics and subtropics.

There are potentially serious consequences on a regional scale for food security because of climate variability and change.

Many models also predict a considerable increase in extreme weather conditions as a consequence of climate change. There may be increased risk of hunger and famine in some locations. Many of the world's poorest people are most at risk, especially those living in subtropical and tropical areas, and dependent on food production systems in semiarid and arid regions. These areas are found in sub-Saharan Africa, south, east and south-east Asia, tropical parts of Latin America and in some Pacific island nations

Atmospheric and oceanic conditions determine the breeding grounds for fish generally and fish production. Globally, climate change is unlikely to affect marine fish production but will probably produce changes at the regional level. Principal changes will be longer growing seasons and lower winter fish mortality. Oceanic changes could lead to migrations in species and affect migration routes, with subsequent changes in fish stocks in the economic zones of some nations. The threat of climate change over decades to centuries caused by human-induced (anthropogenic) increases in greenhouse gases in the atmosphere is a matter of global concern. This concern is being addressed by the UN Framework Convention on Climate Change through which nations have committed themselves to achieve stabilization of greenhouse gas concentrations in the atmosphere "at a level that will prevent dangerous anthropogenic interference with the climate system

THE IMPACT OF CLIMATE VARIABILITY ON FOOD PRODUCTION

CLIMATE variability has always had a significant impact on food production. Reliable climate records have been kept for many regions of the globe only over the last 100 years. Around the mean global surface temperature increase of between 0.3°C and 0.6°C since the late 1 9th century, considerable variability occurs. About 20-30 per cent of the temperature variability from the global trend, especially in the southern hemisphere, is linked to the Southern Oscillation, an irregular variation in the tropical oceans and atmosphere between the Pacific and Indo-Australian areas.

Rainfall in the Sahel from the late 1960s to 1993 was well below amounts received earlier in the century, about half that of the wet 1950s.

Food production is well adjusted to the mean climatic conditions of the region, and can cope with moderate variations. However, climatic variability creates hazards to which agricultural ecosystems are not well adapted. High temperatures exacerbate the effects of drought, damage crops and their establishment, and reduce yields. Low temperatures, frost and heavy snowfall curtail yields and destroy crops. Heavy rainfall and flooding cause inundation and waterlogging of productive land. Drought directly impacts on agricultural yields by reducing plant growth and animal production. High winds cause mechanical damage to crops, soil erosion and land degradation.

A phenomenon that is related to the occasional warming of the eastern part of the Pacific Ocean is the El Niño/Southern Oscillation. El Niño events affect the global climate, particularly in the southern hemisphere.

EL NIÑO AND ITS IMPACTS

Oscillation causes lower agricultural yields and major variations in temperature (both land and marine) and rainfall.

El Niño episodes have strong correlations with:

- Drought in southern Africa India, Indonesia, Australia and parts of the Americas
- Floods in Kenya, Peru, Argentina and the United States of America
- High temperatures in Japan and parts of Canada

The Toll of Chronically Poor and Erratic Rainfall

A ALTHOUGH catastrophic weather phenomena receive wide media coverage, it should be noted that far more agricultural production is lost in pockets of chronically poor rainfall or other adverse weather during otherwise average years. In addition, climate is characterized by persistence, i.e. a tendency for "good" or "bad" years to occur in runs, which highlights the need for storage of food, and particularly affects livestock.

Finally, due to population growth, agriculture had to expand more and more into marginal land, including those with soils with poor water storage capacity. Such areas are more vulnerable to irregular rainfall, resulting in more frequent "drought" even under relatively stable climatic conditions. This increases even further vulnerability to climate change.

Adaptation Strategies

The impacts of climate variability and change require a number of strategies to make food security more robust:

- New varieties
- Adaptation of new crops
- Efficient land management
- Minimum and reduced tillage technologies
- Control and prevention of land degradation and desertification
- Mitigation of the effects of drought
- Improved seasonal climate prediction
- Fisheries stock assessment and management
- Preservation and restoration of wetlands and estuaries.

Global Warming and Future Climate

During the past century human activities have changed the atmospheric concentrations and distributions of greenhouse gases and aerosols.

Concentrations of carbon dioxide, methane and nitrous oxide have grown by about 30, 145 and 15 per cent, respectively. These increases have been from the burning of fossil fuels, land-use changes and agriculture. Greenhouse gases have a warming effect on surface temperatures. In contrast, tropospheric aerosols, resulting from fossil fuel combustion and burning of biomass, have a cooling effect on climate. The balance of evidence now suggests a discernible human influence on global climate and that the warming effect of greenhouse gases is outweighing the cooling effect of aerosols.

It is now believed that global temperatures could increase at a faster rate than they have up to now. Results of advanced computer models project a "best estimate" increase of global mean surface air temperatures by about 2°C, relative to 1990, by 2100 AD. General warming is expected to lead to an increase in high temperature extremes, with decreases in extremes of cold with repercussions on the hydrological cycle with changes in the occurrence of severe droughts and floods. Most climate models indicate an increase in rainfall intensitv leading to more extreme rainfall events.

THE ROLE OF FORESTS IN FOOD SECURITY

Forests contribute directly to the diets of forest dwellers and of many who live far beyond the woods. Forest fruits nuts and berries, for instance, are popular with urban as well as rural consumers. These and many other forest foods add variety and flavour to diets while providing essential vitamins, minerals, fats and proteins. During times of seasonal food shortages or emergencies-caused, for example, by droughts, floods or wars-forest foods also offer vital insurance against malnutrition or famine. Leaves-used as flavouring in soups, stews and relishes-and mushrooms are the most common forest foods. Animal foods include a large variety of both invertebrates, such as edible insects, and vertebrates, including mammals, birds and fish.

Forests for Income

For rural people, especially those with little or no land of their own, forests may provide the main source of cash income. This income does not come from wood harvesting only. Non-wood forest resources can often generate greater, more sustainable incomes than can be gained from the same land when used for agriculture or logging. World trade in rattan, for instance, is worth US$2 000 million annually. In India alone, forest-based industries support 30 million people.

Forests for Livestock

Forests provide fodder and rangeland for 30 to 40 million pastoralists worldwide who herd some 4 000 million cattle, goats and sheep. Trees help to protect pastoral rangelands, providing shade for cattle and crops and thereby supporting livestock production. Nonetheless, while livestock are increasing in number, the area available for grazing is being reduced because of conversion to crop production.

FORESTS AND THE ENVIRONMENT

Forests and trees greatly contribute to maintaining the ecological balance. The integration of trees within agricultural schemes sustains crop production by improving soil fertility. Trees help to control water and wind erosion and they recycle vital nutrients, such as nitrogen, back into the soil. Trees also grow where agricultural crops might fail, allowing production on marginal lands. As they grow, trees absorb and store carbon dioxide (CO^2). Deforestation-especially by burning-releases a great amount of stored CO^2 into the atmosphere, contributing to global warming.

Forests and medicine For 75 to 90 percent of the people in developing countries, natural products represent the only source of medicine. The active ingredients found in 25 percent of prescription drugs come from medicinal plants. Nearly all of the so-called alternative medicines are also based on plant extracts. The estimated value of plant-based drugs is nearly US$45 000 million a year.

Forests and Biological Diversity

Forests are among the most important living genebanks on earth. Many of the foods we consume today originated as wild crops in the forests. Genetic improvement has much to gain from existing wild species, which may possess valuable traits that can be incorporated into their cultivated relatives to make them hardier and more disease-resistant. If deforestation is not controlled, however, it could be the single greatest cause of species loss over the next 50 years.

Forests for Energy

Wood energy is drawing increasing attention as an environmentally friendly source of energy. Wood is still people's main source of fuel for cooking, processing and preserving food, and will continue to be for many years to come. Worldwide, 2 000 million people depend on wood for cooking, a basic step in ensuring proper nutrition. In many developing countries, fuelwood supplies as much as 97 percent of total energy consumption. Wood-based energy systems are the most readily available in many areas and, when properly managed, they are not only versatile and sustainable but also effective in generating income and jobs.

Forests for Habitat

Forests are home to 300 million people around the world who depend on shifting cultivation, hunting and gathering to survive. The needs of forest dwellers have often been overlooked in development plans and their lives are becoming increasingly precarious as population pressures encroach on the land available for shifting cultivation.

Forests and Culture

Traditionally, the importance of forests and trees has been clearly recognized by cultures worldwide. Trees have featured throughout history: in religion and folklore and are often described as God's gift to humans. They are recognized for their regenerative nature and are associated with health, marital harmony and longevity. For these and other reasons, forests are carefully protected by traditional societies.

Forests and Security

The effective integration of forests into agricultural, economic and development schemes-carefully planned according to local needs and circumstances has great potential for increasing food security for present and future generations. On the other hand, the continuing loss of vital forest resources causes damage that is, in many cases, irreversible. By designing and implementing integrated schemes for the management of forests at the national and international levees, governments can strengthen and renew their crucial role in relieving the burden of hunger and poverty throughout the world.

FORESTS AND NUTRITION

Forests make a particularly important contribution to the nutrition of the rural poor, who, more than others, are likely to be dependent on trees for a significant part of their income and food supply. Forest-dwelling hunters and gatherers, the world's 300 million shifting cultivators and millions of smallholder and landless households living near forests, in the savannah or growing trees on their farms and compounds depend on trees as part of their survival strategies.

Forest foods can offer vital insurance against famine during times of seasonal food shortages or emergencies such as droughts, floods and wars. It is common for rural households to depend on forest foods between harvests, when harvested stocks have been consumed but the next crops have still to mature. Women in particular count on these resources for supplementary nutrition, emergency foods, fuelwood for cooking and many other important products they need to ensure the nutritional well-being of their families.

One of the main contributions of forests and trees to household nutritional standards is as income. This income may be used to buy staple foods that usually cannot be produced in large quantities in the home garden. In Peru, a hare hunter can earn the equivalent of US$! 350 a month, compared with a labourer's typical wage of $100.

Food from Trees and Forests

Nearly everyone consumes tree foods in one form or another. Innumerable cultivated trees produce food: fruit and nut trees coconut palms plantains, olives and so on. Among the forest fruits that have gained popularity on the world market are avocados, mangos and guavas. Market forces have galvanized production of these fruits-formerly wild or semi-cultivated forest products-in their countries of origin and have lead to their spread to other areas.

Many households throughout the world grow trees in their home gardens, supplementing their diets with fruits, nuts, edible leaves and other foodstuffs. The fruit of the baobab far surpasses the orange's famous Vitamin C content of 57 mg per 100 g of truit at 360 mg per 100 g, and one variety of jujube reaches levels as high as 1 000 mg per 100 g. Wild leaves contain more riboflavin than eggs, milk, nuts or fish. In Ghana, over 100 wild plant species are valued for their leaves and over 200 for their fruit.

Forest foods are traditionally used to supplement the staple diet, providing vitamins, minerals and proteins that are lacking in starch-based cultivated crop foods.

People living near forest reserves in Nigeria consume as much as 84 percent of their animal protein in the form of game. Studies in Zimbabwe's Communal Areas suggest that well over 90 percent of households routinely consume insect protein, mostly in the form of termites.

Trees such as coconut and palm provide oils that are essential for cooking and numerous other household uses. Mushrooms and truffles are a source of protein, minerals and variety in diets.

Health for Humans, Animals and Plants

Many trees produce chemicals to protect themselves from natural predators. These chemicals often have medicinal properties that are critical in maintaining levels of family nutrition.

For example, the bark of the *Khaya senegalensis is* used for intestinal problems in tropical Africa, while the Copaiba tree of the Latin American tropics produces a substance used as an expectorant. Just one variety of yam, found in Mexico, provides the chemical that is the basis of virtually all oral contraceptives. Folk medicine, which relies heavily on plants and the traditional knowledge about them, is the standard source of medical treatment for at least three-quarters of the world's people; some analysts set the figure as high as 90 percent. India has more than 2 000 known medicinal plants, Malaysia around 1 000 and Brazil at least 3 000.

Forest products provide important remedies for animal diseases, helping to safeguard livestock production. The hardiness and resistance or tolerance to diseases and pests of many cultivated crops also depend on biological diversity-the key to improved crop varieties and animal breeds. Woods and forests, particularly in the tropics, are rich depositories of biological diversity.

Forest Ecosystems

In Addition to their direct contribution to food supplies, trees provide habitats for I animals, insects and plants that indirectly contribute to human nutrition. Mangrove forests, which cover only about 1 600 km^2, are essential to the life cycles of many of the world's major commercial fish species. Shrimp, oysters, crabs and countless other edible species of aquatic animals also feed and breed in these forest ecosystems.

Besides being consumed directly, insects contribute to human diets in a number of ways. Honey is universally valued for its high energy content-more than 280 Calories per 100 g The blossoms of forest trees and plants growing below the forest canopy provide a year-round supply of food for bees in the form of nectar and pollen. In India, village-level bee-keeping yields an estimated 37 000 tonnes of honey a year. Similar products extracted directly from trees include sweeteners such as maple syrup and various sugar substitutes.

4

Impact of Climate Change on Agriculture

Climate change and agriculture are interrelated processes, both of which take place on a global scale. Global warming is projected to have significant impacts on conditions affecting agriculture, including temperature, carbon dioxide, glacial run-off, precipitation and the interaction of these elements. These conditions determine the carrying capacity of the biosphere to produce enough food for the human population and domesticated animals. The overall effect of climate change on agriculture will depend on the balance of these effects. Assessment of the effects of global climate changes on agriculture might help to properly anticipate and adapt farming to maximize agricultural production.

CLIMATE CHANGE AND AGRICULTURE

Despite technological advances, such as improved varieties, genetically modified organisms, and irrigation systems, weather is still a key factor in agricultural productivity, as well as soil properties and natural communities. The effect of climate on agriculture is related to variabilities in local climates rather than in global climate patterns. The Earth's average surface temperature has increased by 1 degree F in just over the last century. Consequently, agronomists consider any assessment has to be individually consider each local area.

On the other hand, agricultural trade has grown in recent years, and now provides significant amounts of food, on a national level to major importing countries, as well as comfortable income to exporting ones. The international aspect of trade and security in terms of food implies the need to also consider the effects of climate change on a global scale.

A study published in *Science* suggests that, due to climate change, "southern Africa could lose more than 30% of its main crop, maize, by 2030. In South Asia losses of many regional staples, such as rice, millet and maize could top 10%".

The 2001 IPCC Third Assessment Report concluded that the poorest countries would be hardest hit, with reductions in crop yields in most tropical and sub-tropical regions due to decreased water availability, and new or changed insect pest incidence. In Africa and Latin America many rainfed crops are near their maximum temperature tolerance, so that yields are likely to fall sharply for even small climate changes; falls in agricultural productivity of up to 30% over the 21st century are projected. Marine life and the fishing industry will also be severely affected in some places.

Climate change induced by increasing greenhouse gases is likely to affect crops differently from region to region. For example, average crop yield is expected to drop down to 50% in Pakistan according to the UKMO scenario whereas corn production in Europe is expected to grow up to 25% in optimum hydrologic conditions.

More favourable effects on yield tend to depend to a large extent on realization of the potentially beneficial effects of carbon dioxide on crop growth and increase of efficiency in water use. Decrease in potential yields is likely to be caused by shortening of the growing period, decrease in water availability and poor vernalization. In the long run, the climatic change could affect agriculture in several ways :

- *productivity*, in terms of quantity and quality of crops
- *agricultural practices*, through changes of water use (irrigation) and agricultural inputs such as herbicides, insecticides and fertilizers
- *environmental effects*, in particular in relation of frequency and intensity of soil drainage (leading to

nitrogen leaching), soil erosion, reduction of crop diversity

- *rural space*, through the loss and gain of cultivated lands, land speculation, land renunciation, and hydraulic amenities.
- *adaptation*, organisms may become more or less competitive, as well as humans may develop urgency to develop more competitive organisms, such as flood resistant or salt resistant varieties of rice.

They are large uncertainties to uncover, particularly because there is lack of information on many specific local regions, and include the uncertainties on magnitude of climate change, the effects of technological changes on productivity, global food demands, and the numerous possibilities of adaptation.

Most agronomists believe that agricultural production will be mostly affected by the severity and pace of climate change, not so much by gradual trends in climate. If change is gradual, there may be enough time for biota adjustment. Rapid climate change, however, could harm agriculture in many countries, especially those that are already suffering from rather poor soil and climate conditions, because there is less time for optimum natural selection and adaption.

Projections

Schneider *et al.*. (2007:787) assessed the literature on key vulnerabilities to climate change. With low to medium confidence, they concluded that for about a 1 to 3°C global mean temperature increase (by 2100, relative to the 1990-2000 average level) there would be productivity decreases for some cereals in low latitudes, and productivity increases in high latitudes. With medium confidence, global production potential was predicted to:

- increase up to around 3°C,
- very likely decrease above about 3 to 4°C.

Most of the studies on global agriculture assessed by Schneider *et al.*. (2007:790) had not incorporated a number of critical factors, including changes in extreme events, or the spread of pests and diseases. Studies had also not considered the development of specific practices or technologies to aid adaptation.

REGIONAL

Africa: Africa's geography makes it particularly vulnerable to climate change, and seventy per cent of the population rely on rain-fed agriculture for their livelihoods. Tanzania's official report on climate change suggests that the areas that usually get two rainfalls in the year will probably get more, and those that get only one rainy season will get far less. The net result is expected to be that 33% less maize—the country's staple crop—will be grown. Alongside other factors, regional climate change-in particular, reduced precipitation-is thought to have contributed to the conflict in Darfur. The combination of decades of drought, desertification and overpopulation are among the causes of the conflict, because the Baggara Arab nomads searching for water have to take their livestock further south, to land mainly occupied by farming peoples.

With high confidence, IPCC (2007:13) concluded that climate variability and change would severely compromise agricultural production and access to food.

Asia: With medium confidence, IPCC (2007:13) projected that by the mid-21 century, in East and Southeast Asia, crop yields could increase up to 20%, while in Central and South Asia, yields could decrease by up to 30%. Taken together, the risk of hunger was projected to remain very high in several developing countries. More detailed analysis of rice yields by the International Rice Research Institute forecast 20% reduction in yields over the region per degree Celsius of temperature rise. Rice becomes sterile if exposed to temperatures above 35 degrees for more than one hour during flowering and consequently produces no grain.

Australia and New Zealand: Hennessy *et al.*. (2007:509) assessed the literature for this region. They concluded that without further adaptation to climate change, projected impacts would likely be substantial: By 2030, production from agriculture and forestry was projected to decline over much of southern and eastern Australia, and over parts of eastern New Zealand; In New Zealand, initial benefits were projected close to major rivers and in western and southern areas. Hennessy *et al.*. (2007:509) placed high confidence in these projections.

Europe: With high confidence, IPCC (2007:14) projected that in Southern Europe, climate change would reduce crop productivity. In Central and Eastern Europe, forest productivity was expected to decline. In Northern Europe, the initial effect of climate change was projected to increase crop yields.

Latin America: With high confidence, IPCC (2007:14) projected that in drier areas of Latin America, productivity of some important crops would decrease and livestock productivity decline, with adverse consequences for food security. In temperate zones, soybean yields were projected to increase.

North America: According to a paper by Deschenes and Greenstone (2006), predicted increases in temperature and precipitation will have virtually no effect on the most important crops in the US. With high confidence, IPCC (2007:14-15) projected that over the first few decades of this century, moderate climate change would increase aggregate yields of rain-fed agriculture by 5–20%, but with important variability among regions. Major challenges were projected for crops that are near the warm end of their suitable range or which depend on highly utilized water resources.

Polar regions (Arctic and Antarctic): For the *Guardian* newspaper, Brown (2005) reported on how climate change had affected agriculture in Iceland. Rising temperatures had made the widespread sowing of barley possible, which had been untenable twenty years ago. Some of the warming was due to a local (possibly temporary) effect via ocean currents from the Caribbean, which had also affected fish stocks. Anisimov *et al.*. (2007:655) assessed the literature for this region. With medium confidence, they concluded that the benefits of a less severe climate were dependent on local conditions. One of these benefits was judged to be increased agricultural and forestry opportunities.

Small islands: In a literature assessment, Mimura *et al.*.

(2007:689) concluded, with high confidence, that subsistence and commercial agriculture would very likely be adversely affected by climate change.

SHORTAGE IN GRAIN PRODUCTION

Between 1996 and 2003, grain production has stabilized slightly over 1800 millions of tons. In 2000, 2001, 2002 and 2003, grain stocks have been dropping, resulting in a global grain harvest that was short of consumption by 93 millions of tons in 2003.

The Earth's average temperature has been rising since the late 1970s, with nine of the 10 warmest years on record occurring since 1995. In 2002, India and the United States suffered sharp harvest reductions because of record temperatures and drought. In 2003 Europe suffered very low rainfall throughout spring and summer, and a record level of heat damaged most crops from the United Kingdom and France in the Western Europe through Ukraine in the East. Bread prices have been rising in several countries in the region.

Poverty Impacts

Researchers at the Overseas Development Institute (ODI) have investigated the potential impacts climate change could have on agriculture, and how this would affect attempts at alleviating poverty in the developing world. They argued that the effects from moderate climate change are likely to be mixed for developing countries. However, the vulnerability of the poor in developing countries to short term impacts from climate change, notably the increased frequency and severity of adverse weather events is likely to have a negative impact. This, they say, should be taken into account when defining agricultural policy.

Crop Development Models

Models for climate behavior are frequently inconclusive. In order to further study effects of global warming on agriculture, other types of models, such as *crop development models*, *yield prediction*, quantities of *water or fertilizer consumed*, can be used. Such models condense the knowledge accumulated of the climate, soil, and effects observed of the results of various agricultural practices. They thus could make it possible to test strategies of adaptation to modifications of the environment.

Because these models are necessarily simplifying natural conditions (often based on the assumption that weeds, disease and insect pests are controlled), it is not clear whether the results they give will have an *in-field* reality. However, some results are partly validated with an increasing number of experimental results.

Other models, such as *insect and disease development* models based on climate projections are also used (for example simulation of aphid reproduction or septoria (cereal fungal disease) development).

Scenarios are used in order to estimate climate changes effects on crop development and yield. Each scenario is defined as a set of meteorological variables, based on generally accepted projections. For example, many models are running simulations based on doubled carbon dioxide projections, temperatures raise ranging from 1°C up to 5°C, and with rainfall levels an increase or decrease of 20%. Other parameters may include humidity, wind, and solar activity. Scenarios of crop models are testing farm-level adaptation, such as sowing date shift, climate adapted species (vernalisation need, heat and cold resistance), irrigation and fertilizer adaptation, resistance to disease. Most developed models are about wheat, maize, rice and soybean.

TEMPERATURE POTENTIAL EFFECT ON GROWING PERIOD

Duration of crop growth cycles are above all, related to temperature. An increase in temperature will speed up development. In the case of an annual crop, the duration between sowing and harvesting will shorten (for example, the duration in order to harvest corn could shorten between one and four weeks). The shortening of such a cycle could have an adverse effect on productivity because senescence would occur sooner.

Effect of Elevated Carbon Dioxide on Crops

Carbon dioxide is essential to plant growth. Rising CO_2

concentration in the atmosphere can have both positive and negative consequences.

Increased CO_2 is expected to have positive physiological effects by increasing the rate of photosynthesis. Currently, the amount of carbon dioxide in the atmosphere is 380 parts per million. In comparison, the amount of oxygen is 210,000 ppm. This means that often plants may be starved of carbon dioxide, due to the enzyme that fixes CO_2, rubisco also fixes oxygen in the process of photorespiration. The effects of an increase in carbon dioxide would be higher on C3 crops (such as wheat) than on C4 crops (such as maize), because the former is more susceptible to carbon dioxide shortage. Studies have shown that increased CO_2 leads to fewer stomata developing on plants which leads to reduced water usage. Under optimum conditions of temperature and humidity, the yield increase could reach 36%, if the levels of carbon dioxide are doubled.

Further, few studies have looked at the impact of elevated carbon dioxide concentrations on whole farming systems. Most models study the relationship between CO_2 and productivity in isolation from other factors associated with climate change, such as an increased frequency of extreme weather events, seasonal shifts, and so on.

In 2005, the Royal Society in London concluded that the purported benefits of elevated carbon dioxide concentrations are "likely to be far lower than previously estimated" when factors such as increasing ground-level ozone are taken into account."

Effect on Quality

According to the IPCC's TAR, "The importance of climate change impacts on grain and forage quality emerges from new research. For rice, the amylose content of the grain—a major determinant of cooking quality—is increased under elevated CO_2" (Conroy et al., 1994). Cooked rice grain from plants grown in high-CO_2 environments would be firmer than that from today's plants. However, concentrations of iron and zinc, which are important for human nutrition, would be lower. Moreover, the protein content of the grain decreases under combined increases of temperature and CO_2." Studies using FACE have shown that increases in CO_2 lead to decreased concentrations of micronutrients in crop plants. This may have knock-on effects on other parts of ecosystems as herbivores will need to eat more food to gain the same amount of protein.

Studies have shown that higher CO_2 levels lead to reduced plant uptake of nitrogen (and a smaller number showing the same for trace elements such as zinc) resulting in crops with lower nutritional value. This would primarily impact on populations in poorer countries less able to compensate by eating more food, more varied diets, or possibly taking supplements.

Reduced nitrogen content in grazing plants has also been shown to reduce animal productivity in sheep, which depend on microbes in their gut to digest plants, which in turn depend on nitrogen intake.

AGRICULTURAL SURFACES AND CLIMATE CHANGES

Climate change may increase the amount of arable land in high-latitude region by reduction of the amount of frozen lands. A 2005 study reports that temperature in Siberia has increased three degree Celsius in average since 1960 (much more than the rest of the world). However, reports about the impact of global warming on Russian agriculture indicate conflicting probable effects : while they expect a northward extension of farmable lands, they also warn of possible productivity losses and increased risk of drought.

Sea levels are expected to get up to one meter higher by 2100, though this projection is disputed. A rise in the sea level would result in an agricultural land loss, in particular in areas such as South East Asia. Erosion, submergence of shorelines, salinity of the water table due to the increased sea levels, could mainly affect agriculture through inundation of low-lying lands.

Low lying areas such as Bangladesh, India and Vietnam will experience major loss of rice crop if sea levels are expected to rise by the end of the century. Vietnam for example relies heavily on its southern tip, where the Mekong Delta lies, for rice planting. Any rise in sea level of no more than a meter will drown several km^2. of rice paddies, rendering Vietnam incapable of producing its main staple and export of rice.

Erosion and Fertility

The warmer atmospheric temperatures observed over the past decades are expected to lead to a more vigorous hydrological cycle, including more extreme rainfall events. Erosion and soil degradation is more likely to occur. Soil fertility would also be affected by global warming. However, because the ratio of carbon to nitrogen is a constant, a doubling of carbon is likely to imply a higher storage of nitrogen in soils as nitrates, thus providing higher fertilizing elements for plants, providing better yields. The average needs for nitrogen could decrease, and give the opportunity of changing often costly fertilisation strategies.

Due to the extremes of climate that would result, the increase in precipitations would probably result in greater risks of erosion, whilst at the same time providing soil with better hydration, according to the intensity of the rain. The possible evolution of the organic matter in the soil is a highly contested issue: while the increase in the temperature would induce a greater rate in the production of minerals, lessening the soil organic matter content, the atmospheric CO_2 concentration would tend to increase it.

A very important point to consider is that weeds would undergo the same acceleration of cycle as cultivated crops, and would also benefit from carbonaceous fertilization. Since most weeds are C3 plants, they are likely to compete even more than now against C4 crops such as corn. However, on the other hand, some results make it possible to think that weedkillers could gain in effectiveness with the temperature increase.

Global warming would cause an increase in rainfall in some areas, which would lead to an increase of atmospheric humidity and the duration of the wet seasons. Combined with higher temperatures, these could favor the development of fungal diseases. Similarly, because of higher temperatures and humidity, there could be an increased pressure from insects and disease vectors. The continued retreat of glaciers will have a number of different quantitative impacts. In areas that are heavily dependent on water runoff from glaciers that melt during the warmer summer months, a continuation of the current retreat will eventually deplete the glacial ice and substantially reduce or eliminate runoff. A reduction in runoff will affect the ability to irrigate crops and will reduce summer stream flows necessary to keep dams and reservoirs replenished.

Approximately 2.4 billion people live in the drainage basin of the Himalayan rivers. India, China, Pakistan, Afghanistan, Bangladesh, Nepal and Myanmar could experience floods followed by severe droughts in coming decades. In India alone, the Ganges provides water for drinking and farming for more than 500 million people. The west coast of North America, which gets much of its water from glaciers in mountain ranges such as the Rocky Mountains and Sierra Nevada, also would be affected.

Ozone and UV-B

Some scientists think agriculture could be affected by any decrease in stratospheric ozone, which could increase biologically dangerous ultraviolet radiation B. Excess ultraviolet radiation B can directly effect plant physiology and cause massive amounts of mutations, and indirectly through changed pollinator behavior, though such changes are simple to quantify. However, it has not yet been ascertained whether an increase in greenhouse gases would decrease stratospheric ozone levels.

In addition, a possible effect of rising temperatures is significantly higher levels of ground-level ozone, which would substantially lower yields.

ENSO (El Niño Southern Oscillation) will affect monsoon patterns more intensely in the future as climate change warms up the ocean's water. Crops that lie on the equatorial belt or under the tropical Walker circulation, such as rice, will be affected by varying monsoon patterns and more unpredictable weather. Scheduled planting and harvesting based on weather patterns will become less effective.

Areas such as Indonesia where the main crop consists of rice will be more vulnerable to the increased intensity of ENSO effects in the future of climate change. University of Washington professor, David Battisti, researched the effects of future ENSO patterns on the Indonesian rice agriculture using [IPCC]'s 2007 annual report and 20 different logistical models mapping out climate factors such as wind pressure, sea-level, and humidity, and found that rice harvest will experience a decrease in yield. Bali and Java, which holds 55% of the rice yields in Indonesia, will be likely to experience 9-10% probably of delayed monsoon patterns, which prolongs the hungry season. Normal planting of rice crops begin in October and harevest by January. However, as climate change affects ENSO and consequently delays planting, harvesting will be late and in drier conditions, resulting in less potential yields.

The agricultural sector is a driving force in the gas emissions and land use effects thought to cause climate change. In addition to being a significant user of land and consumer of fossil fuel, agriculture contributes directly to greenhouse gas emissions through practices such as rice production and the raising of livestock; according to the Intergovernmental Panel on Climate Change, the three main causes of the increase in greenhouse gases observed over the past 250 years have been fossil fuels, land use, and agriculture.

Land use

Agriculture contributes to greenhouse gas increases through land use in four main ways:

- CO_2 releases linked to deforestation
- Methane releases from rice cultivation
- Methane releases from enteric fermentation in cattle
- Nitrous oxide releases from fertilizer application

Together, these agricultural processes comprise 54% of methane emissions, roughly 80% of nitrous oxide emissions, and virtually all carbon dioxide emissions tied to land use.

The planet's major changes to land cover since 1750 have resulted from deforestation in temperate regions: when forests and woodlands are cleared to make room for fields and pastures, the albedo of the affected area increases, which can result in either warming or cooling effects, depending on local conditions.

Deforestation also affects regional carbon reuptake, which can result in increased concentrations of CO_2, the dominant greenhouse gas. Land-clearing methods such as slash and burn compound these effects by burning biomatter, which directly releases greenhouse gases and particulate matter such as soot into the air.

Livestock

Livestock and livestock-related activities such as deforestation and increasingly fuel-intensive farming practices are responsible for over 18% of human-made greenhouse gas emissions, including:

- 9% of global carbon dioxide emissions
- 35-40% of global methane emissions (chiefly due to enteric fermentation and manure)
- 64% of global nitrous oxide emissions (chiefly due to fertilizer use.)

Livestock activities also contribute disproportionately to land-use effects, since crops such as corn and alfalfa are cultivated in order to feed the animals.

Worldwide, livestock production occupies 70% of all land used for agriculture, or 30% of the land surface of the Earth.

ENVIRONMENTAL IMPACT OF AGRICULTURE

The environmental impact of agriculture varies based on the wide variety of agricultural practices employed around the world.

Climate change and agriculture are interrelated processes, both of which take place on a global scale. Global warming is projected to have significant impacts on conditions affecting agriculture, including temperature, precipitation and glacial run-off. These conditions determine the carrying capacity of the biosphere to produce enough food for the human population and domesticated animals. Rising carbon dioxide levels would also have effects, both detrimental and beneficial, on crop yields. The overall effect of climate change on agriculture will depend on the balance of these effects. Assessment of the effects of global climate changes on agriculture might help to properly anticipate and adapt farming to maximize agricultural production.

At the same time, agriculture has been shown to produce significant effects on climate change, primarily through the production and release of greenhouse gases such as carbon dioxide, methane, and nitrous oxide, but also by altering the Earth's land cover, which can change its ability to absorb or reflect heat and light, thus contributing to radiative forcing.

Land use change such as deforestation and desertification, together with use of fossil fuels, are the major anthropogenic sources of carbon dioxide; agriculture itself is the major contributor to increasing methane and nitrous oxide concentrations in earth's atmosphere.

Deforstation development by local villager and smuggler

Genetic Engineering

Intensive farming alters the environment in many ways. Some of the disadvantages of this method of farming include:

- Limits or destroys the natural habitat of most wildlife, and leads to soil erosion
- Use of fertilizers can alter the biology of rivers and lakes.
- Pesticides generally kill useful insects as well as those that destroy crops
- Generally not sustainable-often results in desertification or, in a worst case scenario, land that is so poisonous and eroded that nothing else will grow
- Requires large amounts of energy input to produce, transport, and apply chemical fertilizers/pesticides
- Use of chemicals on fields creates run-off, excess runs off into rivers and lakes causing pollution
- Use of pesticides have numerous negative health effects in workers who apply them, people that live nearby the area of application or downstream/downwind from it, and consumers who eat the pesticides which remain on their food

Irrigation

Irrigation can lead to a number of problems:

- Depletion of underground aquifers through overdrafting.
- Ground subsidence.
  - Groundwater recharge-an ecological restoration, mitigation, and remediation technique.
- Underirrigation gives poor soil salinity control which leads to increased soil salinity with consequent build up of toxic salts on soil surface in areas with high evaporation. This requires either leaching to remove these salts and a method of drainage to carry the salts away.
- Overirrigation because of poor distribution uniformity or management wastes water, chemicals, and may lead to water pollution.
- Deep drainage (from over-irrigation) may result in rising water tables which in some instances will lead to problems of irrigation salinity requiring watertable control by some form of subsurface land drainage.
- Irrigation with saline or high-sodium water may damage soil structure owing to the formation of alkaline soil.
- Runoff causing surface water and groundwater-aquifer hydrologic cycle water pollution.
  - Bioretention-an ecological restoration, mitigation, and remediation technique.

Pollutants

A wide range of agricultural chemicals are used and some become pollutants through use, misuse, or ignorance.

- Pesticide drift
  - soil contamination
  - groundwater and water pollution
  - air pollution *spray drift*
- Pesticides, especially those based on organochloride
- Pesticide residue in foods

- Pesticide toxicity to bees
  - List of crop plants pollinated by bees
  - Pollination management
- Bioremediation

Soil degradation

Main article: Soil degradation

- soil contamination
- erosion
  - sedimentation

Waste

Plasticulture, the use of plastic materials in agriculture, raises problems around how to carry out the recycling of agricultural plastics.

Issues by region

- Hedgerow removal in the United Kingdom.
- Soil salinisation, especially in Australia.
- Phosphate mining in Nauru
- Methane emissions from livestock in New Zealand.
- Some environmentalists attribute the hypoxic zone in the Gulf of Mexico as being encouraged by nitrogen fertilization of the algae bloom.

Sustainable agriculture

The exponential population increase in recent decades has increased the practice of agricultural land conversion to meet demand for food which in turn has increased the effects on the environment. The global population is still increasing and will eventually stabilise, as some critics doubt that food production, due to lower yields from global warming, can support the global population.

Organic farming is a multifaceted sustainable agriculture set of practices that can have a lower impact on the environment

Other specific methods include: permaculture; and biodynamic agriculture which incorporating a spiritual element.

SEASONAL CLIMATE PREDICTION AND AGRICULTURAL MODELS

There is a strong history of integrated climate–crop models to estimate the impacts of climate change scenarios, and adaptive breeding and land use strategies. Advances in climate prediction at a seasonal lead-time have stimulated substantial interest in forecasting crop yields as a means of improving farm management and policy-level interventions in a manner that reduces risk and enhances livelihoods and food security, particularly in the marginal, rainfed, tropical cropping regions that the green revolution largely bypassed.

Farmers experience climate change not as a shifting mean but as climatic variations. Climatic variability at all of its time-scales is, therefore, a current challenge to development. Furthermore, developing flexible, proactive strategies for managing year-to-year climate variations within farming communities and the institutions that interface with them, using advance climate information, is arguably the most concrete step that the agricultural enterprise can take to build resilience to long-term changes in the global climate system. These two realizations appear to be bringing the historically distinct global change adaptation and agricultural development agendas closer together, particularly in Africa.

Several research groups are seeking to advance methodology to integrate crop simulation models with dynamic climate forecast models for application at a range of spatial scales. A range of promising approaches has emerged that may have relevance to management of climate variability and application to climate change projections. In this book, we seek to put such work in context by discussing how integrated climate–crop models operating at a seasonal lead-time might contribute to efforts to address climate-related constraints to agricultural development, with some emphasis on rainfed agriculture in Africa. Section 2 summarizes the role of climatic risk and potential role of seasonal climate prediction in agriculture. Section 3 relates integrated climate–crop modelling to constraints that have been identified to effective use of seasonal forecasts within agriculture. The three subsequent sections propose three areas in which integrated modelling might contribute to more effective use of seasonal climate forecasts for the benefit of smallholder agriculture in the developing countries.

CLIMATE RISK AND AGRICULTURAL DEVELOPMENT

Climate exerts a profound influence on the lives of poor rural populations who depend on agriculture for livelihood and sustenance, who are unprotected against climate-related diseases, who lack secure access to water and food, and who are vulnerable to hydrometeorological hazard. The year-to-year variability of rainfall is a significant constraint to the sustainability of rainfed farming systems in poorer countries of the tropics. This argument is developed more fully in Hansen *et al.* submitted*a*. Climatic extremes, such as drought and flooding, have a direct and often persistent impact on farmers' assets and livelihoods. Perhaps, more important, the uncertainty associated with climate variability creates a moving target for management, and is a disincentive to sustainable resource management, and to the intensification and adoption of innovation that is necessary for secure livelihoods and long-term rural prosperity.... Variability by itself is not necessarily welfare-decreasing if it is anticipated and acted upon.

Surprise, however, has adverse consequences since the optimal *ex post* and *ex ante* choices rarely coincide Rainfall variability tends to be the dominant source of livelihood risk in smallholder rainfed agriculture, particularly in dryer environments. In the face of climatic uncertainty, risk-averse farmers employ conservative strategies, including avoidance of improved technology, under-use of fertilizers and shifting from productive to non-productive liquid assets. In sub-Sahara Africa, where soil nutrient depletion is now recognized as a root cause of declining per capita food production and a critical constraint to sustainable livelihoods, the apparent effect of climatic uncertainty on investment in soils is a particular concern. These *ex ante* strategies, designed to buffer against climatic extremes, substantially reduce average income and marginal productivity of assets, and do so disproportionately for the relatively poor. Despite the tremendous concern about climate change, climate variability has not received as much attention as other development issues, in part because it has been considered part of the environmental baseline that is not amenable to intervention. Climate variations in the months ahead no longer need to be accepted as a total unknown.

The chaotic nature of the atmosphere restricts deterministic prediction of weather events to lead-times of several days. However, year-to-year variations in the atmosphere are influenced by interactions between the atmosphere and the more slowly varying ocean and land surfaces, such as those associated with the El Nino-Southern Oscillation (ENSO) in the tropical Pacific.

Improvements in our understanding of interactions between the atmosphere and its underlying surfaces, advances in modelling the global climate system, and substantial investment in monitoring the tropical oceans now provide a degree of predictability of climate fluctuations at a seasonal (i.e. several months) lead-time in many parts of the world. Goddard *et al.* (2001) provide a useful, recent review of the scientific basis and methodology of seasonal climate prediction. Where the necessary conditions are in place or can be put into place, seasonal climate prediction offers an under-exploited opportunity to manage climate variability: to respond proactively to adverse conditions and exploit favourable conditions.

INTEGRATED CLIMATE–CROP MODELLING AND THE CLIMATE RISK PROBLEM

The potential for seasonal forecasts to reduce the adverse impacts of climate variability and enhance rural livelihoods has motivated a number of pilot studies targeting smallholder farmers in developing countries. Several pilot studies with African farmers have demonstrated a high level of interest and have identified a range of promising livelihood management responses.

They have also identified several obstacles to using seasonal forecasts effectively to reduce the adverse impacts of climate variability and enhance rural livelihoods. I highlight three for which integrated climate–crop modelling has a potential role. The first is a mismatch between farmers' needs and the scale, relevance and transparency of available forecasts.

The second is the cost, risk and learning time farmers face during adaptation and adoption. Third, propose that failure to obtain adequate institutional, financial and political support is also a key constraint. Farm-scale studies have identified several resource constraints that limit responses to advance climate information, but that might be amenable to intervention if additional institutional actors (e.g. suppliers of production inputs and credit) are engaged. Scaling up beyond plot studies will require substantial investment on the part of national agricultural and meteorological services. Providing comprehensive institutional support, including provision of relevant climate information, appropriate technical guidance and intervention in financial services and production inputs (Hansen *et al.* submitted*a*) will require the involvement of a broader range of institutions that have typically been involved in pilot studies.

Several research groups who are working on applications of seasonal climate forecasts have invested heavily in the use of crop simulation models. Although, the use of weather data from analogue years associated with, e.g. ENSO phases, has been the standard approach, interest in coupling crop simulation with dynamic climate forecast models has increased substantially in recent years. A mismatch between the scale of dynamic climate models and crop simulation models complicates the task.

Crop growth depends more on the distribution of weather within a season than on the season averages that forecasters typically provide. Crop simulation models, generally, assume the small-scale of a homogenous plot, and simulate dynamic interactions between weather, management and crop growth and development on a daily time-step. On the other hand, the spatial resolution of the current generation of general circulation models (GCMs) is on the order of 10 000 km^2. Although, GCMs simulate the atmosphere on a sub-daily time-step, the spatial averaging within grid cells distorts day-to-day variability, with potentially serious consequences for simulated crop responses. Fortunately, recent and ongoing research has given rise to several promising approaches to translating seasonal climate forecasts into probabilistic predictions of crop response.

It is clear that applications of seasonal climate forecasts to manage risk are concerned with impacts on, e.g. crops and not climate *per se*. Yet, the most critical opportunities and challenges have more to do with institutional support than technology. If that is the case, then what contribution can agricultural models integrated with seasonal climate prediction models make? I propose three promising contributions: (i) translating seasonal climate forecasts into useful information; (ii) *ex ante* assessment of potential benefits and (iii) fostering and guiding application.

TRANSLATING CLIMATE FORECASTS INTO USEFUL INFORMATION

Hammer (2000) argued that seasonal climate forecasts have no intrinsic value. First, value comes from improved decisions not information. Second, it is not climatic means but impacts within the system being managed that are relevant to decisions. If climate forecasts are to have value, they must modify decision makers' expectations of the production or economic outcomes that relate to goals, within the system being managed. Crop models integrated with seasonal climate forecasts provide a means of translating forecasts of seasonal climate anomalies into forecasts of production impacts. The nature of the decision determines the appropriate spatial scale and lead-time of crop forecast information.

Farm Level Applications

Producers of annual crops must routinely make a range of critical production and livelihood decisions prior to planting that interact with climate, but whose outcome is not realized until harvest several months later. Where predictability is sufficient, seasonal forecasts may provide probabilistic information about crop yields with sufficient lead-time to influence pre-planting decisions. A mismatch between the content, scale, format and lead-time of available operational climate forecasts, and the information that farmers need for such decisions, is the most often cited constraint to effective use. It is also the constraint that is most within the control of climate information providers.

Although, farmers' information requirements are somewhat context-specific, a few generalizations emerge from experience in a range of contexts. Farmers need information that: (i) can be interpreted at a field scale; (ii) includes information about timing beyond three-month climatic means; (iii) is explicit about accuracy; and (iv) is expressed in terms of impacts and management implications within the agricultural systems that they manage.

In contrast, operational climate forecasts are typically expressed as three month climatic means averaged over large areas. When accuracy is communicated, it is typically expressed as shifts in the probability of experiencing outcomes within each climatological tercile, with no information about how the probabilities are derived.

The widespread awareness associated with the 1997 El Nino event stimulated a great deal of interest and debate about the potential value of climate prediction to poor farmers in developing countries. Some expressed doubts about the feasibility of meeting farmers' information requirements. Is predictability of climate and crop response at the farm scale sufficient to be useful?

If not, will responding to forecasts that could be wrong expose farmers to unacceptable risk? Barrett (1998) expressed concern that the level of predictability of crop yields at a farm scale is likely to be inadequate for use by risk-averse smallholder farmers. First, fine-scale spatial variability of rainfall implies that seasonal rainfall predictability is limited to aggregate spatial scales. Second, because crop yield is not a simple function of seasonal total rainfall, the accumulation of errors going from seasonal climatic predictors (e.g. sea surface temperatures), to local seasonal means, to crop response implies that predictions of impacts such as crop response will be less accurate than predictions of climatic means. Barrett called for greater investment in methods for translating climate forecasts into forecasts of relevant farm-level impacts.

Averaging in either time or space tends to increase prediction skill by reducing the random 'noise' component of variability in weather. As Gong *et al.* (2003) demonstrate, the skill of GCM-based seasonal climate forecasts tends to increase with increasing spatial aggregation relative to a single GCM grid cell in several parts of the world.

For the state of Ceará, in northeast Brazil, they also showed that downscaling to individual single stations reduces prediction skill, but that a substantial proportion of the predictability remains. Although limited experience seems to support the generalization that forecasts that are skilful at an aggregate scale show only moderate decline at individual points, there remains a need to evaluate the influence of scale of aggregation on prediction skill systematically in a range of locations.

The argument that predictability of agricultural impacts is necessarily less than that of climatic means overlooks two considerations. First, information (e.g. antecedent rainfall, stored soil moisture) beyond seasonal climatic anomalies can contribute to predictability of crop response. Second, predicting relevant impacts directly from climatic predictors instead of from predicted climatic means reduces accumulation of errors, and potentially incorporates information about rainfall distribution and other relevant meteorological variables that are embedded in climatic predictors, but lost when converting them into seasonal rainfall totals.

In a paper that arguably stimulated much of the interest in using seasonal forecasts to benefit farmers in Africa, Cane *et al.* (1994) showed that ENSO-related sea surface temperatures in the Pacific were correlated more strongly with maize yields (1970–1993) than with rainfall averaged across Zimbabwe. Dilley (1997) found that maize yields in Oaxaca, Mexico, were correlated more strongly with the Southern Oscillation Index than with local rainfall. K. P. C. Rao, the APSRU model to simulate maize yields for the short rains season at Katumani, Kenya, as a function of observed weather and GCM-based monthly hindcasts disaggregated to daily values using a stochastic weather generator. Correlations between predictions and observations were higher for simulated yields than for seasonal rainfall totals, although the analysis did not account for crop model error. By integrating GCM-based seasonal rainfall forecasts into an operational regional wheat forecasting system in Queensland, Australia, Hansen *et cl.* (2004) showed that reported district yields were more predictable than seasonal rainfall totals. They attributed this in part to the influence of observed antecedent rainfall and resulting soil moisture storage on subsequent yields. I anticipate that methodological advances and empirical evidence will address concerns about the predictability of crop response to climate fluctuations. Yet, given the spatial heterogeneity, multiplicity of yield-reducing factors and paucity of data in rainfed farming systems of much of Africa, realistic, site-specific forecasts of crop yields are likely to be elusive for some time.

Early Warning, Market and Policy Applications

Advance information about crop production is relevant to decision-makers operating at a range of scales from field to national or regional, whose decisions impact the welfare of farmers. Institutions responsible for responding to drought or food crises and traders and investors in commodity markets, are interested in anticipating production at relatively large spatial scales. Because of the adverse impacts of variability on commodity prices, the use of advance information about production to manage markets for staple foods to stabilize prices is appealing from the standpoint of food security. Although, experience with using climate information to intervene in markets is still limited, economy-wide modelling in Mozambique suggests considerable potential aggregate benefits of market applications of climate forecasts.

In food-insecure regions of Africa, early warning systems based on remote sensing of rainfall and vegetation, and monitoring of local commodity markets, provide early indication of likely food shortfalls. When a crisis requires external food aid, it can take several months to verify shortfalls, mobilize donors, transport food to the region and distribute it to the affected population. As a result, assistance often reaches the affected people after they have already suffered adverse health effects, divested productive resources or migrated away from their farms. Food aid organizations in Africa are increasingly interested in seasonal climate forecasts because of their potential to increase lead-time. For example, in August 2004, stakeholders concerned with food security early warning and response in East Africa initiated a periodic food security outlook forum, associated with the Greater Horn of Africa Climate Outlook Forum, with the goal of projecting likely food security impacts associated with the climate outlook to inform response.

In contrast to many climate-sensitive decisions at the farm level, market and food security early warning applications can often use forecast information at various points within the growing season.

The combination of increased spatial scale (Gong *et al.* 2003) and usefulness of forecasts at shorter lead-times increases the predictability potentially available for such applications. On the other hand, institutional constraints to responding to food crises are likely to require a higher threshold of forecast certainty than individual livelihood decisions.

Operational crop forecasting systems exist in many regions to support market and policy applications and food security early warning systems. These are often based on monitoring weather and crop conditions during the growing season. In some instances, they incorporate regionally calibrated crop models to simulate growth or water stress up to the current point within the growing season, then sample weather for the remainder of the season from past years to estimate yield forecast uncertainty. Skilful seasonal forecasts provide additional information that can increase the accuracy of within-season production forecasts based on monitoring and simulation alone, particularly early in the growing season. Integrating probabilistic forecasts of food production from integrated climate–crop models into models of household vulnerability has potential to improve aid assessments and targeting at a relatively long lead-time.

EX ANTE ASSESSMENT OF BENEFIT

Ex ante impact assessment seeks to assess the potential outcomes of an innovation in advance of its adoption, while *ex post* assessment seeks to assess actual outcomes following adoption. Because the use of seasonal climate forecasts within agriculture is a relatively new innovation, *ex ante* methods are, in most cases, the only way to estimate their benefits.

Pilot studies have compiled some evidence of use of forecasts for farm decisions, but have, generally, not tried to quantify the resulting production or livelihood benefits. Even after farmers learn to use forecast information routinely, *ex post* assessment of benefits would require multiple years due to the stochastic nature of climate variability and forecast responses—longer than typical funding cycles allow.

Furthermore, there are few, if any, regions in the developing world where rural communities have had access to operational climate information tailored to their needs for sufficient time to allow *ex post* assessment of use and benefits.

Ex ante impact assessment serves two related roles in applied agricultural research: providing evidence of potential benefit of proposed interventions to support mobilization of resources, and providing insight to target interventions where the positive impact is likely to be greatest (Thornton submitted). Resource mobilization has to do with allocation of scarce resources between a particular intervention or institution, and others that compete. Targeting relates to an institution or program's allocation of scarce resources among its own competing activities.

Confidence and Credibility

Increasing competition for dwindling resources for applied research has driven the international agricultural research community to become proactive about both quantifying the benefits of past activities (i.e. *ex post* impact assessment), and providing evidence of the likely benefits of proposed interventions (i.e. *ex ante* assessment).

Likewise, donors increasingly require *ex ante* evidence of benefit before they will invest heavily in new agricultural innovations. The application of seasonal climate prediction is a new innovation that potentially competes for scarce resources with technologies such as crop genetic improvements that have relatively long records of *ex post* evidence of impact. On the positive side, it shares with integrated natural resource management (INRM) a relatively short history, heavy demands on management and context-specific implementation that prevent robust *ex post* impact evaluation (Barrett 2003).

Yet, the broad suite of interventions that fall under INRM are generally well funded within the international agricultural research community. Climate applications face the additional challenge of engaging climate and agricultural institutions that often do not have a history of substantive cooperation.

Although, there are good theoretical reasons to expect that farmers and other agricultural stakeholders should benefit, there are still few well documented *ex post* demonstrations of adoption and benefit in developing countries, relative to many other agricultural development interventions.

Some rather fundamental expressions of doubt about the potential utility to farmers in developing countries appear in the literature, citing examples of lack of use and barriers to use of available seasonal forecasts by smallholder farmers.

Hansen (2004) summarizes some of these concerns in a set of questions: is there enough predictability at the farm scale to be useful? Do smallholder farmers have the capacity to respond to climate forecasts? Will climate forecasts that could be wrong expose farmers to unacceptable risk? Can smallholder farmers with limited education understand probabilistic climate forecasts? Is the application of seasonal climate forecasts inherently biased against the poor? With the exception of farmers' ability to understand probabilistic forecasts, well designed, data-driven *ex ante* assessments can help answer these concerns for particular contexts.

Credible evidence of acceptability and benefit to farmers may contribute to mobilizing funds and influencing the agendas of institutional partners. On the other hand, much of the support for forecast applications for agriculture has come from sources that do not traditionally fund agricultural research and development, and that have not yet demanded the level of evidence that traditional agricultural donors typically require.

Targeting Interventions

The potential to benefit from seasonal climate forecasts lies in the intersection of predictability of relevant components of climate variability, vulnerability (more correctly, sensitivity) to the adverse impacts of climate variability and ability to modify climate-sensitive decisions (Hansen 2002). *Ex ante* impact assessment, using integrated climate–crop–economic modelling, can provide a quantitative basis for selecting priorities for allocating scarce resources among regions, farming systems and interventions. Examples of the use of *ex ante* modelling to target regions or populations seem to be absent from the climate applications literature. There are, however, a few examples of analysis that are relevant to setting priorities for forecast system development and policy.

FOSTERING AND GUIDING RESPONSES: MODELS FOR MANAGEMENT

Crop simulation was initially seen as a way to integrate knowledge of individual processes, obtain insights into interactions, and use predictive ability to test hypotheses. As their ability to simulate complex genotype × environment × management interactions advanced, crop models were increasingly seen as a way to enhance the transferability of results of traditional agronomic research in the face of environmental heterogeneity.

The advances in food security and rural welfare associated with the green revolution in Asia and Latin America have been difficult to reproduce in marginal rainfed regions. Heterogeneity of the environment has been advanced as one explanation for low rates of adoption of improved technology, and weak returns on investment in extension services in Africa relative to other parts of the developing world. 'An important reason for the failure of earlier programmes was their top-down nature and limited recognition of the wide diversity and heterogeneity of farmers and fields as a prime characteristic of livelihoods and farming systems in (less-favoured areas)'.

Because the production outcomes of management are highly dependent on soils, climate and topography and on farmers' goals, assets, social status and access to markets and services, spatial heterogeneity of these variables creates a need to tailor management to local conditions. Experimental methodology developed in the crop sciences to control for the effects of variability in space and time, is not well suited to the task.

Farming systems research (FSR), advanced as a way to understand the context-specific needs and opportunities of farmers, shares with agronomic experimentation the location specificity problem and need to aggregate to recommendation domains in order to scale up results, with an inevitable tradeoff between relevance and cost. The ten-year international benchmark sites network for agrotechnology transfer (IBSNAT) project was developed under the assumption that appropriate use of crop models could compensate for the limitations of traditional research methods in the face of environmental heterogeneity (IBSNAT 1993). Well validated process-oriented models were seen as relatively rapid and cost-effective means of transferring research results to locations other than where they were developed and tested, and tailoring technology to specific environments without having to replicate field research at every location.

The rationale for using system modelling for agrotechnology transfer in the face of environmental heterogeneity is relevant to the use of seasonal forecasts for climate risk management. Climate variability adds a time dimension to environmental heterogeneity. Regionally adapted and tested crop models allow one to quickly explore the production outcomes of a range of management alternatives under a range of climate scenarios (realized or predicted), and for a range of soil conditions.

System modelling is arguably the only tractable way to do so. Although agronomic trials can be replicated in space, at significant cost, to provide information on management outcomes across space, extending replicated trials over enough years to provide robust results across the range of climate variability is not feasible. Furthermore, adaptive climate risk management is not a packaged technology, but an information input with implications for potentially many aspects of the farming and livelihood system. Because of differences in resource endowment, goals, livelihood strategies and risk tolerance, these applications are likely to be more context-specific than many agronomic technologies.

Farm Management Decision Support Systems

Although, modelling tools that came out of the IBSNAT project and similar efforts during the 1980s and early 1990s targeted researchers, the goal was to use models as '...the means by which knowledge of systems and their performance is made portable and accessible to users whose livelihood and welfare depend on this performance' (IBSNAT 1993). Yet, the mechanism for transferring the resulting knowledge to farmers was not always clear. Increased on-farm use of PCs in developed countries raised the prospect of developing model-based decision support systems (DSS) to deliver the benefits of modelling to farmers more directly through support of tactical farm management decisions.

There have been several attempts to develop and deliver agricultural simulation models via farmer DSS, primarily in Australia and the USA (McCown 2002). To address the problem of model complexity, most provide simplified user interfaces to crop models, or databases of pre-run simulations. PC-Yield addressed the data availability problem by packaging DSS software with a subscription to daily field-specific weather data updates via the Internet. The FARMSCAPE project provided on-site weather stations and soil characterization for client farmers. Limited experience suggests that significant early and ongoing stakeholder participation is also a necessary condition for success.

Despite some modest successes, uptake of model-based farm DSS has, generally, been disappointing. A review of crop model applications in developing countries brought a growing awareness to the forefront, that crop simulation models have not fulfilled early expectations as a tool for transferring technology to farmers.

From a review of 14 DSS projects, McCown (2002) provides a thoughtful analysis of reasons for the low level of farmer adoption, and suggests several niches where DSS might play a significant role in farm decision-making. One of the key lessons is that, while farmers might be willing to use a DSS as a tool to assist in low-level, routine tasks, they tend to resist any proxy—human or software—for their own management process.

Two other observations about farm DSS are significant to this discussion. First, several authors have noted instances where interactions and experimentation around model-based DSS have challenged farmers' perceptions, and stimulated learning and the formulation of new heuristics (i.e. rules of thumb). Once the new heuristics are learned, the DSS is no longer needed. Second, there appears to be a trend toward delivering the knowledge embodied in model-based DSS through expert intermediaries, rather than directly to farmers via the software.

From Decision Support to Discussion Support

The shift in focus away from the traditional notion of DSS toward the use of modelling to stimulate dialogue, highlight options and tradeoffs, and foster co-learning and consensus building lead to the relatively new notion of models as 'discussion support systems'. 'In this 'mutual understanding' relationship, intervention intent shifts from educating and persuading to recognition of and respect for other ways of viewing the world....Intervention emphasis shifts from *prescribing* action to *facilitating* learning in actions' (McCown 2002).

This transition in thinking about the role of agricultural simulation models parallels an ongoing shift within the broader agricultural development community away from a linear model of technology development and transfer, towards increasing recognition that farmers are not passive recipients but innovators who actively experiment and repackage technology to meet their needs and circumstances.

The farm DSS projects that McCown (2002) evaluated are all in developed countries. To what degree can this experience translate to smallholder farmers in developing countries? Limited experience suggests that the prospects are quite good. In a set of workshops with farmers in two villages in Zimbabwe,

Carberry *et al.* (2004) used APSIM crop simulations as a basis for discussion about a range of farm management questions.

Despite initial scepticism on the part of the research team and participating farmers, the farmers found the simulation results to be credible and relevant. The simulation model facilitated virtual experimentation, allowing researchers to respond quickly to questions that participating farmers raised about crop response to fertilizer, management of a limited supply of manure and impacts on competing crops of planting delays forced by labour shortage.

The researchers concluded that the model facilitated a high level of farmer–researcher dialogue and debate between farmers, challenged farmers' perceptions in a manner that led to learning, and stimulated interest in on-farm testing of innovations proposed by the farmers. In the context of climate risk management, researchers used the APSIM model effectively with a group of farmers in western Tamil Nadu, India, as a basis for discussing and debating possible management responses to ENSO-based climate forecasts.

Shifts in aggregate crop area statistics were consistent with farmer discussions about the 2002 climate forecast and crop model results. Gadgil *et al.* (2002) responded to a request from farmers by using the PNUTGRO model to evaluate climatic risk as a function of planting date for rainfed groundnut in southwestern Andhra Pradesh, India. The farmers appeared to value and learn from crop model results that supported a later planting date than normally recommended (Gadgil personal communication).

Model-based Recommendations?

Although, crop models have contributed significantly to discussions about climate applications between researchers and collaborating groups of farmers, the cost of such intensive interactions is high relative to the number of farmers impacted. I am aware of several researchers who are interested in using crop models as a basis for formulating advisories for broad distribution within farming communities. The trend in the USA and Australia towards use of crop models by expert intermediaries who advise farmers (McCown 2002) seems to support such an approach.

Just as DSS have, in come cases, prompted learning and formulation of new heuristics that eliminated further need for the DSS among farmers (McCown 2002), it seems likely that crop models integrated with seasonal forecasts may serve more as a vehicle researchers and farmer advisors to learn principles of climate risk management through accelerated experience and experimentation that they can then transfer through their interaction with farmers.

AGRICULTURE AND FOOD SECURITY

As heads of state and government gather in Rome for the World Food Summit, they can look with satisfaction on the progress that has been made in increasing food production and food security, with concern on the high levels of hunger and malnutrition that persist, and with dismay on the prospect that future progress will be slow and uneven. After 30 years of rapid growth in agricultural production, the world can produce enough food to provide every person with more than 2 700 Calories per day a level which is normally sufficient to ensure that all have access to adequate food, provided distribution is not too unequal.

Yet more than 800 million people in the developing world suffer from chronic undernutrition. Lack of essential energy and protein stunts the bodies, minds and hopes of some 200 million children. Over the past few years, world grain stocks have dwindled to dangerously low levels, highlighting the fragility of food supplies in a world where the population is expected to reach 7 billion people by the year 2010, almost double the 3.7 billion of 1970.

Achievements and Lessons of the Past

IN THE EARLY 1960s, global food supplies for direct human consumption stood at only 2 300 Calories per person per day, very unequally distributed. In developed countries the average was already 3 030 Calories per day. In the developing world it languished below 2 000. Probably more than half the people in the developing world suffered from chronic undernutrition.

Then over 30 years, the world population more than doubled. But agricultural production increased even faster. By 1994, global food supplies for human consumption had climbed to 2 710 Calories per person per day. And the percentage of chronically undernourished people in the developing world had been reduced to 20 percent. These gains resulted from a number of factors including:

- widespread use of new, high-yielding crop varieties and technologies. The package of technologies referred to as the green revolution, including increased use of irrigation, fertilizer and pesticides, increased yields for millions of farmers, although with some negative social and environmental impacts.
- increased reliance on food imports. During the 1970s alone, net imports of cereals by developing countries more than tripled-from 20 million to 67 million tonnes.

Increased cereal yields in developing countries (kg/ha)

Progress for Some, but not for All

Despite gains in food production and food security on a world scale, many countries and whole regions failed to make progress in recent decades. Sub-Saharan Africa produces less food per person today than it did 30 years ago. The number of chronically undernourished people in the region has more than doubled since 1970, from 96 million to over 200 million.

For the most part, countries endowed with better resources to begin with scored rapid gains in food production. On the other hand, yields generally stagnated in those countries that started with very low yields. Wheat yields in the ten most productive countries jumped from 2.65 to 5.12 tonnes per hectare.

But average yields among countries at the other end of the scale edged up only from 0.47 to 0.76 tonnes per hectare. After achieving significant growth in per caput food production during the 1960s, numerous developing countries failed to make progress over the past two decades. The majority of them registered outright declines between 1972 and 1992.

Looking Forward-Continued Gain, Continued Pain

Looking ahead to the year 2010, world agricultural growth is expected to slow but should still outpace population growth. As a result, food availability in the developing countries will improve to an average above 2 700 Calories per person per day.

But not all regions and countries will share equally in these gains in production and nutrition. The situation in Africa south of the Sahara will deteriorate further, while progress in South Asia will be painfully slow. By the year 2010, the number of chronically undernourished people in sub-Saharan Africa may still be some 264 million, or 30 percent of the population.

Environmental Constraints

IN THE PAST, expansion and intensification of agriculture have often damaged the very resources essential to farming-such as soil, water and the genetic diversity of crops-as well as the wider environment.

Soil erosion and other forms of land degradation rob the world of 5 million to 7 million ha of farming land every year. Clearing forests or growing crops on steep slopes or on large fields without protection against the wind can lead to erosion.

Waterlogging and salinization caused by poor drainage have sapped the productivity of nearly half the world's irrigated lands. Some 30 million ha have been severely damaged and an additional 1.5 million ha are lost each year. Excess use of mineral fertilizers and pesticides can pollute surface and: groundwater sources. Nitrates from fertilizers and feedlot wastes have contaminated groundwater in many countries and have been identified as a health risk, especially for infants. At the same time, in some countries the use of too little fertilizer depletes soil nutrients and contributes to soil degradation.

Loss of genetic diversity has accelerated with the spread of intensive agriculture and high-yielding crop varieties to large parts of the developing world, replacing the traditional diversity of crops with monocultures.

Deforestation accelerated during the 1980s, with more than 15 million ha of tropical forests lost each year, mainly to provide land for agriculture. Agriculture also contributes significantly to release of greenhouse gases that have been linked to global warming. Some 30 percent of carbon dioxide emissions result from deforestation and other land use practices such as rangeland burning and agriculture may account for as much as 90 percent of nitrous oxide emissions.

PLAN, PROTECT AND PRODUCE

The per caput availability of agricultural land in developing countries is projected to nearly halve between the late 1980s and 2010, from 0.65 to about 0.4 hectares. Even this figure will shrink further by 2050. It is critically important to optimize the uses to which land is put, assisted by sophisticated techniques of land-use planning. Land that is designated for agricultural use will have to be carefully protected, using a range of conservation techniques, from the degradation that now results in the loss of an estimated 5 to 7 million hectares of good land each year.

Most land users do not have the time, the resources or the inclination to adopt new, and perhaps risky, practices to tackle problems that they probably cannot even see. So emphasis must be placed on involving farmers from the start in developing and adopting measures that not only conserve the soil but also offer short-term, tangible benefits-such as increased yields or easier work.

Matching the Land to the Use

Sound land-use planning has been made much easier by the advent of micro-computers, the development of databases and the use of Geographic Information Systems.

The diagram below summarizes the essential steps in optimizing the choice of crop for any given plot of land, down to a 1 0-km square. These steps involve matching the requirements of individual crops (step 1) with existing conditions on the ground: climatic requirements (2a) and soil requirements (2b). Overlaying these two inventories then creates a land inventory which includes information on both climate and soil (3). Constraints on crop yield are then added on, together with information about pests and harvesting difficulties (4). Finally, data on soil constraints are added, resulting in a land-use recommendation about what crop should be grown, what inputs will be required, and what crop management techniques should be used.

The Causes of Land Degradation

Human activities have often led to degradation of the world's land resources. Damage has occurred on 15 percent of the world's total land area 13 percent light and moderate, 2 percent severe and very severe. There are four main types of land degradation.

The commonest form of degradation, water erosion is causing massive damage in nearly all developing countries. It occurs where steep land is being unwisely farmed and where gently sloping land is left exposed to the effects of heavy rain. In the United States the annual loss of topsoil still averages 12 tonnes per hectare, and an estimated 50 million tonnes a year of plant nutrients are washed away with it.

Land stripped of vegetation and exposed to strong winds can be quickly blown away-as much as 150 tonnes can be blown off one hectare in an hour. Wind erosion caused the famous dust bowls in the Great Plains of the United States in the 1 930s. The cure for wind erosion is to ensure good ground cover and windbreaks (such as hedges).

Soil may be damaged if it is worked with heavy equipment in wet weather or when it is compacted round water holes in pasture land. Biological damage occurs when soils are deprived of their nutrients, organic matter or humus. Deep-rooting crops are needed to cure physical damage, and crop rotation and good farming practices to cure biological damage. When poorly drained land is irrigated, the sun evaporates the water, leaving behind its salts. After several years, the soil becomes highly saline and affects plant growth. If drainage is very poor, the soil may also become waterlogged. It is estimated that about 40 million out of 200 million irrigated hectares are waterlogged, affected by salt, or both. The area of land being abandoned every year for these reasons is roughly equal to the amount of land being reclaimed and irrigated.

FOOD SECURITY AND THE ENVIRONMENT

In order to meet minimum requirements of a growing population, food production will need to double over the next 30 years. Yet the natural resources required to produce this additional food such as soil, water and the diversity of crops and livestock-are finite and vulnerable to degradation.

Between 1950 and 1995, for example, rapid population growth cut in half the amount of cultivated land per person-from more than half a hectare to barely a quarter.Because only about 11 percent of the world's land is really suited to agriculture, the amount of arable land per person will continue shrinking. By the year 2020, for example, Southeast Asia will have only 0.09 hectares per person-an area barely one-tenth the size of a soccer field.

Per caput water availability is also falling rapidly. In Africa, for example, the amount of water available per person has dropped almost 75 percent since 1950-from over 20,000 cubic metres a year to a little over 5,000 cubic metres. Experts define countries where the amount of water available for all purposes, including agriculture and industry, amounts to less than 1,000 cubic metres per person per year. More than 230 million people-mostly in Africa and the Near East-now live in such countries.

The Price of Expanded Production

Pushing against resource limits to increase food production can damage or degrade natural resources in many ways:

Soil degradation-Expansion of agriculture onto less suitable land exposes fragile soils to the dangers of erosion and nutrient depletion. Human-induced degradation already affects almost 2 billion hectares, or 15 percent of the world's soils.

Deforestation-During the 1980s, more than 15 million hectares of tropical forests were lost each year, mainly to provide land for agriculture.

Drainage of wetlands-Felling and drainage of mangrove forests and other coastal wetlands destroys spawning and feeding grounds for fisheries. About 95 percent of the world's marine production originates from coastal ecosystems.

Loss of biodiversity-The conversion of forests and other natural habitats to food production has been the primary reason for the rapid loss of biological diversity that threatens between 5 and 20 percent of some groups of vertebrates and plants with extinction.

Overfishing-almost 70 percent of those stocks of marine fisheries for which assessments are available are being fished at levels close to or beyond the maximum sustainable yield.

Intensive Production-Promise and Peril

Applying intensive production techniques to increase output from Lands already under cultivation could both provide enough food to meet the needs of an expanding population and relieve pressure on marginal Lands and vulnerable ecosystems. Research stations typically obtain yields more than double those achieved by farmers under similar conditions.

But intensive food production can also take a heavy toll on the environment. Poorly managed irrigation can lead to salinization and waterlogging. Some 30 million hectares of irrigated Land have been severely damaged by poor drainage and accumulation of salt in the soil.

Reliance on a few high-yielding varieties of plants and Livestock has eroded biodiversity within the limited number of species used for agriculture, increasing vulnerability to pests and diseases.

Thirty percent of all breeds of Livestock have less than 20 breeding males or Less than 1000 breeding females remaining. Intensive aquaculture systems, such as cage culture of salmon and Large-scale shrimp culture in coastal areas, can cause excessive nutrient enrichment of water bodies, degradation of wetlands and the loss of biological diversity from the introduction of exotic species.

How to Reduce Environmental Impacts

Environmentally sound food production systems must achieve three aims: increase production and productivity, reduce pollution and resource degradation, and be socially and economically viable.

Among hundreds of attractive possibilities, the following will have priority:

- the prevention of soil erosion with live hedges, grass strips, orchard trees, simple bench and ridge terraces, contour ploughing, strip cropping, limited tillage, green manuring, windbreaks and mulches;
- improving the management of irrigated areas, in particular by improving drainage to the 11 million hectares of waterlogged irrigation land in Asia;
- large-scale promotion of integrated plant nutrition systems, which provide crops with the nutrients they need at the optimal return to the farmer;
- large-scale promotion of integrated pest management systems, which use biological and other techniques to control crop pests with a minimum use of pesticides;
- development of intensive methods of livestock production, of biogas units for use of animal wastes, and of diets to reduce methane emissions from cattle;
- improved fishery management to allow marine stocks to recover, as well as intensive development of aquaculture and inland fisheries;
- the development of non-wood forest products as sources of income;
- fuelwood plantations around homesteads and in pert-urban areas;
- the use of agroforestry to diversify production, increase productivity and stabilize soil and water resources; and
- policy adjustments to foster biodiversity through techniques such as mixed use buffer zones to protect existing areas, and the maintenance of crop diversity through crop rotations and sequences.

Securing Food within Nature's Limits

Scientists believe that technical options are available to provide enough food for future populations without harming the environment.

Keys to achieving this in practice will be:

- the efficient use of resources-that is, converting scarce resources into useful products in a way that is economically viable but that minimizes impact on the environment during production, processing and marketing;
- the use of planning and implementation frameworks to facilitate and diffuse the responses provided by science and technology to the demand for more food. an approach to governance that promotes dialogue with diverse interest groups and shares decision-making authority and control over allocation of resources to district and local levels, while simultaneously discouraging corrupt or inefficient practices.

The political and administrative framework for achieving these goals should have at least four main elements:

- introduction of ecologically-sound, participatory land-use planning to identify and mitigate the environmental impacts of increased food production;
- social and economic policies that encourage food producers to manage their soil fertility and moisture, pest populations and biological diversity through integrated management systems. In many cases, success will depend on first addressing social or economic constraints such as equitable land tenure and access to capital, unemployment and the marginalization of women;
- investment in human capital and rural infrastructure by integrating agricultural research, education and extension and training agricultural advisors to help farmers apply environmentally-sound food production methods;
- continuous environmental assessment, monitoring and evaluation of the impacts of food production practices, and feeding this information back to policy-makers and producers.

The Role of Government

Unlike many other sectors, governments have a special role to play in promoting rural development and environmentally sound agriculture. Governments should:

- support environmentally-based practices through incentives that promote the efficient use of inputs and encourage the full use of human resources
- reduce subsidies that lead to adverse environmental impacts introduce water pricing policies and institutional changes to increase the efficiency of water use in all sectors
- develop policcs to promote the best land-use practices and the equitable distribution of resources
- transform smallholder agriculture into modern, competitive and productive enterprises by investing in sustainable agricultural and rural development
- assess food production potential in and around cities, and produce more food near to where it is consumed
- improve infrastructure so that farmers can deploy quality seed, fertilizer and equipment, and equip extension staff to promotc sound environmental management practices

5

Global Climate Change and Food Security in a Growing World

Global climate change is one of utmost international concerns. There is a perception among many that global climate change is simply global warming. In fact, global climate change is an integrated system of several atmospheric phenomena and their products. At the surface, concentrations of greenhouse or radiative gases such as carbon dioxide, chlorofluorocarbons, methane and nitrous oxide have clearly increased since the onset of the industrial revolution. These trace gases, in addition to warming the surface air temperature by trapping some of the energy from the outgoing radiation, when transported into the stratosphere (10-15 km above the surface), destroy the beneficial ozone layer naturally present at that height. Such a loss in the thickness or thinning of the ozone layer will permit the increased penetration to the surface of deleterious wavelengths of solar radiation (Ultraviolet or UV [B-band], 280-315 nanometers, 1 nanometer = one billionth of meter), with much concern for consequent increases in the incidence of melanoma or skin cancer.

Average global air temperature has increased by about 0.8° C above pre-industrial levels and a 2001 report by the Intergovernmental Panel on Climate Change projected a rise from 1.4° C to 5.8° C by the year 2100. While this prediction is extremely important, there is a significant amount of spatial variability in the air temperature. Local climate in different geographic areas may very well become warmer and drier, cooler and wetter or remain unchanged. Any change in the climate is expected to manifest itself as increases in the frequency of extreme events such as hurricanes, blizzards, heat waves and the number of days without precipitation during the plant-growing season (drought).

Increases in air temperature can accelerate crop growth and consequently shorten the growth period. In cereal crops for example, such changes can lead to poor vernalization (e.g., hastened flowering) and reduced yield. There is also evidence that since the 1950s, in North America, in China and in the former Soviet Union, nighttime temperatures have increased much more than the daytime values (because of increased cloud cover due to air pollution and formation of hygroscopic, cloud-forming aerosols in the atmosphere), with the potential to reduce reproductive development in many crop species and consequently, their seed yield.

In developed countries, agriculture is supported by a complex system of research; education, finance and farm supply overlying the agricultural potentials of the arable soils. Public policy and agricultural management will attempt to develop strategies for maintaining crop production in areas with best soils, in spite of shifts in climate. Of equal or greater importance than the direct effects of rising air temperatures is the indirect effect on the hydrologic cycle, leading to shifts in the dependence on irrigation, where water is available. For example, projected drier summers in parts of the USA corn-belt will probably result in a shift from the production of corn to grain sorghum. This has serious economic consequences. Currently USA ranks #1 in the world in corn production (41% of the global production) and the area of its cultivation is on the rise, particularly since it is the largest source for ethanol (through fermentation) used as fuel in automobiles.

In as much as changes in air temperatures will have an impact on crop production, so will increases in the surface concentrations of carbon dioxide and ozone and elevated levels of ultraviolet-B radiation. Most unfortunately, much of our knowledge on these effects is based on experimental studies directed to changes in one variable at a time. Increases in the carbon dioxide concentrations are expected to increase the biomass in many crop species (particularly C3 plants such as soybean and rice, in comparison to C4 plants such as corn and sorghum). However, as seen in the greenhouse production of horticultural crops such as lettuce, increases in biomass may not always translate to acceptable nutritional quality of the consumed product, due to the increases in the accumulation of starch in the foliage at the expense of soluble carbohydrates and decreases in the protein content, unless nitrogen fertilization is practiced. In as much as the beneficial effects of increasing carbon dioxide concentrations on crop production are frequently cited, increasing levels of surface ozone (generated from precursor pollutant emissions, primarily from fossil fuel combustion) and ultraviolet-B radiation produce deleterious effects. Rapidly growing number of studies show that the adverse effects of ozone and ultraviolet-B radiation offset the beneficial effects of carbon dioxide. Since all three variables are on the rise (accounting, however, for their spatial variability), questions remain as to the outcome of their joint effects, superimposed on other climate variables such as shifts in air temperature and soil moisture availability and biotic factors (incidence of pathogens and pests).

While plant canopies serve as a sink for carbon dioxide during photosynthesis (daytime), they are a source during the night due to respiration. Furthermore, soils are a larger source for carbon dioxide due to increased microbial respiration and litter or biomass decomposition under increasing temperatures. Equally importantly agricultural emissions of greenhouse gases are governed by the use of nitrogen fertilizers (increased nitrous oxide emissions from the soil as a greenhouse gas) and animal husbandry (increased ammonia emissions from manure leading to atmospheric nitrogen fertilization by deposition, for example, in precipitation). Those are major concerns in the context of the contribution of agriculture to the climate change issue (warming air temperatures due to the former or shifts in biodiversity due to the latter). In addition, rice paddies are a major source of methane (a greenhouse gas). As populations grow in Asia (by some 29% in 2030), so will the area under rice production, to sustain the food supply.

Clearly the issues associated with deteriorating air quality are a global concern. Satellite data document the spread of aerosols all the way from West Africa to northeastern India to China. India and China rank among the top countries in net human consumption of primary food production. India also ranks at the top in the withdrawal of more than 40% of its total available fresh water supply, in comparison to China (20-40%) and the USA (10-20%). By the year 2050, a majority of the global population is projected to be at a high risk of suffering from water stress. Currently Asia supports more than one half of the global population, with a projected increase of 29% by the year 2030. In comparison, population is expected to increase in Africa by 65%, North America by 26%, and South America by 31% and in contrast, a decrease by 6% is predicted for Europe. The increases in the populations of Asia, Africa and South America are projected to be largely due the birth rates while increases in the US population would be mainly due to immigration.

It is very educative to examine the status of the present and projected global agricultural production within these overall scenarios. Currently the ratio of rural to total populations is for: the world-52%, China-65%, India-71% and the USA-20%. Similarly the ratio of agricultural to rural populations is for: the world-80%, China-94%, India-73% and the USA-10%. These are telling statistics of the major dependence of the two most populous countries in the world (China and India) and in addition, some others, on intense human labor for food production and sustainability, compared to the US.

China, India and the US account equally for some 40% of the total area in the world under crop production. Yet the agricultural production in metric tons per capita of the total population is for: the world-0.26, China-0.29, India-0.20 and the USA-1.4. The large difference between the statistic for the US and the others is due mainly to the use of complex and highly mechanized and managed crop production systems in the US, compared to the emphasis on manual labor elsewhere.

In the US these types of statistics have led to some adverse, shortsighted consequences. There has been a progressive decline in the number of individual farmers and a converse increase in corporate mega farming. In addition fluctuations in the commodity prices, the so-called surplus food supply and imports of foreign plant products have worked negatively against the profitability of individual US farmers and thus, the decline in their numbers.

The genetic base of domesticated or cultivated plants is very narrow compared to their wild relatives. Thus, many currently grown crops are considered to be genetically depauperate. Elite lines and hybrids derived from such germplasms are designed to yield well under relatively narrow and well-defined growing conditions. However, superior genotypes are used heavily in various crop-breeding programs, often resulting in considerable relatedness among cultivars grown across large geographic areas, although some cultivars may have more narrow distribution than others.

In general, the narrow genetic base and specific goals used in the breeding of virtually all modern crops make it unlikely that crop breeders will be able to accommodate large and rapid changes in the climate. On the other hand if climate change occurs gradually, production agriculture will be able to adapt to such changes as long as farm resources are not limiting. Nevertheless, if indirect selection of crops to climate change is practiced, it will prove to be an inefficient process. Thus, there will be an increasing need for regions able to sustain high crop production in the future to distribute their surplus food supply to others subjected to adverse impacts, particularly to populations in dire need. That might prove to be a critical determinant of future world populations.

The US agriculture is influenced by: (a) increased urbanization, (b) increasing population migration from rural to urban communities, (c) farming by increased mechanization and consequently decreased dependence on labor, (d) increased area under cultivation of crops developed through the application of biotechnology and consequently better disease, pest and weed control, (e) gain of higher yields and (f) farm consolidation through mergers (mega-corporate farms). In contrast, factors influencing food security in the developing countries include: (a) increasing population, (b) rapidly growing urbanization, (c) decreasing crop land, (d) decreasing farm resources, (e) continuing crop loss, (e) declining crop production and (f) declining biodiversity.

The number of mega cities (greater than 10 million population per city) has increased from 2 in 1950 to 28 in 2004. In 2001, the numbers of poor people (living on $1 or less per day) were concentrated primarily in East Asia, Sub-Saharan Africa and South Asia. During 1998, as equivalents of 1990 $, significant long-term growth in GDP (Gross Domestic Product) per capita was predominantly in Western Europe, Japan, US, Canada and the Oceania.

Based on 2003 statistics, according to the Organization of Economic Cooperation and Development (OECD), additional foreign support needed for developing countries to reach 0.5 level of GDP in billions of $, among all developed countries, the US and Japan were the worst in giving aid. In contrast, Sweden and the Netherlands were the most generous with no additional aid required to reach the 0.5 GDP level. Thus, there is a major gap among the main nations of wealth and those that need support for sustainability of their society and their agriculture.

In the final analysis, scientists will continue to study the critical and important issues of the effects of adverse air quality and climate change on crop production. Unfortunately, some scientists have and will use socio-political reasons to further their own cause.

Fortunately, in general, those types of activities are transient by nature (e.g., the rise and fall of the acidic precipitation research program in the US during the 1980s and 90s). At the end, sustaining the future global populations through food production and food security would require scientific integrity and a much broader and holistic understanding of the many coupled, but complex facets of our society and their feedbacks to the continuing process of environmental change and its impacts.

SUSTAINABILITY OF FOOD SECURITY IN ASIA

Ensuring food for all, today and in generations to come, is one of the greatest challenges facing the world community. Food security is defined as the ability of people to meet their required level of food consumption at all times; it is considered by many to be a basic human right. However, about 1.1 thousand million people in low-income, food-deficit developing countries cannot meet such basic needs. Among them, more than 800 million live in rural areas, depending directly on agriculture for their food supply, employment and income. Therefore, boosting the rural economy, particularly through increased agricultural production, is one of the chief means of alleviating poverty and increasing food security.

Food security consists of three major components: availability (associated with production and trade); accessibility (associated with income and wealth); and utilization (associated with health and nutrition) (Asenso-Okyere, Benneh and Tims, 1997). While there seems to be a consensus among analysts that current global food production is adequate to avoid widespread famine and malnutrition, the overall positive trends disguise the disparities in production and distribution of food between regions. The disparities are described by Rosegrant, Agcaoili-Sombilla and Perez (1995) as a two-tiered system of food security, in which rich and rapidly growing economies enjoy abundant, affordable food supplies, while poor, slow-growing countries suffer from food scarcity and malnutrition. This means that the food security problem is, in the main, not one of shortage but of imbalance and distribution.

Another aspect of food security is sustainability. The concerns are: "can food production continue to keep up with demand in generations to come?" and "is the prosperity of the current generation at the expense of the future?" Some analysts believe that the rapid growth in agricultural production in the last few decades has occurred at great environmental cost (Anderson, 1994). That is, over-exploitation has resulted in natural resources being depleted and the environment being damaged. Indeed, the greater intensity of use of land and water resources and chemicals has created problems such as soil salinization, soil erosion, water pollution, pest resistance, etc. As a result, there are signs of declining rates of growth in yields. For example, it has been shown that the average annual growth rate of paddy rice yield in the world declined from 2.42 percent in 1974-82 to 1.78 percent in 1982-90. The corresponding figures were 2.62 and 1.66 percent for Asia and 4 and 1.6 percent for China. Similar results were found for other crops, including wheat, maize, sorghum and other coarse grains.

Similarly, externalities from agricultural production, and related environmental or "green" issues such as climate change, preservation of wilderness areas and biodiversity, animal welfare and food safety, have received increasing attention in the discussion of agricultural policy in recent years.

These concerns suggest that sustainable food security is not only about meeting the increasing and changing demand for food now, but about protecting the environment for future generations. Whether and how this is to be achieved depends on a number of economic, social and political factors, both at the national and international levels. Socioeconomic factors with potentially significant effects on future developments in the world food situation include: population and income growth, demographic changes and urbanization on the demand side, as well as technological change and productivity growth on the supply side. Therefore, future agricultural production and productivity growth depend on, among others, a combination of agricultural, environmental, trade and macroeconomic policies at the global level.

Although food security issues are multi-faceted, the discussion here focuses on food availability and production in Asia and the Pacific as a first step towards resolving such issues. Particular attention is paid to the role of investment and agricultural productivity in meeting the challenge of sustainable food security.

Seven member countries in this region were selected for in-depth examination: Australia, the United States, China, India, Indonesia, Japan and South Korea. These countries are chosen because of their importance in the food balance both in the world and the region. For example, China and India are predicted jointly to account for more than 30 percent of the estimated global increase in cereal demand (718 million metric tons) between 1993 and 2020. The estimated demand increase from China has raised concerns over China's ability to feed itself and the impact of changes in China's trade position on global food balances and prices. Indonesia is chosen for similar reasons. Together, these three countries account for nearly 70 percent and 40 percent of the population in Asia and in the world in 1996, respectively.

In addition, Australia and the United States are chosen because of their role as major food exporters to the region. Japan and South Korea, on the other hand, represent (newly) industrialized countries that are major food importers. These differences among the selected countries in the stage of economic development, resource endowments and government policy are central to identifying factors in affecting agricultural productivity growth and the role of government policy.

PRODUCTION AND PRODUCTIVITY GROWTH IN AGRICULTURE

When evaluating the performance of a production unit or the agricultural sector, it is common to use production (the level of output), productivity (output per unit of input) or efficiency (actual output relative to the potential output or best practices) as indicators. Although these measures are closely related, they can yield different rankings in measuring performance. In general, productivity is the most commonly used measure, be it measured in terms of total factor productivity (TFP) or in partial terms such as labour productivity (output per labour) and yield (output per hectare) for its relative ease in calculation and interpretation.

In the following sections, changes over time in output and productivity growth in different regions are compared and the causes for variations are discussed.

Agricultural Development and Input Use

Agricultural output and productivity vary greatly with the stage of economic development, resource endowments, government policy and agronomic-ecological conditions.

However, there is a similar path in agricultural development over time and across countries. Pingali and Heisey (1996) categorized the technological transformation of cereal crop production system into three distinct phases:

i. the land-augmentation phase;
ii. the labour-substitution phase; and
iii. the knowledge-and management-intensity phase.

The basic assumption is that the transition from one phase to another is determined by growing factor scarcity, first for land, then for labour and finally for other factors of production, such as machinery and management skills.

The first phase is characterized by area expansion being the main source of output growth, as was seen during the pre-Green Revolution era of the 1950s and 1960s. However, as opportunities for area expansion decline over time, cropping intensity is increased, along with increasing use of water, fertilizers, pesticides and high yielding varieties. This was indeed the case during the Green-Revolution period in the 1970s and early 1980s.

Such intensive production results in an increased demand for labour and mechanization, as the production system moves from single-cropping to double-and triple-cropping with increased application of purchased inputs. Eventually, production reaches the point of diminishing marginal returns to further intensification, as was the case in the late 1980s, the post-Green Revolution phase. Here, better technical knowledge and management skills are used to substitute for traditional inputs.

Variety selection, fertilizer timing and placement, water management and pesticide application are some areas in which productivity has improved with reduction in unit cost of production. The model just outlined is used in the following analysis as the basic framework to explain the changes in input use and in productivity between the 1960s and the 1990s. First, it is applied to various regions in the world, then to the developing and developed countries, and finally to the selected countries in Asia and the Pacific.

FACTORS AFFECTING PRODUCTIVITY GROWTH

In explaining productivity growth, economists originally limited themselves to the role of conventional inputs such as land, labour, physical capital, water and chemical inputs. However, the failure to explain productivity growth adequately led them to examine the role of human capital and public goods, such as education, agricultural research and extension and publicly provided infrastructure. Public policies that have a strong link to agricultural productivity such as policy reforms were also examined.

The rationale for considering research is the belief that investments in research result in increases in the stock of knowledge, which, in turn, either facilitate the use of existing knowledge or generate new technology. Technological advances, whether resulting from changes in input quality or how inputs are combined, lead to productivity gains. Education, training and extension also increase productivity by increasing people's knowledge and skill base, which are essential for technology adoption and efficient use of inputs. Public infrastructure, on the other hand, increases productivity by facilitating the exchange of goods and services.

Technological Change

Technological change is recognized by many as one of the most important sources of productivity growth. It refers to the changes in the production process that come about from the application of innovation and newly acquired scientific knowledge and technical and management skills. Technological change increases agricultural productivity either by shifting the production frontier upward so that more measured output can be produced with the same amount of inputs or by moving closer to the production frontier so that the same amount of output can be produced with a smaller amount of inputs. Better organizational and management skills not only improve input-output combinations but enable producers to respond more quickly to changing market circumstances.

While generation of new technology or knowledge comes from investments in research and development, adoption of technology involves investments by the potential users in both physical and human capital. Therefore, adoption of technology depends principally on their applicability and expected returns of the innovation. However, there may be a long lag between development, adoption and productivity gains. Chavas and Cox (1992) found the lag to be up to 15 years between making an investment in research and having an effect on productivity. However, after taking effect, the benefits from an innovation may persist for thirty years or more.

The lag between generation of new technology and its widespread adoption by farmers has important policy implications. First, the adverse effects of reduced public funding to agricultural research and extension on productivity may be under-estimated if the lagged effects are not accounted for. Secondly, the complementarity between research and extension should be taken into account. The former helps the development of new technology, while the latter helps speed up the rate of diffusion and adoption of new technology. Extension can be done more effectively by identifying factors that contribute to technology adoption. As an example, innovators in a farming community can be identified and targeted for extension services.

Since better-educated farmers are found to be more likely to adopt new technology, human capital is a pre-condition for technology adoption and hence productivity growth. Further, if adoption of new technology requires additional investments, lack of access to credit and additional inputs may prevent or slow down technology adoption. Finally, because potential users of new technology often differ in the agronomic-ecological conditions in which they operate, new technology may require adaptive research before it can be transferred successfully to different locations. These impediments to technology adoption mean careful planning and provision of necessary infrastructure are essential to capture the full benefits of new technology.

Agricultural Research and Extension

Many researchers have explored the roles of research and extension in promoting agricultural growth. Rosegrant and Evenson (1992) found that in South Asia, public research accounted for 30 percent of the output growth, and extension for about 25 percent, with corresponding rates of return being 63 percent and 52 percent, respectively. Pray and Evenson's (1991) survey of Asia found the rates of return to national research investment ranged from 19 to 218 percent, returns to national extension investment from 15 to 215 percent, and returns to international research investment from 68 to 108 percent.

Evenson and McKinsey (1991) found that public investment in research accounted for over half of the output growth in India and extension contributed about one-third. The calculated internal rates of return were 218 percent for public research and 177 percent for extension. However, they found that little output growth was attributable to infrastructure. Jamison and Lau (1982) also found that physical capital had little impact on production or profits, as compared to farmer's education and extension services.

Fan (1996) found that public research expenditures accounted for about 20 percent of total production growth in Chinese agriculture during the period 1965 to 1994. The annual rates of return to agricultural research investment in China ranged from 44 percent to 83 percent.

Fan (1996) concluded that the rapid growth in agricultural output in China during the 1980s and 1990s was the result of public investments in R&D as well as the institutional and market reforms that began in 1979. He concluded that increases in agricultural research were justifiable; not only did they stimulate additional output growth, but the rate of return to agricultural research was much higher than commercial interest rates.

Despite the high rates of returns from public research investments, agricultural research intensity (ARI), measured as a percentage of Chinese agricultural GDP, was found to have declined from 0.56 percent for the period 1958-1965 to 0.43, 0.44, 0.39 and 0.40 percent, respectively, for 1966-1976, 1977-1985, 1986-1990 and 1991-1993 (Fan, 1996). Lin (1998) reported that, as part of the overall market reform, the Chinese Government had reduced its fiscal appropriation for agricultural research, shifting funding from institutional supports to competitive grants and cost recovery. As such, it can be expected that an increasing proportion of research activities will move from the public to the private domain.

Other studies on output growth have also shown a high payoff from agricultural research and extension. The results indicate that the rate of return on research, in most cases, ranged from 15 to 50 percent for both developed and developing countries, but some estimates were as high as 218 percent. The wide disparity among the estimates raises questions regarding the sensitivity of these estimates to the commodity of interest and the use of different time periods and methodologies.

Estimates for Asian countries appear to be higher and show a much wider variation than those of studies in the United States. This could be due to the diverse nature of Asian agriculture, which differs from country to country in economic, social and agronomic-ecological conditions. Because of inconsistency in the data and methodology used, it is not possible to make direct comparisons across countries or over time. Nevertheless, the general conclusion that R&D yields relatively high returns seems indisputable.

Human Capital

Human capital refers to knowledge, experience and skills possessed by people involved in the production process. It is influenced directly by education, training and extension. Its importance lies in the fact that it has a significant impact on the adoption and the utilization of technology, which in turn, affect the allocation of resources and productivity. A well-trained and well-educated labour force is said to be in a better position to assess changing conditions and make necessary adjustments. This ability is becoming ever more important in an increasingly deregulated and global economy where changes in the commodity markets are frequent and quick responses are required.

The concept of investment in human capital covers not only investments in formal schooling and post-school and on-the-job training, but also investment in the form of improved health and family care. Social capital, on the other hand, refers to one's ability to utilize social networks and institutions. Social status, education and the range of social institutions available can influence one's social capital. Social capital is important in that it affects access to physical capital, land title, credit and cooperatives, all of which have implications for resource allocation and, hence, productivity.

Women appear to suffer most severely from having limited access to human and social capital in some developing countries, although a larger proportion of women than men are engaged in agriculture. For example, women account for 70 to 80 percent of household food production in sub-Saharan Africa, 65 percent in Asia, and 45 percent in Latin America and the Caribbean.

As such, it has been suggested that empowerment of women and gender equality are important factors for raising productivity and promoting food security in developing countries. Jahnke, Kirschke and Lagemann (1987) also found that low adoption of high yield varieties (HYV) in Africa is attributable to lack of appropriate technology development and few extension services directed to women. These findings suggest that acknowledging the critical role of rural women in Asia and providing them with greater access to resources and human capital are crucial in promoting sustainable agriculture and food security.

MARKETS, CLIMATE CHANGE, AND FOOD SECURITY

In 2009, chronic and abrupt food security crises continue to plague many regions around the world, despite the productive capacity to feed every person adequately. Food security, the ability of all people to have enough food for an active and healthy life, has not been attained for all for many reasons, including broad issues of poverty, natural resource disparities, unequal global trading arrangements, and poor or corrupt government(s), among others. In 2008, the Global Hunger Index found that West Africa is a region with some of the most severe hunger in the world (1). This book will explore the relationships among global environmental change, food prices, and food insecurity in West Africa, and the role that technology can play in addressing these problems. The use of technology in agriculture has transformed food production in many parts of the world during the past century. Irrigation, improved seeds, chemical fertilizers and pesticides, and the use of large machinery have massively increased worker productivity and crop yields. These industrial production systems, coupled with tightly integrated shipping and transportation networks, grain storage, and processing systems have kept global food prices steady or declining since 1950, despite massive increases in global population.

Technological change has not reached most West African region farmers, however. In that region, farms are small, primarily cultivated with hand tools, planted with seeds with low yield potential, and use little or no chemical fertilizer. Consequently, most small farms are only able to attain yields which are less than one-seventh (~14%) of those regularly achieved in industrialized systems. In most of the region, purchasing food takes up 50% or more of most households' income. As global demand for food doubles by 2050, the regions that are already food-insecure today are likely to be put under further pressure as the price of food rises.

Climate change is likely to further threaten the ability of the region to compete in a global food system. Although the likely impact of climate change on rainfall in the region is currently unclear, increases in average temperature will undoubtedly reduce yields in tropical countries as well as in many of the key production areas of the world. Changes in climate, coupled with the likely doubling of the local population (in West Africa) and an addition of at least two billion more people to feed globally in the next two decades, make it very likely that food prices will return to and surpass the levels seen in 2008. The advent of large-scale use of food commodities in biofuels means that the surplus previously seen in the U.S. is rapidly disappearing. These elements will put a significant pressure on markets that are thus likely to again produce high commodity prices in the near future.

West Africa is a semiarid region with a rapidly growing population and a very low gross domestic product. In contrast to South and East Asia, which have seen a reduction in the number of food-insecure people in recent years, the number of poor and food-insecure people in Africa is still rising and is likely to continue to rise because of the lack of economic and agricultural growth that can feed the increasing population. A significant portion of the world's extreme poor, who live on less than $0.50/day, reside in the region.

Many farming families have diversified their income sources, working in rural markets, livestock production, crafts, and wage labor markets. Although this has increased cash income and to some extent has also improved the standard of living, it has also driven most farmers in the region to be net purchasers of food from the market. In fact, despite its agricultural orientation, the entire West African region is a net food buyer, importing even local food staples such as millet and corn.

West African farming households experience significant interannual variability in food production and prices. Local food prices are influenced by a diversity of factors, including social unrest, macro-economic policies of the governments, food and income assistance often from multiple sources, regional price and crop production variations, as well as demand and other market factors. However, when weather reduces agricultural production over large areas, the resulting widespread reductions in supply cause significant increases in local food prices.

In addition to annual variation, prices of food staples also exhibit a distinct seasonal pattern. The two main reasons for this are a lack of storage capacity and the limited access of rural producers to export channels. An inability to store forces farmers to sell most of their surplus in the months after harvest (September"December), and to purchase imported grain during the "hungry season" (June"August) when their own stocks are depleted. Access to international markets is a partial substitute for stockpiling, as food can be imported and exported in the same way that stocks can be drawn-down or built-up. But due to costly export procedures and overall low volumes potentially available for export, selling food on the world market is not an option for rural farmers. (Storage and integration with other markets is the reason prices for basic storable foods such as rice, wheat, beans, etc., show relatively little intra-annual variation in developed countries.) The simultaneous influx of grain on local markets reduces the prices that farmers receive at harvest, whereas the scarcity of food during summer translates to high prices. Thus preharvest grain prices are significantly greater than postharvest prices.

Because most poor and food insecure farmers in the region do not invest in the agricultural technology needed to boost overall yields, production remains only at subsistence levels. Many small farmers produce little more than they consume throughout the year, and many are net buyers of the crops that they produce. Farmers in Burkina Faso, for example, sell only 10"20% of the cereals produced, mainly after harvest, consuming the rest within the household or exchanging them with other needy households for goods and services, then purchasing food on the market if they run out of stocks.

For the purpose of welfare analysis related to food prices, it is important to distinguish sellers and buyers. In all markets, sellers benefit from a price increase (all else equal), whereas buyers lose, and vice versa. In the context of subsistence-level farming households in West Africa without access to storage, the differentiation into net sellers and net buyers is a little more complicated. On one hand are consumers who buy all of their food on the market and producers who produce much more than they consume and are able to sell grain year-round (provided they have storage facilities). The former are clearly net buyers, whereas the latter are net sellers. However, most rural households produce some grain, sell part of it, but then buy the same type of grain on the market later in the year.

Note that there are two types of net buyers: by *volume*, who buy a greater quantity than they sell; and by *value*, who spend more money on food than they earn by selling. To illustrate the latter, suppose the common scenario in which prices in the summer are double that of postharvest. Take a household producing 110% of its total calorific demand: if it sells 30% postharvest for income, it then needs to buy back 20% in the summer (110% " 30% + 20% = 100%); due to price fluctuations, the household is a net buyer by value given a loss of (+30% “ 2[20%]) = “10%. Thus, in this book, we combined these types of buyers together with pure consumers as “net buyers”.

Using this definition, the effect of an exogenous crop price increase is positive for net sellers and negative for net buyers. If crop prices increase due to a bad harvest, net buyers still unequivocally become more food-insecure, as the amount of money they need to buy food increases relative to their income. The effect on net sellers, however, is ambiguous and depends on the relative magnitudes of the price increase and output decrease. They profit if the price increase is relatively larger than the output decrease, and vice versa. It is therefore possible that both net buyers and net sellers can lose from a bad harvest.

INTEGRATION WITH GLOBAL MARKETS

As in many regions around the world, West African markets have recently become more integrated with each other and with the global commodity markets. There is clearly no perfect correspondence among these prices, but there is certainly some correlation. There is a correlation between local grain prices and the lagged world corn price for some countries, and there is also some evidence for cointegration between local and world prices. However, the strength of the cointegration is rather weak.

Rapidly expanding urban markets in West Africa rely on global commodities for affordable food. Efficient global commodity markets have made rice imported from China, Malaysia, and Indonesia extremely competitive with corn, millet, and sorghum grown locally, but this is only the case for urban markets. Because there is a high cost to move grain from the interior of the continent to the capital cities and ports on the coast, local food prices in rural areas tend to be sensitive to climate variability. When rural markets have a deficit and prices are high, grain is imported from the capital city and thus local prices are affected by global fluctuations. In this sense rural markets are integrated asymmetrically into world markets: grain flows in from abroad when prices are high, but not the other way around. This makes the world price (plus transportation costs) a determinant for peak prices during the hungry season, but not for prices after harvest (unless harvest is unusually low). As evidence for such an asymmetric integration note the fact that West African countries only import but do not export grain, and the pronounced intra-annual variation of local prices.

Integration into world markets benefits net buyers as it lowers peak prices, while decreasing the profits of net sellers. Because there are many more net buyers than net sellers, integration into world markets has generally improved food security in West Africa. Yet at the same time, the dependence of local prices on world prices makes local food prices vulnerable to shocks from the world markets. For example, the increase in global corn (maize) prices in 2008 had a strong influence on the price of grain in the rural, informal commodity markets in West Africa, despite their relative isolation. The period of high global prices had the immediate consequence of sharply increasing the number of hungry people while boosting the income of only a few relatively well-off farmers.

CLIMATE CHANGE AND AGRICULTURAL PRODUCTIVITY

The Intergovernmental Panel on Climate Change (IPCC) 2007 report estimated that warming global temperatures are likely to reduce West African agricultural production by up to 50% by 2020. The impact of climate change on rainfall is far less certain, particularly because global climate models often have difficulty reproducing West Africa's complex monsoonal rainfall, which is dominated by waves of moisture moving east across the continent. Certainly large changes in the global water cycle are anticipated with dynamic changes in the atmosphere due to increasing temperatures, but exactly how these changes will affect West Africa is unclear.

West Africa will not be the only region suffering from a changing climate. Primary grain producing areas in semiarid regions of Australia, the U.S., and regionally in southern Africa will all be significantly impacted by drought and water scarcity. Food production is unlikely to increase further in these regions while the global demand for food will likely double in the next four decades, resulting in higher food prices in the long run.

It is increasingly likely that the world's major industrialized countries will adopt some kind of global greenhouse gas mitigation policy. Although the cost of not mitigating emissions is likely to be far higher in the long run than the immediate impact of carbon controls, in the near term, such mitigation policies will likely increase the cost of energy. Industrial agriculture, which uses high levels of fertilizer and complex transportation systems, is highly reliant on petroleum products. The result is a relationship between petroleum and corn prices on the international market.

This linkage between food and fuel spells trouble for the capital-poor countries that will need to buy food from the international market when they are affected by drought, flood, or economic crisis. The world will eventually adjust to the rising cost of carbon-based fuels, but in the next few decades it is likely that the link between food and fuel will challenge West African nations' ability to finance food imports. Thus a critical priority should be to increase the productivity of local agricultural systems that produce far less than they could.

TECHNOLOGY TO INCREASE LOCAL PRODUCTION

Former World Bank economist William Easterly points out that despite foreign countries spending billions to end poverty in Africa between 1960 and 2003, poverty has risen steadily over the past five decades. Providing affordable technology, financial assistance, high-yielding agricultural seeds, and fertilizer can only dramatically improve yields in the region if the technology is provided at an appropriate scale and through institutions that are properly supported and developed. The poverty of farmers, traders, and their customers in urban areas in West Africa is a primary source of the problem of food insecurity and low productivity. This poverty, as is pointed out by Broad and Cavanaugh in their 2006 article, is caused by "a complex, multidimensional maze of power relations" that has at its roots massive inequality regarding access to resources, power over marketing, and structural issues in the economies themselves. Simply trying to implement a 1960s style green revolution in Africa may increase production but is unlikely to improve food security, as it is the poorest with the least land and fewest resources that are food-insecure. Further, widespread implementation of water-intensive agricultural systems imported from the West are unlikely to be sustainable in the long term for these poor, semiarid countries.

Technology to improve agricultural productivity in the region needs to be small scale, tailored to the region, and sustainable in the long run without huge corporate or International Monetary Fund-style loans. Local farmers need to be empowered through appropriate policies that give them rights to improvements they make to land, the trees they nurture, and the resident water. Local research agencies, such as the Nigeria-based International Institute of Tropical Agriculture (IITA) and its funder Consultative Group on International Agricultural Research (CGIAR), can produce low-cost strains of maize, millet, and sorghum that are disease resistant and higher yielding exactly for the farming practices used in West Africa. Another promising way to improve the lives of West African farmers would be to provide small-scale storage facilities that would make it unnecessary for small-scale farmers to sell their crop after harvest and buy back that very same type of crop at much higher prices later in the year.

Other examples of technology that can reduce long-term vulnerability include mobile phone fund transfers. These transfers can move a dollar or two from one local customer to another to provide funds for agricultural transactions with virtually no fee. Programs that provide microloans for agricultural inputs coupled with crop insurance programs, paid out when satellite remote sensing shows crop failure, can provide both loan coverage and funds to support the household after crop failure. Community-based natural resource programs, such as the one that has dramatically increased tree cover in Niger, provide other ways that both empower the farmer and local community: raising incomes of the poorest while enabling the country to remain debt free. Technology can thus contribute to improving the food security of the region while adapting to a changing climate.

WARMING OF THE INDIAN OCEAN THREATENS EASTERN

Sustainability science often examines trends and the interaction of trends through the lens of "use-inspired basic research". We present here an analysis of rainfall and agricultural capacity trends inspired by our research supporting earlier early warning for the U.S. Agency for International Development's Famine Early Warning System. Most of this work has focused on monitoring and predicting emerging drought conditions in eastern and southern Africa, one way of improving adaptive capacity recommended by the Intergovernmental Panel on Climate Change (IPCC). In 2003, however, a routine attempt to use early-season (March to April) rainfall as a predictor of late-season (September to October) crop production produced a disturbing discovery: substantial rainfall declines had occurred within critical crop-growing areas in Ethiopia. The location and timing of these trends made them dangerous.

Further analysis suggested links to drought across much of eastern Africa during the long-rains season and potential anthropogenic links to the central Indian Ocean. In addition to climate analysis, this work also included evaluations of population, agriculture, and water security. We find that in eastern and southern Africa, the combination of declining per-capita agricultural capacity and increasing aridity is exacerbating vulnerability and rural poverty.

Declining investments in rural development, rapidly increasing rural populations, the depletion of soil nutrients through erosion, and the cultivation of most cultivatable areas limit agricultural productivity growth. Low per-capita agricultural production and rural poverty go hand in hand, slowing progress toward Millennium Development goals (MDGs). A recent overview of these goals indicated differential progress on different fronts. Education and economic conditions have improved. Population growth remains high (2.3% per year). Progress on hunger and health has been halting. Our concern is that post-1980 rainfall declines during the main eastern African long rains (March–April–May, MAM) and the main southern African summer rains (December–January–February, DJF) may be contributing to African food insecurity. We believe that these declines may be associated with anthropogenic warming in the Indian Ocean. If so, these precipitation declines, acting in concert with declining agricultural capacity, likely constitute a prime example of societally dangerous climate change.

In this report we quantify the likely impact of observed precipitation and agricultural capacity trends by using empirical food-balance indicator models. These models estimate the millions of undernourished people as a function of population, cropped area, seed use, fertilizer applications, and main growing-season precipitation. These models show that continued declines in rainfall and per-capita agricultural capacity will produce increasing food insecurity. We next use observations and climate model simulations to argue that recent declines in eastern and southern African growing-season rainfall are linked to anthropogenic warming in the Indian Ocean. This link to global warming implies that these precipitation declines are likely to continue or intensify. For eastern Africa, this result is at odds with the most recent IPCC assessment, which anticipates precipitation increases.

For southern Africa, this result is consistent with previous analyses, which anticipate rainfall declines. Here we argue that warming in the south-central Indian Ocean (0–15°S, 60–90°E) has a similar effect on near-coastal eastern and southern Africa during boreal winter and spring. In each season, oceanic warming seems to reduce onshore moisture transports while increasing continental atmospheric stability. This may explain recent drought tendencies in gauge data, satellite-observed precipitation, lake levels, and vegetation indices in densely populated water-insecure regions of eastern African. If a common anthropogenic Walker-cell-like disruption has caused declines in both southern and eastern African rainfall, then this disruption is likely to persist. Furthermore, recent climate-change impact assessments, based on optimistic precipitation simulations over eastern Africa, may underestimate yield reductions. Our food-balance modeling of millions of undernourished people, however, suggests that these impacts could be mitigated by agricultural development.

MODELING THE IMPACTS OF AGRICULTURAL CAPACITY AND RAINFALL

Over the past 25 years the population of food-insecure eastern and southern Africa has doubled while per-capita cropped area has declined by 33% and the millions of undernourished people increased by 80%. Today, one in three small children is dangerously underweight, and 40% of 308 million people are undernourished. Average national per-capita cropped-area values are often below 1,000 m^2 per person.†† Food aid has become chronic, with 2005 World Food Program aid valued at U.S. $200 million. Poor farmers in these countries, often trapped in cycles of displacement, division, and degradation, depend on rain-fed agriculture. Per-capita crop production is an important metric of food availability and security. Limited technological inputs create a strong dependence between national average cropped area and national average production ($r = 0.95$).

Recent agricultural capacity trends tend to be dominated by cropped-area and population-growth increases.** In general, increased food production has matched growing population through increased labor inputs and through extensification, with area under cultivation increasing by 50% over the past 25 years while population has almost doubled. Seed and fertilizer use has also lagged population growth. Unfortunately, since 1990, overseas agricultural assistance has declined from 12% to 4% of total foreign aid, and only 4% of African public spending goes to agriculture.

This declining investment in agriculture has contributed to stalling increases in agricultural inputs. As the gap between population growth and structural agricultural components continues to grow, vulnerability and rural poverty will increase, amplifying the impact of agricultural droughts. These droughts have seemed to be more severe in recent years, and main growing-season rainfall** has declined by H"15% across eastern and southern Africa, in step with recent increases in radiative forcing. The interaction of agricultural and rainfall trends may be represented by empirical models estimating the millions of undernourished people.

Food-security analysis. Rainfall, population, cropped area, seed use, and fertilizer use for eastern and southern Africa. Rainfall is expressed as a percentage of the 1951–1980 average. The other variables are expressed as percentages of 1979–1981 averages. Global radiative forcing is shown with a stippled line on an inverted axis. The black vectors denote recent observed rainfall and agricultural capacity tendencies. Agricultural data were obtained from the Food and Agriculture Organization. Empirical food-balance model results expressed as percentages of the millions undernourished in 2000.

The five components of national per-capita production (rainfall, population, cropped area, and seed and fertilizer use) can be combined into two variables: rainfall and per-capita agricultural capacity. Agricultural capacity represents the slowly varying nonweather component of a national food balance and is a function of cropped area and seeds and fertilizer divided by population with units of per-capita crop production (kg per person per year). The main growing-season rainfall and per-capita agricultural capacity trends for 10 eastern and southern African nations. Somalia has been excluded as a result of limited data. The downward-pointing arrows indicate countries that experienced key growing-season rainfall declines between 1979 and 2005 (Ethiopia, Kenya, Burundi, Tanzania, Malawi, Zambia, and Zimbabwe). Note the geographic clustering of observed rainfall declines along Africa's eastern seaboard. Countries with left-pointing vectors (Ethiopia, Uganda, Zambia, and Zimbabwe) have experienced 1994–2003 declines in per capita agricultural capacity. In these countries population has grown faster than agricultural infrastructure, leading to increased rural poverty and vulnerability to climatic shocks.

In these semiarid countries a strong dependence on rain-fed smallholder farming practices results in quasilinear relationships between grain yields, seasonal rainfall receipts, and food deficits. Hence, agricultural capacity multiplied by percent normal rainfall is strongly related to per-capita production. The inverse of this measure (food imbalance) is related to food insecurity.** For each country (except Ethiopia, because of data limitations), the food-imbalance measure was regressed against "millions of undernourished" statistics obtained from the United Nations Food and Agriculture Organization. These regressions give us a pragmatic means of translating changes in rainfall, cropped area, and seed and fertilizer use into an index of food insecurity that is grounded empirically by historic observations. The resulting model performed well at a national/interannual scale for eastern and southern Africa (r = 0.86, P = 1.6 × 10^{-5}). To stress the semiquantitative nature of these projections, we present our results as percent changes from a 2000 baseline, which also allows comparison with the MDG of halving the number of undernourished people by 2015.

WALKER-CELL-LIKE ANOMALIES MAY EXPLAIN OBSERVED RAINFALL DECLINES

Will the observed rainfall declines persist, increasing levels of undernourishment? Fueling this concern is the strong covariance between global temperatures (r = 0.82) and south-central Indian Ocean (0–15°S, 60–90°E) sea surface temperatures (SSTs). Both have risen dramatically since the 1980s, along with radiative forcing, and tropical Indian Ocean SSTs recently reached their highest value in 120,000 years. Although anthropogenic warming has occurred in all oceans, this warming has been larger in the Indian Ocean. Recent careful analysis identified an 0.5–1.0°C 1960–1999 SST increase in the Indian Ocean Thermal Archive. This study also finds that most World Climate Research Program Coupled Model Intercomparison Project (CMIP3) models recreate this tropical warming tendency, strongly implicating greenhouse gas and aerosol emissions in the recent observed warming. Modeled CMIP3 increases in southern tropical Indian Ocean temperatures are strongly linked to trends in equatorial Pacific zonal wind stress and southward shifts in the latitudinal position of the subtropical gyre. Warmer oceanic SSTs have produced substantial increases in precipitation over the tropical Indian Ocean, indicated by both satellite (13%) and reanalysis (28%)

data sets. This convection releases energy in the atmosphere, influencing the regional weather via a Walker-cell-like circulation anomaly. This mechanism may have been responsible for the 1984 Ethiopian drought.

A warming Indian Ocean disrupts moisture transports and African rainfall. (*A*) Time-series of Goddard Institute for Space Studies (GISS) global temperatures and Kaplan Indian Ocean SSTs. (*B*) Pixel-by-pixel bivariate regression coefficients linking seasonal standardized precipitation** and seasonal standardized Global Precipitation Climatology Project precipitation over the southwest Indian Ocean. The red arrows show the general location of lower tropospheric (850 hPa) westward wind maxima. (*C*) First canonical correlates for each season. Results have been screened for significance ($P < 0.1$). The blue shading denotes the core of the westward transports, with mean 850-hPa wind speeds of >4 $m{\cdot}s^{-1}$. (*D*) CAM diabatic forcing experiment results. Arrows indicate simulated moisture-transport anomalies ($kg{\cdot}kg^{-1}{\cdot}m{\cdot}s^{-1}$). Blue-red shading indicates diabatic heating anomalies ($K{\cdot}day^{-1}$).

The statistical connection between increased oceanic precipitation and continental rainfall. Both data sources have been normalized; hence, a regression coefficient of ⁻0.6 associates a 1-SD increase in oceanic precipitation with a ⁻0.6-SD decrease in African rainfall. The latitude of negative associations shifts with the march of seasons, following the thermal equator and path of maximum onshore moisture transports (shown schematically with arrows).

The connection between seasonal moisture transports and central Indian Ocean warming (represented by precipitation) can be explored empirically by canonical correlation analysis (CCA). CCA is a statistical technique that finds dominant patterns of covariability in two sets of multivariate data. The two sets of data examined were seasonal 1950–2005 zonal reanalysis moisture transports over Africa's eastern seaboard (20°N–20°S, 25°E–45°E) and seasonal tropical Indian Ocean precipitation (15°N–15°S, 55°E–90°E). Tropical oceanic precipitation is linearly related to diabatic atmospheric heating, which can produce east–west Walker-cell-like circulation anomalies. Our hypothesis is that these anomalous circulations control decadal rainfall fluctuations that endanger food-insecure countries along the eastern seaboard of Africa.

In each season, we find that the first canonical correlate identifies a first CCA pattern describing shared Indian Ocean precipitation and moisture-transport variations. This approach produces a time series describing covariant Indian Ocean precipitation (CC_P) and moisture transports (CC_M). Increasing tropical Indian Ocean precipitation (blue circles) is associated with atmospheric ridging and anticyclonic moisture circulation over eastern Africa (arrows), which disrupt the main onshore moisture flows (shown with blue shading). University of Delaware precipitation deficits for the strongest six oceanic precipitation events are shown with red boxes. Although only boreal spring results are shown here, the patterns for other seasons are similar; a Walker-cell-like dipole emerges as the dominant (first canonical correlate) relationship. The transport correlations indicate reduced onshore moisture fluxes between 0 and 15°S. This region supplies 66% of Indian Ocean-sourced zonal moisture transport into tropical Africa, and 83% of the annual mean zonal moisture transport entering tropical Africa originates in the Indian Ocean. The northern flanks of the CCA patterns are associated with transport anomalies flowing from the drier Sahelian regions. Thus, changes in central Indian Ocean precipitation are correlated with transitions between dry continental and moist oceanic air masses over tropical Africa.

At low (decadal) frequencies, correlations between the CC_M and CC_P approach unity, and the zonal transport indices are negatively correlated (*r* H" "0.9) with regional rainfall. In total the CCA-identified transports can explain 85% of the low frequency variations in eastern MAM, southern DJF, and Sahelian June–July–August (JJA) rainfall. All three seasons/regions experienced a 1960–1970 decline in observed rainfall and CCA transport forcing, in synchrony with anthropogenic 1960–1970 increases in Indian Ocean heat content. A second heat-content increase in the early 1980s was associated with MAM and DJF transport disruptions and drying tendencies in southern and eastern Africa. Slower increases in JJA transport disruptions, combined with north/south shifts in Atlantic SSTs, have likely led to a modest recovery in Sahelian rainfall, albeit with continued declines across the eastern Sahel and southern Ethiopia.

To examine the influence of diabatic heating on moisture transports in a simulation framework, we have also conducted experiments with the National Center for Atmospheric Research Community Atmosphere Model, a fully nonlinear atmospheric model with explicitly resolved moist processes. An additional diabatic heating term is added over the central Indian Ocean, which increases the local rainfall, as in the work by Barlow *et al.*. The added heating is sinusoidal in latitude and longitude for a half period over the domain "20°S to 5°N and 50 to 100°E with a magnitude of 0.02 W·kg^{-1}. This southern central Indian Ocean domain was chosen to match our previous observational analyses and the early assertion that enhanced cyclonic activity helped create the tragic 1984 Ethiopian famine.

A clear influence on moisture transport over the interior of Africa is observed, in good agreement with the expectations of simple Gill-type dynamics, and is associated with decreases in local rainfall. These MAM circulation anomalies are similar to previous modeling results for JFM, and the observed low-level circulation anomalies associated with warm Indian Ocean warming seasons for boreal spring. Thus, although the relevance of the simple Gill model might be questioned, especially because it neglects the mean wind, the general link between increased central Indian Ocean precipitation and decreased onshore moisture transport seems robust even in a full atmospheric model.

In summary, the strong, probably anthropogenic, warming of the south-central Indian Ocean increases maritime precipitation, which is statistically and dynamically related to continental rainfall declines and moisture-transport reductions. Nonlinear climate simulations driven by diabatic heating over the Indian Ocean produce similar transport anomalies. In this context, what do projected 21st-century climate changes suggest over the Indian Ocean and tropical Africa?

CLIMATE-CHANGE SIMULATIONS SUGGEST CONTINUED INDIAN OCEAN WARMING

In this section we present a multimodel analysis of CMIP3 precipitation simulations. If the consensus of these models suggests continued increases in oceanic precipitation, then we should be concerned that continued continental rainfall declines, will lead to increased undernourishment unless mitigated. We selected 11 models having both 20th-century and 21st-century climate simulations. Because near-term (2000–2030) projections of radiative forcing are quite similar across the various emission projections, the various 21st-century scenarios were combined.

CMIP3 MAM precipitation simulation results. (*A*) A time (1950–2100) versus longitude plot of CMIP3 ensemble means averaged between 15°N/S. At each 5° longitude box, the 150 years of precipitation values were translated into *z* scores (SDs, ό). Red shades indicate drier conditions. Blue shades indicate above-normal precipitation. (*B*) A time versus probability plot showing the multimodel ensemble probability density functions (PDFs) for the south-central Indian Ocean (0–15°S, 60–90°E). (*C*) Summary of changes in frequency of above-"normal" precipitation and correlation of precipitation changes in individual climate models with the multimodel ensemble means for this same region.

We begin by analyzing east–west (zonal) tropical precipitation tendencies. A time-longitude plot of temporal *z* scores (SDs, ό) of the CMIP3 ensemble means averaged between 15°N/S. In this plot the 1950–2100 MAM multimodel means were averaged between 15°N and 15°S at 5° intervals between 20°E and 160°E. The time series at each longitude was translated into *z* scores (SDs) and plotted with red (blue), indicating reduced (enhanced) precipitation. As greenhouse gas forcing increases with time, beginning in the 1970s, precipitation increases across the Indian Ocean and declines across tropical Africa. This timing is broadly consistent with observed increases in oceanic SSTs and reductions in continental rainfall. We can analyze scatter surrounding the CMIP3 climate-change consensus by translating the 132 individual precipitation simulations into time-varying probability distribution functions

(PDFs),**. The multimodel ensemble precipitation PDFs over the tropical Indian Ocean (0–15°S, 60–90°E). As greenhouse gasses and aerosols accumulate in the atmosphere, the Indian Ocean warms, and oceanic precipitation increases, presumably producing moisture-transport variations and tropical African rainfall declines similar. The PDFs are tight and trend strongly, increasing steeply after the mid-1970s, in step with radiative forcing increases and observed African rainfall declines, so that by late in the 21st century the ranges of precipitation projected are quite different from historical ranges. Indian Ocean precipitation changes for the 11 different individual models (*x* axis) along with the correlation between each model's multisimulution mean time series and the ensemble mean (*y*). All models exhibit positive correlations, so that the models were unanimous in projecting increases in MAM atmospheric warming (i.e., precipitation) over the tropical Indian Ocean. The frequency with which MAM central Indian Ocean precipitation totals in 2031–2050 exceeded the average rainfall total for 1951–1970 increased by >20% in 10 of the 11 models.

SUMMARY AND CONCLUSIONS

Two independent, but interacting, post-1980 tendencies have contributed to food insecurity in eastern and southern Africa. First, population growth has exceeded increases in agricultural infrastructure and cultivated area. Second, there has been a tendency for main growing-season rainfall to decline. Empirical and model-based explorations support assertions that Walker-cell-like disruptions of atmospheric circulations and moisture transports link a warming Indian Ocean to a drier eastern African seaboard. Multimodel CMIP3 ensembles suggest greenhouse gas and aerosol emissions have contributed substantially to this observed late 20th-century warming. Anthropogenic climate change has probably produced societally dangerous increases in eastern and southern African food security. These conclusions, in general, agree with the most recent Fourth IPCC finding that semiarid Africa may experience large-scale water stress and yield reductions by 2030.

The work presented here, however, differs in approach from the IPCC analysis, focusing on empirical relationships rather than raw CMIP3 precipitation simulations. These raw simulations have implied that eastern Africa might become wetter while southern Africa becomes drier. We question the fidelity, in general, of continental precipitation simulations, especially over the extremely complex terrain of east Africa. Global models suppress important local mechanisms and vary substantially in their ability to represent the transient systems that draw kinetic energy from the mean circulation, overcoming stability inhibitions and producing organized mesoscale convection. Even monthly reanalysis precipitation fields have almost no skill ($R^2 < 0.2$) compared with observations in eastern Africa. Given this uncertainty, we believe that the observed quasilinear negative relationships between central Indian Ocean warming and east African rainfall represents the mostly likely outcome. These anthropogenic drought tendencies may be indicative of other "Indian Rim" and South American countries as well, because similar precipitation reformulations also suggest 21st century main season declines, with the result that main growing-season droughts may disproportionately affect tropical and subtropical countries. Global assessments of anthropogenic precipitation and yield changes may be underestimating these drought signals. The climate-change impacts in low-income nations have been almost completely driven by emissions from middle-and high-income countries. Although more research, and better climate models, will be required to settle quantitatively issues of attribution, the social and economic disruptions associated with anthropogenic drought may add substantially to these impacts.

Vulnerability arises through a complex interplay of exposures, sensitivities, and resiliencies that can either dampen or amplify the impact of climatic shocks. The recent IPCC assessment identifies many means of enhancing adaptive capacity in Africa. Improved forecasts and earlier early warning can help, as can improving existing rain-fed agriculture through farm management, as can enhanced biotechnological inputs. Recent research has suggested that investments in African agricultural development will lead to substantial propoor economic growth. Our analysis suggests that the continuation of recent tendencies will be likely to result in continued increases in undernourishment; but this is not a *fait accompli*. The range of possible human outcomes is large and depends primarily on the choices that we make. By 2025 rates of child malnutrition, for example, could range from 9.4 to 41.9 million. Our agricultural capacity models suggest that a 15% increase in yields per decade (equivalent to a 2 kg per person per year increase in agricultural capacity) could come close to achieving the MDG of halving the number of undernourished people, albeit by 2030 rather than 2015.

Although notable achievements in economic growth and education have been made since 1999, recent progress on hunger in Africa has been very slow and has fallen short of keeping pace with the relatively rapid population growth. The past few years have seen an increased governmental appreciation of the role of agricultural development, but public investments in agriculture and international donor assistance have lagged behind MDG commitments. More and higher quality assistance and agricultural polices, guided by objective policy design and better governance, can help eastern and southern Africa achieve sustainability transition. Investments in agricultural capacity seem warranted, given the large financial and humanitarian costs of business as usual in a changing climate system. These investments may also be just, given the strong evidence for anthropogenic drought and the disproportionate emissions by middle-and high-income countries.

6

The Effects of Climate Change on Food Production

As the Earth's climate continues to warm at an escalating rate, the production of food will be affected around the globe. Food production potential and food security may be at risk as rising temperatures will force farmers to move toward the poles, rising oceans submerge arable land, and rainfall becomes more sporadic. Some studies suggest that a higher atmospheric concentration of carbon dioxide, a gas necessary for photosynthesis, will benefit crops to such an extent that it might outweigh the other factors (Pearce, 2005). However most scientists agree that the net effect of higher temperatures will be a decrease in overall agricultural production. It is impossible to determine the exact effects of climate change on weather patterns, temperature, and precipitation because of the complexity of these natural cycles, so it is difficult to definitively say how yields will be effected by global warming.

The loss of arable land as a result of climate change could be devastating in many areas of the world. Already, some areas of the world are losing farmland due to desertification. Farmers have been driven out of the southern areas of Spain because the average surface temperature in the country has risen 1.5 degrees Celsius, comparatively more than the 0.8 degree increase globally since 1880. Rainfall in the United States is expected to decrease 20 percent by 2020, and 40 percent by 2070, according to United Nations projections (Rosenthal, 2008).

As temperatures continue to rise globally and rainfall patterns change, larger areas of the world will fall victim to dangerously severe droughts and floods more frequently.

The threat of desertification should not be underestimated, especially in areas in the developing world. The United Nations Secretary, General Ban Ki-moon, has declared it "one of the world's greatest environmental challenges." Desertification today puts at risk the livelihoods of 1.2 billion people who live in over 100 different countries (Greenpeace, n.d.).

One reason that desertification is difficult to address adequately is because it is the result of a range of different causes, both related and unrelated to climate change. In much of the discussion about desertification and climate change, the two topics have been generally considered separately. Desertification has been seen as the product of unsustainable farming habits or simple cyclical droughts of unusual severity, where climate change has been seen as a global issue with other repercussions. Measures taken to adapt to desertification have been generally focused on managing resource use on the local level, while the discourse surrounding climate change has been focused on reducing fossil fuel use and the pollution that results, but in the future, we may need to further intertwine these issues to find more effective solutions (Erikson, 2001).

As the climate continues to warm, temperatures will fluctuate more and established weather patterns will start to change – in some places it is evident that they already have. In a double heat wave in California in 2006, temperatures soared for 3 weeks, exceeding 100 degrees for 20 out of 21 consecutive days. In that double heat wave, Fresno County, California alone was dealt $85 million in losses in just beef, dairy and poultry production. In Europe in 2003, a heat wave killed over 35,000 people and scientists predict that by 2040, Europe could experience heat waves of this magnitude as often as every other year (Ibid.). Beyond the direct damage inflicted on entire populations of people, the resulting sudden loss in productivity could potentially continue to cause damage for years after a heat wave this severe. What does this loss of productivity mean for the general population of non-farmers is that the dependability of the food supply will fall into question, and across the board decreased supply will lead to increased prices and mass starvation and malnutrition in the poorest and hardest-hit areas.

While global warming is a significant stress factor for many species relied upon for global food production, it may actually speed the growth of weeds that interfere with agriculture. In a study conducted in Orange County, California, researchers studied the ability of wild mustard – among the most widespread weeds in the area – to adapt to the new environmental conditions brought on by global warming. Published in January 2007 by scientists from UC Irvine's Department of Earth System Science, data showed that in just a few generations the weed was able to respond to the pressures of natural selection. Common weeds tend to have a few things in common: they tend to grow and reproduce faster and in larger numbers than most other plants. This is a great benefit for environments that benefit those who can adapt quickly to a changing environment. Arthur Weis, professor of ecology and evolutionary biology at UC Irving and one of the authors of the study predicted, "Climate change could result in a big increase in the number of weedy species growing in our natural habitats – to the detriment of slower-evolving, longer-lived native species, like the redwood" (Brennan, 2008). Because the characteristics responsible for the success of weeds in these conditions are common to weeds around the world, the results of this study can probably be generalized to larger areas. Recent research also suggests that glyphosate, the most widely used herbicide in the United States, loses its efficacy on weeds grown at the increased carbon dioxide concentration levels predicted in coming decades.

Rising temperatures will continue to increase the ranges of invasive pests of all types as they are able to move to areas that were previously too cold for their survival. According to World Wildlife Fund Invasive Species Policy Officer Julie Kirkwood, studies in Australia show that already, invasive species are responsible for more than $4 billion in costs for the Australian economy alone. More than 70 percent of world's population lives on coastal plains, and in colder regions, milder temperatures near the sea make the land more conducive to farming. As rivers approach the ocean, they become wider and saturate the land more fully, reasons that made many farmers choose these regions. Over the 20th century, sea level rose between 10 and 20 centimeters and in 2001, the Intergovernmental Panel on Climate Change predicted that sea levels would rise from anywhere from 9cm to 88cm with a "most likely" estimate of 50cm by 2100, making a great deal of land uninhabitable, at least without the use of sea walls and the pumping of seawater.

While the rising sea levels that are predicted for the next 90 or so years are likely to prove highly destructive, the melting of the Greenland ice sheet is already accelerating and, if it melts completely, could put massive areas of inhabitable land underwater. According to the IPCC:

For years, many have predicted that the increased levels of carbon dioxide in the atmosphere that results from respiration and the burning of fossil fuels would increase the yield of crops and would negate any negative effects from global warming. For years, controlled indoor studies have shown that plants do respond well to increased carbon dioxide concentrations, but new studies conducted in the United States, China and Japan, have shown somewhat troubling results. What makes these studies different from previous ones is that they did not isolate the crops indoors, carbon dioxide was simply piped into the air surrounding crops grown outside. In these Free-Air Concentration Enrichment experiments (FACE), researchers found that the real life results from the same amount of carbon dioxide enrichment showed only half the benefit as compared to comparable indoor studies. But these studies went one step further and included a factor not considered in the others – the increased concentration of ozone in the air that is predicted as a result of higher temperatures. Researchers found that a 20% increase in ozone levels cut yields by 20%. Increases of ozone concentration at this level have been predicted for Europe, the US, China, India, and large areas of the Middle East by 2050. If these results prove to be correct, the detrimental effect of the increased ozone concentration would more than negate the benefit of carbon dioxide fertilization, leading to a 10%-15% reduction in the world's crop yields (Pearce, 2005).

As we move forward into an escalating spiral of increasing temperatures and the changes in atmosphere and precipitation patterns that result, farmers will be forced to move into new areas. Yields will be lower and dangerous spikes in temperature could wipe out entire crops if they coincide with flowering. We will need new solutions for guaranteeing a consistent production of food if we are to adapt to our changing planet.

THE FOOD FOOTPRINT AND AGRICULTURAL GREENHOUSE GAS EMISSIONS

Large scale food production, which has been developed over the last century, has many adverse effects on the environment and is a significant contributor to climate change. The most obvious way food production leads to climate change is the burning of fossil fuels which releases greenhouse gases into the atmosphere.

Since the industrial revolution, the three most significant anthropogenic sources of greenhouse gases have come from the burning of fossil fuels, land use, and agriculture. In fact, agriculture and the industrial processes involved with it are the source of almost one quarter of global greenhouse gas emissions. Greenhouse gases are emitted in several different ways. Deforestation releases CO2, methane is release from cattle and rice patties, and fertilizers release nitrous oxides.

Almost all food production is inherently linked with agriculture, which serves as the basis for most produced food items. One of the environmental issues associated most heavily with agriculture is deforestation, and subsequently, desertification. Deforestation occurs when forest land is cleared for use in raising crops or livestock. With less plant matter per unit area, more carbon dioxide, which would normally be used during photosynthesis, is contained in the atmosphere. This results in a broken down environment with much less biodiversity. Currently, about one-third of anthropogenic CO2 released in the air comes from deforestation activities, mostly in the tropical and subtropical regions of the world.

Seven Effects of Climate Change :

1. The drying of previously moist soil: The lack of canopy to protect the moist soil causes increased sun exposure resulting in the water evaporating into the atmosphere and causing dry, cracked dirt. Soil is now no longer as fertile.
2. Temperatures become more extreme: The shade caused by the canopy allows for more moderate temperature in the forest, without this shade temperatures increase significantly causing desert like temperatures.
3. The most humid regions become more desert like: Because of the drying of the soil and the inability of the soil to keep the moisture this dry soil will become desert sand causing more dust storms which ruins the soil.
4. Less recycling of water: One of the ways the moisture is usually transfered to the atmosphere is through the foliage to fall on the adjacent coasts and then on the inland forests but once these inland forests are destroyed, it will have a dramatic effect on the water cycle.
5. Effects on the carbon dioxide exchange: The rain forests are second to oceans as the "sink' that holds carbon dioxide from the atmosphere.
6. Increased desertification: Increasing deforestation is directly resulting in the increase of desertification. It is estimated that desertification is threatening 20% of the world's population.
7. Soil erosion: Deforestation contributes to run off of rain fall, which depends on the soil characteristics.

Deforestation and Agriculture

These issues have resulted in significant impacts on agriculture and food supply's of different regions in the world. Although deforestation has direct effects on agriculture, nevertheless the effects of deforestation have the largest impact. A problem with the removal of forests, especially near rivers and lakes, is that the moisture that the trees absorb normal from these water sources is no longer absorbed and this results in flooding. The crops and sometimes the villages of many people living in rural areas of the third world are destroyed by these floods that are caused by the lack of trees along their riverbanks and near their villages. Kenneth Nyasulu, Director of Forestry in the Ministry of Natural Resources, Energy, and Environment of Malawi, stated that "As forests are removed, the soil is left bare. This is washed away, leaving the land unproductive" (Mweninguwe. 2005). Malawi is a region in southern Africa that is leading in deforestation per year. The Department of Forestry reported that around 50,000 ha are lost each year due to deforestation. This number will continue to increase because deforestation is not a long term solution because after a few years of cultivating, the soil becomes exhausted and bare, and the cycle begins again with more trees being cleared and more CO2 being released into the atmosphere. Deforestation has significant impacts on the dry seasons of many tropical forests, especially the amazon. It was found that here is more rainfall over deforested areas in the wet season and a reduction of the dry season precipitation over these areas compared to the forested areas. Nevertheless the precipitation that could be over the forested areas is now no longer as large and areas the do not necessarily need the precipitation are receiving this rain.

This CO2 recently has had enormous impacts on the crops of the world. The annual global losses of wheat and corn is equal to the entire amount that Argentina produces each year. This goes against many assumptions that claim that agriculture will thrive due to the warming globe and increase CO2. Since 1981 the annual value of lost crops worldwide is about $5 billion (Hoffman. 2007) Different forms of agriculture will steadily decrease if the global heating trend continues. Not only will small villages experience the affects of global warming attributed to deforestation but also the more developed countries such as the US, who is one of the leaders in CO2 emissions annually.

Adaptation, Mitigation, and Food Security

There is a consensus among scientists and policy makers around the globe that a rise in temperature is an undeniable part of our future. Many scientists believe that this change has been fuelled, in part, by our agricultural methods, which release heat-trapping greenhouse gases into the atmosphere and clear the planet of its natural forests. In the face of these realities, our challenge is to produce the food required to feed our growing population of 6.7 billion, while simultaneous reducing the impact food production has on climate change. We must adapt our agricultural system to allow for the imminent changes in temperature and weather patterns and create new methods of farming that will prevent further warming.

Adaptation

Adapting our food producing systems to continue to feed our growing numbers while under effects of climate change will be no easy task; yet maintaining a constant or rising level of agricultural production will be necessary to prevent starvation on a global scale. Certain steps can be taken to try and adapt both individual crops, and the agricultural system as a whole to these changes. The first way of doing this is by advancing the technology and methodology of food production itself while changing the methods and areas used for growing crops, raising livestock, and harvesting seafood. For agricultural production, this means adjusting water use by using water conservation and better irrigation technologies in dry climates. In wet climates, or climates effected by extreme rainfall or extreme storm events predicted as part of climate change, effective water management methods are needed to prevent water-logging, erosion, and nutrient loss. Altering the timing and location of crop planting, can also have an effect. It is recommended to keep livestock consumption and local feed production (pasture, grain, etc.) equal, to rotate grazing areas, and alter forage species and animal breeds in response to local conditions. It is also important to ensure adequate water supplies. Unfortunately, there is an outer limit to the effectiveness of such adaptation; heat tolerant livestock tend to have lower levels of productivity (Ibid.)

The next major change we can make is to reintegrate and reorganize food production systems to take advantage of shifts in climate. This falls under the realm of planned adaptation according to the IPCC (Ibid.). Moving agricultural industries in response to climate change will likely be necessary and require government support. Major investment and development of irrigation technologies may be necessary on a national or global scale. Areas that rely on one or few crops as their primary food supply will find adaptation more difficult than countries with varied food supplies (such as the United States and Most of Europe) when threatened by climate change. Lobell projects that South Asia and Southern Africa are at the greatest risk considering their production habits and the climate models. These areas will require large scale adaptation efforts to continue providing enough food for their people.

On the marine front, considering the current poor state of our fisheries, adaptation to climate change involves putting less pressure on fisheries by increased regulation. Reducing the level of fishing is the suggested method of reducing stress on species threatened by climate change by allowing for them to adapt.

Finally, it should be mentioned that increased levels of carbon dioxide have led some to propose that yields will be favorably affected by increased photosynthetic production. Indeed, some experiments have shown this to be the case ; however, other research questions the validity of this effect as well as the nutritional value of the grain produced. Seneweera and Conroy found that while rice produced in higher states of CO2 was firmer when cooked, the concentrations of vital nutrients iron and zinc were reduced. Rice grown with enriched CO2 and higher temperatures has also been shown to have a lower protein content and general quality. This has poor implications for nutrition in heavy rice consuming cultures, which also may have limited diets. Finally, research has questioned the validity of crop increases across the board due to raised concentrations of atmospheric carbon because current studies show only about half the originally predicted benefits. When this is coupled with a predicted ground-level atmospheric ozone, the results show a loss in Photosynthesis and a twenty percent reduction in yield. Therefore, it will likely not be possible to depend on the increase of atmospheric carbon dioxide as a defense against the impacts of climate change.

Mitigation: Eliminating the Effect of Food Production on the Climate

Agriculture accounts for between 10-12% of total human greenhouse gas emissions, with 60% of methane (CH_4) emissions, and 50% of all human nitrous oxide (N_2O) emissions. While food production's share of greenhouse gasses is small overall, its share of both nitrous oxide and methane is large. These gasses have a far higher effect than carbon dioxide which is by far the most prevalent gas. Methane is about 21 times more effective at trapping heat than CO_2 (EPA, 2007), and nitrous oxide is far more than that, being 310 times more effective than CO_2 (EPA, 2006). From this, we can see that the effect of food production, while by no means the single source of Global Warming Potential (GWP), has a major effect. In addition to adapting our agricultural system to continue to provide us with secure sources of food in a warmer world, we must also adjust our agricultural practices and implement technology to reduce the affect of food production on the problem of Climate Change itself. Mitigation practices fall under several categories; reducing emissions, enhancing removals, and avoiding (or displacing) emissions. The first category involves changing practices to put less GHG's into the atmosphere. Changing feed practices for livestock and altering the method of nitrogen application to crops are two examples of practices that would reduce emissions of methane and nitrous oxide respectively (Ibid.).

Enhancing removals deals with improving the carbon sequestering potential of food production. According to the IPCC's Third Assesment report (2001), agricultural ecosystems have a high carbon storage potential, mostly in organic matter within the soil. Processes that increase photosynthesis and slow re-release of carbon via plant respiration or erosion will affect this result. Such stores of carbon are referred to as "carbon sinks". While sequestering other gasses is possible on a more limited level, the primary sequestering potential for CO_2- is sometimes at a cost of more emissions of other GHG's; such as methane or nitrous oxide. Once again, the methods and technologies used are expected to vary widely by local climate and geographical conditions. The final method, avoiding or displacing emissions, involves using agricultural bi-products and crops as a source of energy and replacing fossil from fossil fuels or other sources. These "biofeedback" energy sources still release GHG's, however they gain benefit from the fact that the carbon used was recently removed from that atmosphere (an active part of the carbon cycle), and not from fossil fuels, where it was stored underground for centuries. With this sort of energy source, the only 'new' carbon introduced to the cycle is that used to produce and process the energy source (Ibid.). Other options, such as using methane from animal waste products to power generators, takes methane that would otherwise be emitted directly to the atmosphere and uses it to generate electricity (DOE, 2002).

Reducing emissions from croplands, especially of methane and nitrous oxide, can often be effected by altering the way the crops are managed. Crop management can also effect how much carbon is taken in by the plants. Adding nutrients to the soil, for example, can improve the carbon gaining potential of the plants. But too much fertilizer can be a bad thing, increasing the emissions of N_2O. Precise regulation of fertilizer application can greatly reduce excess N_2O emissions; as can strict control of leaching. Periodically draining rice paddies could help control high methane emissions. Unfortunately, this could cause a spike in N_2O production from those same fields. Many of these practices have tradeoffs; either in terms of increased emission of another greenhouse gas, or damage to ecosystems in other ways. Loss of forests (a better carbon sink than croplands), due to increased agricultural production would clearly be a bad thing; while increased efficiency of production on current cropland (with possible spike in emissions) could slow the inevitable growth of agricultural lands, and prevent emission-high deforestation. Implementation of all of these practices must consider these factors and many more. A long view is needed; many of these practices change over time (Ibid.).

The majority of research on agricultural mitigation has been in the field of soil carbon sequestration. The IPCC Second Assesment Report (1996), estimated that 400-800 million metric tons of carbon could be sequestered in global agricultural soils per year, with saturation (and the end of sequestering) occurring after 50 to 100 years. Further, it was estimated that by using 10-15% of agricultural land to grow "energy crops", i.e. crops for ethanol or biodeisel, could offset 300-1300 million metric tons of carbon (or 1100-4800 metric tons of CO2) per year from fossil fuels, by capturing previously emitted carbon and burning it again. Simply turning crop residue (i.e. stalks of plants, straw, etc.) into biogas, or direct burning it, could contribute 100-200 million tons of carbon (400-700 Mt CO_2), without disrupting food production .

ENSURING GLOBAL FOOD SECURITY

There are many ways to affect climate change and secure our future food supply. However, the future is very uncertain. The IPCC makes recommendations, sometimes contradictory, but in the end, much of this is new ground. The IPCC recommendation is to use agriculture for producing biogas, but widespread production of ethanol in developed countries, along with incentives by national governments to produce ethanol, has been discovered to be a major contributor to the large rise in food prices in 2007 and 2008 by World Bank Economists and others. For reasons probably unrelated to Climate Change, China is undergoing severe agricultural decline. They have lost one fifth of their agricultural land since 1949 due to soil erosion and economic development (CIA, 2008). China's imports of grain are growing as their population grows and environmental problems impact agriculture (Siver, 2008), and they are projected to have a grain production deficit on the order 40 million tons per annum. With China and other industrialized nations with grain deficits hunting for scarce food exports, the rise in prices is hitting poorer nations particularly hard. Countries with grain surpluses have been halting exports to guarantee food to their own populaces, as surplus food becomes scarcer. African nations are among the hardest hit; Mauritania has seen a 67% increase in the cost of wheat, a 117% increase in the cost of cooking oil, and a 25% increase in the cost of rice (the three key ingredients for food in the nation). Mauritania currently has a roughly 45 day supply of these commodities; and producing nations are being stingy with imports (Faiola, 2008). Wealthy importers such as Malaysia and Singapore are hording food and banking against even higher prices. People are starting to leave their homes in search of work and food (Ibid.) Even the United States is feeling the crunch; the price of wheat flour has doubled in just a few months, probably linked to a 24 million acre drop in wheat planting since 1981; some of which is due to the production of ethanol, and corn and soy for export (Morgan, 2008).

With all of these shortages happening now, we can only wonder what climate change is going to do to an already dire situation. It may be true that climate change is already be affecting production in a limited way, but by all accounts, it will get far worse despite our best efforts. What will the world look like then?

Food supplies and poverty levels have been significant global issues for centuries. The concept of achieving total food security, defined as "access by all people at all times to enough food for an active, healthy life," is one of the most challenging goals for humanity. However, with the recent onset of global climate change, providing enough food to sustain human populations is becoming increasingly difficult. Most models show that global warming will reduce agricultural output, leading to shortages in many developing countries. With less supply come higher costs, and in turn less availability to already impoverished regions. Studies show that the number of hungry people in developing countries will increase by 1% for every 2-2.5% increase in prices. In 1980, there were an estimated 500 million people at risk of hunger. In 2060 this number is projected to be around 640 million, ignoring the effects of global change. The increase in cost due to lower yields is expected to increase this statistic by anywhere from 60 to 350 million people.

For researchers modeling the impact of climate change on poverty levels, agriculture has been the most significant variable. This is because many of the staple crops used to feed human populations are naturally more vulnerable to climate shifts. Studies have predicted agriculture's role in reducing poverty will decrease, leading to around 600 million additional people with inadequate food supplies. There is some debate as to whether small or large-scale farming would adapt better to global warming. While small farming are generally thought to be good adapters, they would not fare as well long term in a shifting environment, as they cannot afford to take risks.

In creating a viable and enduring agricultural system for the 21st century and beyond, great care must be taken to craft agricultural systems that take into account the dual problems of increasing population and food demand, and climate change. As can be seen above, the problems are multivariable, interrelated and profound; and there is no clear answer facing us at this time. But at the same time, these problems are not going away, and much work and research is still needed to see us through. Though most research considers a growing population a given of these agricultural problems, we feel that governments singularly and as a whole should begin to consider widespread population control measures. Population is growing, especially in developing countries, some of which are the hardest hit by the growing food crisis, and curtailing growth would reduce much of the strain to continue expanding agricultural production in the face of climate change and adverse effects such as deforestation. We believe that by implementing moderately strict population control along with these solution and mitigation practices, we stand a good chance of being able to feed our people for the next century. Humans have always faced the problem of feeding themselves, but never has the scope of the situation been so wide, and the solutions so grand and inspiring.

Conservation vs Food Production: a False Dichotomy

It is tempting, given the question's use of the term "conserving ecosystems," to focus this answer on the 14% of the terrestrial system that is protected. Such a response, however, would miss the elephant in the room. To conserve ecosystems in a changing climate, we must instead focus on how they are used and managed in the remaining 86% of land cover. Food production currently dominates that use, with 40 percent of the Earth's land cover managed for crop production and pasture.

To date, the focus on managing ecosystems for food production has resulted in significant benefits for humans. The Millennium Ecosystem Assessment found that globally human well-being has improved over the past 50 years, as measured by the UN human development index. We live longer, are better nourished, literacy rates have risen along with educational attainment, and per capita GDP is rising.

Yet, as human well-being has improved, the health of ecosystems has declined. Humans have degraded the majority of ecosystem services" "capture fisheries, freshwater, pollination and many more" "while enhancing a few food services. Food production is a major force behind every direct driver of ecosystem degradation identified by the Millennium Ecosystem Assessment in 2005.

Food production as a major driver of ecosystem degradation. Habitat conversion: Approximately 43% of tropical and subtropical forests and 45% of temperate forests have been converted to croplands. Over exploitation: 70% of global freshwater use is by agriculture, reducing its availability for other uses. Invasive species: The introduction of aquatic alien fish species has led to the extinction of native species in many parts of the world. Pollution: Only a fraction of nitrogen applied as a fertilizer is typically used by plants, the rest ends up in inland waters and coastal systems, creating eutrophication and dead zones. Climate Change: Agriculture directly contributed to around 14% of global greenhouse gas emissions in 2005 and drives additional emissions through its role in deforestation.

Minqin Oasis in Western China, for example, historically served as a natural barrier against the dryness of the Tengger and Badain Jaran deserts. In the 1950s Chairman Mao implemented a national plan to boost food production, entailing cultivation, deforestation, irrigation, and reclamation. The long-term consequences on other ecosystem services such as erosion control and freshwater were devastating. As a result, the Minqin oasis has been swallowed by deserts, leading to abandonment of once productive land. In the U.S. midwest region, the production of crops, livestock, and biofuel has degraded coastal ecosystems. In the Gulf of Mexico, nutrient runoff from farmland has created a dead zone approximately the size of New Jersey which has degraded fisheries and is expected to worsen with climate change.

Can this paradox of improving human well-being by increasing food production at the expense of other ecosystem services that humans depend on continue? Scientists worry that time lags may exist between the degradation of ecosystems and the resulting effects on human well-being. And that these may lead to tipping points past which damage to ecosystems is irreversible. The Millennium Ecosystem Assessment identified several examples of irreversible ecosystem change, such as the sudden collapse of chronically over exploited North Atlantic cod stocks in the late 1980s. As climate change impacts exacerbate food production stresses on ecosystems, it is conceivable that such collapses become commonplace, with enormous implications for food security, especially in the developing world where two billion rural poor depend on ecosystems for sustenance and livelihoods. For example, the Amazon provides critical water and climate regulation services that the region's agricultural sector depends upon for its survival. Yet scientists fear that ongoing deforestation combined with climate change could bring the Brazilian Amazon to a tipping point beyond which it experiences widespread dieback and transitions into savanna-like vegetation. The reductions in rainfall would devastate efforts to raise crops and cattle in the region.

AVOIDING ECOSYSTEM SERVICES TIPPING POINTS

To conserve ecosystems in the face of climate change, confronting the elephant-the way we meet our needs for food-must be a prime focus. And our approach to conserving ecosystems must ensure that they are not pushed beyond dangerous tipping points. Future approaches to conserving ecosystems must tackle the three interlinked challenges of climate change, ecosystem services degradation and rising demand for food..

Climate change

Climate change affects the quantity and quality of food and

other ecosystem services. Moderate warming (1-3Â°C) is expected to benefit agriculture in mid to high latitudes, but to decrease yield of cereals in low latitudes (medium confidence). The loss of ecosystem services is likely to be a major source of surprises from climate change. While ecosystems have adapted before in response to shifts in climate, their resilience this time is undermined by existing and growing human pressures. Future food production must therefore reduce its pressure on ecosystems and plan for the unexpected, such as changes to freshwater, natural pest regulation and pollination services.

Ecosystem service degradation

The majority of ecosystem services globally have been degraded, including those that underpin food production. Crops, livestock and aquaculture are among the few ecosystem services that have been enhanced. The degradation of ecosystems services is expected to grow significantly worse in the first half of the 21st century, with climate change possibly becoming the dominant driver by the end of the century.

Doubling of food demand

The focus on increasing food production needs to continue, if we are to sustain previous gains in human wellbeing, feed a growing population and lift millions out of poverty. But increasing food production at the expense of other ecosystem services and climate change cannot be sustained indefinitely. Approximately 13 million ha of forest, for example, are lost annually, primarily as a result of the expansion of land used for food and fuel. Deforestation is a significant cause of climate change and results in the loss of ecosystems services that are critical inputs to agriculture, including erosion control, climate regulation, pollination and water regulation. Yet, projections estimate conversions of an additional 120-240 million ha by 2030, much of it in Latin America and Sub-Saharan Africa and much of it for food production.

Food Production and Climate Resilience

Addressing the intertwined challenge of meeting rising

demand for food and conserving ecosystems in a changing climate will not be easy. It will require policy makers at all levels of society adopting different approaches to conserving and managing ecosystems that factor in climate change and other drivers of ecosystem change. Two such approaches are described below: 1. integrate climate change and ecosystem service risks in decisions that affect ecosystems and 2. reconcile food production and conservation goals.

Integrate climate change and ecosystem service risks in decisions. Future ecosystem use decisions, particularly those that involve food production, should assess the risks associated with their dependence and impact on ecosystem services and how these risks will be altered by climate change. This comprehensive tool identifies the direct drivers of ecosystem change, including climate change, in a particular setting, and assesses both risks and opportunities stemming from a decision's dependence and impact on ecosystem services. It can be applied by policy makers working in different sectors and at multiple scales, from field to forest or watershed from to national to regional and local levels.

Reconcile food production and conservation goals. Future approaches to food production must first and foremost recognize its interdependence on a basket of ecosystem services and develop strategies to sustain them in the face of climate change. To achieve this, food security experts need to work alongside agriculturists and biologists to maximize food production while minimizing further ecosystem and biodiversity loss. Three key strategies can help meet this goal:

Restore degraded lands

There is an urgent need to halt the expansion of food production into natural ecosystems in order to conserve ecosystem services and biodiversity. Globally, over one billion hectares of land is believed to have restoration potential for increased human use-a global combined area greater than China. More work is needed to determine which of this is suitable for food production, taking into account water availability, climate change and social factors. Restoring even a small part of this for food production would help reduce pressure on natural ecosystems. In Indonesia, for example, the World Resources Institute is seeking to develop a scalable model for diverting new oil palm plantations that would otherwise replace virgin forests onto degraded land. This ensures that oil palm plantations can keep expanding to meet demand" "generating local revenues and jobs while reducing deforestation. Similar opportunities exist to divert the expansion of cattle ranches in the Amazon region to degraded lands.

Increase productivity on existing farmland

While intensification doesn't immediately come to mind when thinking about conservation, it is nevertheless a key strategy to reduce stress on natural ecosystems. The challenge is to find ways to produce more food without unwanted ecosystem trade-offs. As noted by Shivaji Pandey, Director of FAO's Plant Production and Protection Division at a 2009 Congress on Conservation Agriculture in New Delhi. "In the name of intensification in many places around the world, farmers over-ploughed, over-fertilized, over-irrigated, over-applied pesticides. In doing so we also affected all aspects of the soil, water, land, biodiversity and the services provided by an intact ecosystem. That began to bring yield growth rates down." Food production needs to be redesigned to be both more productive and synergistic with other ecosystem services. Public subsidies and tax incentives, for example, should be used to compensate farmers for managing their lands in ways that sustain beneficial ecosystem services to society. To contend with climate change, farmers need location-specific information on ecosystem services and changing climate conditions. This should be combined with research on how improved practices can address climate constraints on crops. For example, rainfall may remain plentiful in parts of Africa but be concentrated in shorter time periods. Ways to minimize run-off and soil erosion and store water to extend growing seasons will thus be important.

Manage demand for food

Opportunities for managing demand for food in both developed and developing countries include changing diets, reducing food waste and advancing programs that encourage sustainable food production. The world's livestock sector is growing at an unprecedented rate driven by rapid growth in demand for animal protein as a result of population growth, rising incomes and urbanization. Animal protein requires more land, water, and energy to produce than plant protein. Education programs can help consumers make informed choices on the environmental and health benefits of food choices. There is also a need to spur and scale up demand for sustainably produced food. This can include promoting the use of certification and labelling programs for sustainably produced agriculture commodities.

MANAGEMENT FOR ENVIRONMENTAL PROTECTION

As discussed previously, irrigated agriculture is a major contributor to the salinity of many surface-and groundwaters. The agricultural community has a responsibility to protect the quality of these waters. It must also maintain a viable, permanent irrigated agriculture. Irrigated agriculture cannot be sustained without adequate leaching and drainage to prevent excessive salinization of the soil, yet these processes are the very ones that contribute to the salt loading of surface and groundwaters.

But surface and groundwater salinity could be reduced if salt loading contributions from the irrigation processes were minimized or eliminated. The protection of water resources against excessive salination, while sustaining agricultural production through irrigation, requires the implementation of comprehensive land and water use policies that incorporate the natural processes involved in the soil-plant-water and associated geohydrological systems.

Strategies to consider in coping with increasing salinity in receiving water systems resulting from irrigation include:

- eliminating irrigation of certain polluting lands;
- intercepting point sources of drainage return flow and diverting them to other uses;
- reducing the amount of water lost in seepage and deep percolation;

- isolating saline drainage water from good quality water supplies.

Only the last two strategies are discussed herein, primarily the last one.

Minimizing Deep Percolation and Intercepting Drainage

As discussed earlier, minimizing leaching always reduces the salt discharged from the rootzone. Additionally, deeply percolating water often displaces saline groundwater of higher salinity or dissolves additional salt from the subsoil. Reducing deep percolation will generally reduce the salt load returned to the river as well as reduce water loss. The "minimized leaching" concept of irrigation which reduces deep percolation should be adopted and implemented to reduce salinization of water resources associated with irrigation projects, especially in projects underlain by salt-laden sediments. In addition, saline drainage water should be intercepted. Intercepted saline drainage water can be desalted and reused, disposed of by pond evaporation or by injection into some isolated deep aquifer, or it can be used as a water supply where use of saline water is appropriate. Desalination of agricultural drainage waters for improving water quality is not generally economically feasible even though it is to be implemented for the return flow of the Wellton-Mohawk irrigation project of Arizona, USA. The high costs of the pretreatment, maintenance, and power are deterrents. Only in extreme cases, or for political rather than technical reasons, is desalination advocated.

Isolating and Reusing Drainage Water for Irrigation

While there is an excellent opportunity to reduce the salt load contributed by drainage water through better irrigation management, especially through reductions in seepage and deep percolation, there are practical constraints which limit such reductions. But the ultimate goal should be to maximize the utilization of the irrigation water supply in a single application with minimum drainage. To the extent that the drainage water still has value for transpirational use by a crop of higher salt tolerance, it should be used again for irrigation.

Drainage waters are often returned by diffuse flow or intentional direct discharge to the watercourse and automatically "reused." Dilution of return flows is often advocated for controlling water salinity. This concept has serious limitations when one considers its overall effect on the volume of usable water, and it should not be advocated as a general method of salinity control.

The preferred strategy to control the salinity of water resources associated with irrigated lands is to intercept drainage waters before they are returned to the river and to use them for irrigation by substituting them for the low-salinity water normally used for irrigation at certain periods during the irrigation season of certain crops in the rotation. When the drainage water quality is such that its potential for reuse is exhausted then this drainage should be discharged to some appropriate outlet. This strategy will conserve water, sustain crop production and minimize the salt loading of rivers that occurs by irrigation return flow. It will also reduce the amount of water that needs to be diverted for irrigation. This strategy is discussed in more detail in the next section.

As indicated in the preceding section, the ultimate goal of irrigation management should be to minimize the amount of water extracted from a good-quality water supply and to maximize the utilization of the extracted portion during irrigation use, so that as much of it as possible is consumed in transpiration (hence producing biomass) and as little as possible is wasted and discharged as drainage. Towards this goal, to the extent that the drainage water from a field or project still has value for transpirational use by a crop of higher salt tolerance, it should be used again for irrigation before ultimate disposal.

It is the intent of this section to describe an integrated strategy of management that will simultaneously facilitate the successful use of saline waters for irrigation, minimize the harmful off-site effects of drainage discharge on the pollution of water resources and maximize the beneficial use of the total water supply available in typical irrigated lands and projects. This strategy illustrates how the information and principles given in the preceding sections of these guidelines can be integrated towards the goals of sustaining irrigated agriculture and protecting soil and water resources.

To the extent practical, water diverted and applied for irrigation should be minimized using the principles and methods previously discussed. Unavoidable excessive, usable resulting drainage water should be intercepted and isolated from good-quality water supplies and used within dedicated parts of the project as a substitute for part of the freshwater given to the crops. The "dual rotation, cyclic" management strategy of Rhoades (1984a, b, c) can be used to enhance the feasibility of reusing such saline drainage waters for irrigation. In this system, sensitive crops (such as lettuce, alfalfa, etc.) in the rotation are irrigated with "low salinity" water (usually the developed water supply of the irrigation project), and salt-tolerant crops (such as cotton, sugarbeets, wheat, etc.) are irrigated with saline drainage water or the shallow groundwater created by over-irrigation in the project. For the salt-tolerant crops, the switch to saline water is usually made after seedling establishment; preplant irrigations and initial irrigations being made with low-salinity irrigation water. The secondary drainage resulting from such re-use should also be isolated and used successively for crops (including halophytes and tolerant trees) of increasingly greater salt tolerance. The ultimate unusable drainage water should be disposed of to some appropriate outlet or treatment facility. The feasibility of this "dual-rotation, cyclic" strategy is supported by the following: The maximum possible soil salinity in the rootzone resulting from continuous use of saline water does not occur when this water is used only for a fraction of the time.

Alleviation of salt build-up resulting from irrigation of salt-tolerant crops with the saline water occurs later when a salt-sensitive crop (s) is irrigated with the low-salinity water supply, or during off season periods of high rainfall. Proper preplant irrigation and careful irrigation management undertaken during germination and seedling establishment are made using the low-salinity water supply to leach salts accumulated from saline irrigations out of the seed-area and from shallow soil depths.

Data obtained in modelling studies and in field experiments support the credibility and feasibility of this "cyclic" reuse strategy. Results of an experiment to test the feasibility of the cyclic, "dual-rotation" reuse strategy are reviewed to clarify and illustrate the concept and to demonstrate its credibility. The strategy was tested in a 20 ha field experiment on a commercial farm in the Imperial Valley of California. Two cropping patterns were tested. One was a two-year, successive-crop rotation of wheat, sugarbeets and cantaloupe melons. In this rotation, Colorado River water (900 mg/l TDS) was used for the preplant and early vegetative growth stage irrigations of wheat and sugarbeets and for all irrigations of the melons. The remaining irrigations were with drainage water of 3500 mg/l TDS (Alamo River water). The other cropping pattern tested was a four-year block rotation consisting of two consecutive years of cotton (a salt-tolerant crop) followed by wheat (a crop of intermediate salt-tolerance) and then by two years of continuous alfalfa (a relatively salt-sensitive crop). Drainage water was used for the irrigation of cotton after seedling establishment; beginning with the wheat crop, only Colorado River water was used. From Watsuit calculations, it was hypothesized that the crops irrigated with the drainage water would yield fully when established with Colorado River water and from other calculations that sufficient desalination of the soil would occur when irrigating with Colorado River water to achieve a good plant stand and to keep the soil from becoming excessively saline over the long-run.

No significant losses in the yields of the wheat and sugarbeet crops occurred in either cycle of the successive crop rotation from substituting drainage water (even in the greater amount; 65-75 percent; treatment cA) for Colorado River water for the irrigation of these crops after seedling establishment. The mean yield of cantaloupe seed obtained in the cA plots was about 10 percent lower than the control, but the difference was not statistically significant. The yields of the fresh-market melons (numbers of cartons of cantaloupes obtained by commercial harvest operations) in 1985 was higher in the Ca and cA treatments than in the C treatment, but they were not significantly different. Hence, no significant yield loss was observed from growing cantaloupes using Colorado River for irrigation in the land previously salinized from the irrigation of wheat and sugarbeets using drainage water.

In the block rotation, there was no loss in lint yield in the first cotton crop (1982) from use of saline drainage water for irrigation, even when it was used for all irrigations, including the preplant and seedling establishment periods (treatment A). There was no significant loss in lint yield in the second cotton crop (1983) grown in the block rotation from use of drainage water for the irrigations given following seedling establishment which was accomplished using Colorado River (the recommended strategy treatment, cA). But there was a significant and substantial loss of lint yield, as expected, where the drainage water was used solely for irrigation (the "extreme-control" treatment, A). This loss of yield was caused primarily by a loss of stand that occurred this second year due to excess salinity in the seedbed during the establishment period. No loss in yield of the wheat grain or alfalfa hay crops occurred in the block rotation associated with the previous use of drainage water to grow cotton on these lands when they were subsequently grown with use of Colorado River water for irrigation. The qualities of all of these crops were never inferior, and often were superior, when grown using the drainage water for irrigation or on the land where it had previously been used. These quality data are given elsewhere.

The average amounts of water applied to each crop and over the entire four-year period, the successive and block rotations, respectively. These data include all water applied, including that used for preplant irrigations and land preparation purposes. That substantial amounts of drainage water were substituted for Colorado River water in the irrigation of these crops without yield loss.

The estimated amounts of water consumed by the crops through evapotranspiration and lost as deep percolation, individual crop and by succession of crops for both rotations. It was assumed that consumptive use was the same in all treatments, since no substantial losses of yield resulted in any treatment. These data show that the saline drainage water was successfully used for irrigation without resorting to high leaching. Data on levels of soil salinity and sodicity in the seedbeds and rootzones are given in Rhoades *et al.* (1989b). Their levels were kept within acceptable limits for seedling establishment and the subsequent growth of the individual crops grown in the rotation when the recommended strategy was employed. These results along with the high crop yields and qualities obtained in this test under actual farming conditions support the credibility of the recommended cyclic, dual-rotation (crop and water) strategy to facilitate the use of saline waters for irrigation.

In this cyclic strategy, steady-state salinity conditions in the soil profile are never reached, since the irrigation water quality changes with crop type in the rotation and with time in the irrigation season. Consequently, a flexible cropping pattern which includes salt-sensitive crops can be achieved. The intermittent leaching which occurs using this strategy is more effective in leaching salts than is continuous leaching (i.e. imposing a leaching fraction with each irrigation) for the reasons given earlier. Another advantage of the strategy is that a facility for blending waters of different qualities is not required.

In order to plan and implement a successful practice involving the use of the cyclic, dual-rotation strategy for irrigating with saline waters, various other considerations must be addressed. The intention here is not to provide a step-by-step process that must be followed nor a rigid set of criteria to address these considerations, since most management decisions are subjective and case specific, but to discuss some of the factors that should be considered and to provide some rough guidelines for selecting appropriate management practices.

Perhaps the most important management decision to make before implementing a reuse practice is crop selection. A list of other criteria that should be considered in the selection of crops for a reuse practice. In most cases, it is recommended that crops of high tolerance to salinity be selected when saline drainage water is to be used for irrigation. However, crops of intermediate tolerance (e.g. alfalfa, melons, tomatoes and wheat) may also be used in some cases, especially if the crop quality is sufficiently benefitted. For example, drainage water (EC 4-8 dS/m) significantly increased the protein content of wheat and alfalfa, soluble solids in melons and tomatoes, total digestible nutrients in alfalfa, and improved colour and netting of cantaloupe, and improved peelability in processing tomato. While improved plant quality should not be the major factor in adopting a reuse practice it may be an important factor in crop selection. Use of saline water to irrigate crops of intermediate tolerance to salinity is feasible, of course, only after seedlings have been established by good quality water.

Economics is also an important selection consideration, since it would be senseless to grow a high yielding crop without a marketable product and the potential for a positive cash flow. In the San Joaquin Valley in California, there is negative correlation between crop tolerance to salinity and economic value. It is unfortunate that there are not many crops that are both tolerant to salinity and have a high economic value. Asparagus is tolerant to salinity and has a high economic value, but harvesting is labour-intensive and costly.

The cyclic, "dual-rotation" reuse strategy described above presupposes the availability of two water sources; the saline water to be utilized and the other a water of low salinity. Such reuse requires that the saline water be readily accessible for irrigation. Possible sources can be the drainage waters that are being discharged in pipes or canals from the irrigation project or that present in the underlying shallow groundwater system. Rainfall may also be the source of good-quality water, if it occurs at required times during the year to meet crop needs periodically and to leach excessive accumulations of soluble salts from the rootzone.

There are many different situations where the use of saline water for irrigation in the recommended strategy could be practical. One situation is where high quality water is available during the early growing season but is either too costly or too limited in supply to meet the entire seasons requirements. This situation is common in parts of India and Pakistan, for example. Where high-quality water costs are prohibitive, crops of moderate to high salt tolerance could be irrigated with saline drainage or groundwater, especially at later growth stages with economical advantage, even if this practice resulted in some reduction in yield relative to that obtainable with a full supply of fresh water. Use of saline water for irrigation reduces the amount of high-quality water required to grow crops and hence expands the water-resource base for crop production.

Another situation conducive for such reuse is one where drainage water disposal, or a means of lowering an excessively shallow water table, is impractical due to physical, environmental, social or political factors. Reuse of the drainage water for irrigation in this situation decreases the volume of drainage water requiring disposal or treatment, and the associated costs. Furthermore, a reduction in the drainage volume also reduces the salt loading of the receiving water. Many growers in the San Joaquin Valley of California are presently undertaking reuse of drainage water, at least as a temporary solution, in order to reduce drainage volume and to meet recently imposed discharge restrictions related to protection of the quality and ecology of receiving water systems.

A difficulty in adopting the cyclic, "dual-rotation" strategy may exist on small farms where the drainage water produced on-site is too little or does not coincide with peak crop-water demand. In the San Joaquin Valley in California, farms are often sufficiently large but peak drain water flow occurs from January to June when most crops would require high quality water. Sole use of drainage water later in the season may not be feasible if the flow rate needed for irrigation exceeds the flow rate from the drains.

To avoid this limitation, surface storage reservoirs can be constructed to store the drainage water until its use is required. An option is to plug the subsurface drains and allow the soil to act as the reservoir. The latter option would not take land out of production for water storage purposes. However, regardless of where the drainage water is stored, a drainage water collection and irrigation system should be designed and operated with "reuse" in mind in order to implement this strategy most efficiently.

One method of collecting sufficient quantities of drainage water is to install a network of interceptor drains in areas with shallow water tables. A submersible pump could be placed in collector sumps as a means to access the drainage water. The size of the area that can be irrigated using such "drainage water" will vary, of course, depending on the capacity of the drainage system. To surface irrigate effectively, at least 10 litres/min/ha is required. Another way to collect drainage water is to install a network of shallow wells in strategic shallow water table areas. The wells can be connected to a common drainage manifold to facilitate collection and distribution. Consultation with irrigation and drainage engineers is advised before installing any drainage water collection system for irrigation use.

The long-term feasibility of using drainage water for irrigation in order to reduce drainage volume would likely be increased if implemented on a project or regional scale, rather than on a farm scale. Regional management permits reuse in dedicated areas so as to avoid the successive increase in concentration of the drainage water that would occur if the reuse process were to operate on the same water supply and same land area (i.e. in a closed loop). With regional management, certain areas in the region can be dedicated to reuse while other areas such as upslope areas, are irrigated solely with high quality water as usual. The second-generation drainage water from the primary reuse area is discharged to other dedicated reuse areas where even more salt-tolerant crops are grown, or to regional evaporation ponds or to treatment plants. Ideally, regional coordination and cost-sharing among growers should be undertaken in such a regional reuse system.

A novel means of "treating" saline waste waters before their ultimate disposal is to use them to irrigate specific crops that have the ability to accumulate large quantities of undesirable constituents (e.g. Se, Mo, NO_3, B, etc.) in the plants, in order to help reduce adverse ecological effects of disposal. The feasibility of biofiltration, the term used to describe this process, has been demonstrated by Cervinka *et al.* (1987), and Wu *et al.* (1987). They found that mustard, some grasses and certain native plant species found in California are effective in accumulating substantial amounts of Se in their shoots. This alternative "reuse" practice is most attractive where: (i) drainage disposal problems exist related to a potentially toxic trace constituent, (ii) a bioaccumulator with economic value exists, and (iii) other treatment processes are either unavailable or too expensive.

An alternative reuse strategy that is often advocated is to blend water supplies before or during irrigation. Blending may be appropriate provided the drainage or shallow groundwater is not too saline *per se* for the crop to be grown. However, in many cases this approach is inappropriate for the reasons. If the blending strategy is adopted, there must be a controlled means of mixing the water supplies. Shalhevet (1984) and Meiri *et al.* (1986) described two blending processes (i) network dilution, and (ii) soil dilution. With network dilution, water supplies are blended in the irrigation conveyance system. With soil dilution, the soil acts as the medium for mixing water of different qualities. A network blending system must be designed and installed if the blending strategy is to be adopted. The theory and design of dilution control systems and their use in irrigation networks has been developed by Sinai *et al.* (1985; 1989).

The cyclic strategy is preferred over the blending strategy in that (i) more salt sensitive crops can be included in the rotation, (ii) a blending facility is not required, and (iii) there is less danger in losing "usable water" for the crop. However, the cyclic strategy will require larger quantities of drainage water during the irrigations where it is used (since the water is not blended) and thus a storage system may be required in order to supply sufficient water for an effective irrigation. In summary, the "cyclic" strategy has more potential and flexibility than does the "blending" strategy, although the latter strategy is easier to implement in some cases.

Another concern besides excessive salinity build-up as regards the long-term feasibility of using saline water for irrigation is that of soil permeability and tilth. The likelihood of these problems increase as SAR increases and as electrical conductivity decreases. Therefore, adverse effects are most likely to occur during the periods of rainfall and irrigation using low-salinity water on soils previously irrigated with sodic, saline water. Such problems occurred at an experimental "reuse" site in California following pre-season rains and pre-irrigation with 0.3 dS/m canal water where sodic, saline water [9000 mg/l TDS; SAR = 30 $(mmol_c/l)^{½}$] had been used for irrigation for four consecutive years (Rolston *et al.* 1988). The consequence was impermeable, crusted soils and poor stand establishment. Whether such a problem will occur, or not, depends upon whether the EC of the high quality water is less than the threshold value, given the SAR of the saline water. Some combinations of the two waters are not permissible. This problem can often be controlled by the use of amendments and appropriate tillage practices as discussed.

Soil salinity under the cyclic strategy will fluctuate more, both spatially and temporally than in soils irrigated with conventional water supplies. Therefore, predicting plant response will be more difficult under these conditions. Hence, long-term effects on soil salination should be monitored using the techniques described earlier. Management must be adjusted to keep the average rootzone salinity levels within acceptable limits for the crop being grown, considering its stage of growth.

Many saline waters contain certain elements, such as boron and chloride, that can potentially accumulate in plants, especially woody, perennial ones, to levels that cause foliar injury and a subsequent reduction in their yield. In such cases, toxicity may produce more long-term detrimental effects than does salinity. Since boron is adsorbed by the soil it requires longer to build to toxic levels in the soil solution and it requires more leaching to remove its excessive accumulations than does salinity.

Thus long-term accumulation in the soil of potential toxicants must be considered, since toxic effects may not become evident for years and may be more difficult to eliminate. Water containing excessive concentrations of B or Cl should not be used to irrigate perennial crops, since (i) these crops are generally more sensitive to specific-ion effects (ii) they represent a long-term investment, and (iii) they will have a long time opportunity to accumulate toxic levels. This same concern applies to growing perennial crops in the presence of a shallow groundwater that contains solutes potentially toxic to the plant.

Another consideration as regards use of saline water for irrigation is the potential of the plant to accumulate certain elements (such as Se, Mo, heavy metals) that are toxic to consumers of the crops (humans and animals). For example, in the San Joaquin Valley of California, drainage water in several locations contains unusually high levels of Se (^{3} 50/m g Se/1). Although Se is essential to humans and animals in small amounts, excessive amounts can cause Se toxicosis. In the San Joaquin Valley, melons and processing tomatoes irrigated with drainage water containing 250 to 350 m g Se/ l accumulated elevated levels of Se in the fruit (250 to 750/m g/kg, dry wt.) that, while not an immediate health hazard, might become so to one whose diet was mostly restricted to such food. Many forages and native plant species have the potential to accumulate excessive amounts of Se (Wu *et al.* 1987). Since grazing animals consume larger quantities of plant mass than do humans, they have a greater potential for being "poisoned" in this manner.

Since plants vary in their ability to absorb and translocate toxic elements, crops that accumulate large quantities of toxic elements in the edible animal organs should also be avoided when using saline waters containing such elements for irrigation. Fleming (1962) found that Se concentrations were higher in *Cruciferae* (cabbage, cress, radish, rape and turnips), *Liliacea* (onion), and *Leguminosae* (clover and peas) than in *Compositae* (artichoke and lettuce), *Gramineae* (barley, oats, rye grass, and wheat), and *Umbelilferae* (parsnip and carrots) when grown on seleniferous soils in Ireland.

It is also important to understand how the toxic constituent is partitioned within the plant. In most annual fruit and vegetable crops selenium accumulates more in the leaves than in the fruit, but exceptions exist. If the saline water in question contains high levels of a potentially toxic element, the user should obtain expert advice.

FOOD SAFETY IN FRESH PRODUCE

Will Daniels began his presentation with a brief description of Natural Selection Foods. With its Earthbound Farm brand, it is the Nation's largest grower, packer, and shipper of organic produce, with products in 80 percent of all grocery stores across the country. The company produces a total of about 2.2 million pounds of leafy green fresh salads every week and distributes its produce internationally and as far away as Asia.

On what Daniels described as a "fateful" September 14, 2006, the California Department of Health Services (CDHS) informed Natural Selection Foods that the company had been implicated in a nationwide outbreak associated with fresh cut bagged spinach. The next day, with little to no information except that it had been implicated (among several other companies at that point) Natural Selection Foods issued a voluntary recall. Prior to September 14, the government had told the company only that the leafy greens industry in general was on high alert and that the government planned to act early and quickly in the event of any foodborne illness associated with bagged greens. Indeed, they acted quickly.

When Natural Selection Foods was implicated, thousands of samples were collected in both the field and the production facility as part of both government and company investigations. Matches were traced to a field that had supplied spinach on the production day associated with consumer infections. However, the source of the contamination was about a mile downwind of the field, with no clear indication of how the contamination had reached the field itself. Not having that crucial information and without a kill step in their process, Natural Selection Foods was forced to examine the entire spectrum of food safety risk(s) and begin developing a multi-hurdle approach to enhancing food safety which, today, represents a significant improvement in Natural Selection Foods' safety management system.

Daniels provided an overview of five of the major programs that Natural Selection Foods has established over these past two years as part of its new multi-hurdle approach:

- *Seed to Harvest:* Natural Selection Foods has developed a new plan for enhanced GAPs, including :
  - o conducting pre-season ranch assessments of the history, topography, adjacent land use, and other relevant features of all potential ranches;
  - o testing all seeds, fertilizers, water and other inputs for O157:H7 enterohemorrhagic *E. coli* (EHEC) and *Salmonella* and preventing all inputs from entering the field without certification that they have tested negative;
  - o during planting, testing water at shorter intervals than required by the California Leafy Green Products Handler Marketing Agreement; and
  - o practicing regular GAP harvest audits and ensuring compliance in workers' practices.
- *Raw Material Firewall:* The company instituted a raw product test and hold program about two weeks after the September 14, 2006, outbreak, whereby 100 percent of all leafy greens are now sampled from and prevented from entering the process stream until negative results are achieved. In addition to testing for EHEC and *Salmonella*, Natural Selection Foods recently added a *Shigella* screen.
- *In the Plant:* The company has made several enhancements in its packing facilities, for example the use of laser sorters in an effort to reduce foreign materials. The laser sorters identify materials that do not contain chlorophyll and reject them from the process stream. This not only allows the wash systems to focus on the salad itself and not extraneous material, it also reduces consumer complaints about foreign materials in their salads. During the first month of having laser sorter across all processing lines, Earthbound Farm saw a 70 percent reduction in such complaints, which was remarkable given that foreign material complaints comprise about half of all complaints. Now, mostly just weeds still pass through. Additionally, in the wash system, the company has added dunk reels for increased

contact time, enhanced filtration time, and added an extra wash step.

- *Finished Product Firewall:* The company added a finished good test and hold program in February 2007, whereby all finished goods are sampled for select pathogens and not released until negative results are achieved.
- *Gaining Deeper Knowledge:* Natural Selection Foods is now using its test data (e.g., from its *Raw Material Firewall* and *Finished Product Firewall* programs) to develop a deeper understanding of what is needed to prevent outbreaks. Importantly, however, Daniels emphasized that testing is not the answer to food safety. The *Raw Material* and *Finished Product* firewalls, for example, are not intended to provide a solution to food safety, rather as a means to "get to the answers" more quickly.

While this multi-hurdle approach to food safety represents a fantastic step forward for Natural Selection Foods, Daniels emphasized that it does not address the multitude of problems that arise after a product leaves the farm and processing facilities—that is, during distribution, storage, retailing and consumption.

Food safety does not stop at the farm, nor does it stop in the processing facility. In fact, what happens after products leave the farm probably amounts to more than 50 percent of the food safety continuum, Daniels said, which raises questions about what additional hurdles could be put in place further downstream with the ultimate goal of consumer protection. Daniels reiterated one of Taylor's key messages: that "real collaboration" among different stakeholders responsible for food safety at various points along this food-to-table continuum is lacking. Too many institutions are still operating like "stovepipes." In order to achieve progress and reduce risks, these different sectors need to start collaborating. He argued, "Collaboration, rather than competition, among those striving for improved food safety could achieve real results." Right now, audits serve as one of the primary mechanisms for communication between different segments of the farm-to-table spectrum (e.g., buyers rely on audits to guarantee that what they are purchasing is safe). But as Daniels asked, "Can audits ensure safety?" He argued that while food safety audits serve as good verification that operators have functional food safety programs, it is really up to the individual operator to ensure that their food safety systems are functioning well. Likewise, further downstream, individual distributors, retailers and consumers need to be responsible for food safety at their respective positions along the food safety continuum. Audits, like other tests, are not preventive measures. Not only are audits not preventive, they are costly. Natural Selection Foods goes through multiple audits yearly, often repetitively for different buyers. Multiple audits cost resources and time, which may be better spent on finding new answers to food safety issues. Daniels remarked that the same "stovepipe" mentality is at work among research institutions as well. While several universities and trade associations are devoting many resources in an attempt to solve some of these issues, many of these efforts are duplicated. More national-level coordination is needed to reduce the redundancy so that we can find answers more quickly and effectively. Moreover, most of the research is being conducted on foodborne illness in the United States, even though many of these issues are not unique to this country. Nor are they unique to the fresh produce industry. Research results often have more wide-ranging implications than are realized.

Finally, Daniels commented on the large quantity of industry-generated data and how these data have been used against companies in the past (e.g., to implicate a company in an outbreak with which they might not have otherwise been associated). Government needs to take the lead in creating a trusted, safe environment where data sharing and research collaboration would quicken the pace of concrete, applicable advancements in food safety.

Daniels then gave two examples of the type of safety data being generated at Natural Selection Foods:

1. In both initial reactives (Raw IR) and molecular confirmation (Raw MC) positives of raw product during

the summer months, when operations are conducted in the Salinas, California, area (as opposed to the winter months, when operations are moved down to Yuma, Arizona). Daniels remarked that this spike raises questions about whether the company should be spending more of their test and hold monies during the summer months.

2. A low level of molecular confirmation positives of organic spinach when measured per million of pounds received, or MC/M Lbs Rec (as opposed to molecular confirmation, or MC, incidents). Daniels explained that the low normalized level for spinach is important given that spinach is Natural Selection Foods' single largest individual ingredient, comprising about 30 percent of the company's received products (i.e., if spinach was not such a large volume product, the high number of incidents, without taking into account volume, would be more alarming than it is). Daniels also pointed to the high rates for organic cilantro, parsley, and dill, noting that herbs are known to carry a higher risk and that the company has taken additional measures to protect them. He said that the spike for conventional freesia was probably an anomaly and that it was a very low-volume item at the time. When these data were generated, Natural Selection Foods was a mixed operation (i.e., mixed organically and conventionally grown products). Today, the company is 100 percent organic.

Daniels then moved on to the topic of government transparency, commenting on how an FDA official had expressed "surprise" early on during FDA's investigation of the more recent *Salmonella* Saintpaul outbreak that Florida tomatoes could end up on the West coast. Upon hearing that remark, it dawned on Daniels that the food safety continuum needs not only better collaboration but also greater transparency. In particular, government needs an industry group that they can really turn to for quick answers during outbreak situations in order to relieve some of the extreme pressure they are under to protect consumers. Too often, outbreaks generate misinformation and media frenzy, which in turn, cause a decline in consumer confidence. This type of misinformation also often leads to the allocation of resources to the wrong places. Having a mechanism in place for government agencies to find quick answers would also alleviate some of the pressure that industry is under during outbreak situations. During the *Salmonella* Saintpaul outbreak, Natural Selection Foods spent an inordinate amount of time reassuring customers that they were distributing neither tomatoes, cilantro, nor jalapeño peppers. Likewise, efforts need to be directed toward helping industry understand government actions and processes better (e.g., during tracebacks).

Daniels concluded by posing the question, "How do we move forward?" He highlighted four necessary steps:

1. Recognize that pathogens exist in our environment and that, in fact our food safety systems control them "99.9 percent of the time." Natural Selection Foods processed fresh produce for 24 years without an incident.
2. Realize that we are all in this together and that one segment's efforts alone are not going to solve the problem or reduce consumer concern.
3. Develop national standards and standardized audits (with one audit verifying compliance for all buyers). Standardizing does not mean adopting a one-size-fits-all approach, rather implementing good agricultural and manufacturing processes and having a hazard analysis and food safety plan in place for that particular operation.
4. Collaborate! Companies need to work together as an industry to make our produce safer; they need to create a secure environment where research efforts can be coordinated, applied, and improved; industry and government need to work together such that coordinated efforts can result in quicker conclusions; and we need to develop better trust by establishing transparency and an open dialogue between industry and government.

RISK MANAGEMENT FOR THERMALLY PROCESSED FOODS

Don Zink began by commenting that thermally processed foods are essentially and technically "completely safe" and, as such, illustrates what can be accomplished with respect to food safety and risk management when "all of the pieces are in place." When failures occur, they are due to mechanical or human errors, not incomplete knowledge about how to manage the risks.

Zink clarified that he would be focusing primarily on commercially and completely sterile products, which comprise just one end of a range of thermally processed foods. Complete sterility is the more extreme: It involves killing even the most heat-resistant thermophilic organisms. Commercial sterilization is not as extreme: It does not necessarily mean that there are no viable microorganisms in the canned product and, in fact, some thermophilic microorganisms usually survive the commercial sterilization process. Rather, it simply means that under the intended conditions of storage and consumer use, those microorganisms are no longer going to continue to grow. Commercial sterility is the standard used today for low-acid canned foods. At the other end of the scale are blanched and pasteurized foods. Blanching is a very mild heat treatment primarily used in the frozen foods industry to fix color and inactivate enzymes that cause undesirable oxidation reactions; blanching may or may not kill some pathogens, depending on how it is done. Pasteurization is usually interpreted to mean that a heat or other form of treatment has been used to destroy harmful microorganisms.Completely sterile and commercially sterile foods arguably have the best safety record of any category of processed foods.

It is difficult to put a number on their safety record, Zink said, given variability in safety and how foodborne disease is monitored around the world. That said the likelihood of contracting botulism or another serious foodborne illness from this type of product is probably less than 1 in 100 billion. Zink identified three major factors that contribute to the safety of canned foods:

The underlying science is defined and complete. While there are still some unknown things, we do understand and have understood for a long time the nature of several critical processes:

a. The physics of heat transfer. Methods to measure the rate of heating among various foods were developed more than 50 years ago, so we know how foods heat, how different foods heat differently (e.g., dried beans heat differently than diced carrots) and how heat is transferred into a container from a piece of processing equipment. We also have well-developed methods for verifying the adequacy and uniformity of heating.

b. Thermal bacteriology. While there is always some worry that a new, heat-resistant "superbug" is going to emerge, we understand the nature of the bacterial flora that exists now. We have identified all of the important target bacteria for heat processing, we have studied their heat resistance and inactivation kinetics, and we have established target values for what kind of inactivation we must have in order to make products safe. Interestingly, all of the heat-resistant microbial organisms of public health concern are actually less heat-resistant than spoilage organisms, which means that foods need to be heated even more than necessary (from a heat processing perspective) in order to kill the spoilage organisms.

c. The engineering of heat processing equipment. We know how to design systems that heat food, we have well-established standards for the design and construction of retorts, and we have excellent process control capabilities.

d. Development of tools for accurately and continuously measuring the process. While new microwave and other technologies are being developed for this purpose, we have other tools available that give us an excellent fundamental understanding of what is going on. In fact, the basic critical variables in thermal processing are relatively easy to measure and document (i.e., temperature, time, flow rate, pH, water activity [a_w], viscosity, thermal diffusivity, heat and temperature distributions).

We have well-developed packaging systems. Zink remarked that it doesn't do any good to produce a safe food if you can't keep it safe before it is in consumer hands.

a. We have a very long history with the metal can and glass jar, with the former dating back to Napoleonic times. So the packaging technology is well worked out—so well worked out that it is possible to request from a vendor a certain type of container for a certain amount of material, longevity, thermal resistance, etc., and the vendor can meet that request. For example, if you wanted a metal can that lasted 20 years, we could do that. Today, most metal cans typically last up to about four years. Similarly, if you wanted a glass jar that could survive any amount of trauma, again we could do that, although it would

b. be heavy and expensive. We have had substantial experience with flexible pouches and cardboard laminates as well. While they may not date back to Napoleonic times, these types of packages have been on the market for decades.

c. We have well-established durability standards for all types of common packaging, including standardized testing protocols that could be used to determine whether your product has a reasonable chance of holding up in the marketplace.

We have well-educated consumers.

a. Nearly every consumer is familiar with the metal can, with the vast majority of consumers understanding that swelling or leakage means that there is some kind of problem. Most consumers are also aware that a badly dented can is suspect. There is some concern, however, that there may be a downward trend in this area, with fewer consumers being aware of potential problems. Not only is there a lot of new packaging entering the marketplace (and taking the place of the metal can), there is less food safety education occurring in the home.

b. That said, consumers seem to be transferring what they know about the metal can to some of these other forms of packaging. If a consumer sees a swollen pouch, for example, he or she might suspect that something is wrong.

c. Either way—with both canned and other types of packaged foods—mechanical or human errors are to some extent caught by consumers.

In conclusion, Zink re-emphasized that the main value of considering the food safety record of thermally processed foods is to contrast it with other types of foods (e.g., fresh produce), and identify and understand those components that give the former a much better safety record. One of the most important components is science. Technically, complete food safety requires a complete understanding of how all the variables contribute to potential contamination problems and a complete understanding of how to build the tools needed for interrupting those routes of contamination (as well as the tools needed for measuring and controlling the process).

NATURAL ENVIRONMENT AND FOODS

Among the nine reported species of Carnobacterium, only two species, C. divergens and C. maltaromaticum, are frequently isolated from various sources. Four species, C. alterfunditum, C. funditum, C. gallinarum and C. mobile, have been isolated a few times from at most three sources. Three species, C. inhibens, C. pleistocenium and C. viridans, have only been isolated from one source, but it should be noted that Carnobacterium spp. related to, for example, C. inhibens have been described. Carnobacterium spp. appear to have both the temperate and polar aquatic environments as habitats including live fish, marine sponges, Antarctic lakes, Arctic and Antarctic sea water as well as the deep sea, aquous alkaline tufa columns from Greenland, and freshwater habitats from the temperate clima zone, including a Sphagnum pond and rivers in the northwest region of Spain.

Although C. maltaromaticum and/or C. divergens have been isolated from tropical fish products, including smoked surubim, a Brazilian tropical freshwater fish, and from vacuum-packed tuna caught in the Indian Ocean and processed in Sri Lanka, it cannot, at least in the latter case, be excluded that this is due to contamination associated with repackaging in Denmark.

The presence of carnobacteria has also been demonstrated in the terrestrial environment, including a field treated with whey, Canadian winter soil, permafrost ice, a compost pile, a collapsed horse manure pile, the larval midgut of a moth species, and other sources. It appears that the temperate/polar aquatic and terrestrial environments are both natural habitats.

Carnobacterium divergens and C. maltaromaticum possess traits that may play a role in their survival in these surroundings. One study has reported that a Carnobacterium sp. soil isolate related to C. maltaromaticum survived 48 serial freeze-thaw cycles better than Escherichia coli and an Enterococcus sp. soil isolate, but worse than a few other soil isolates, including an Acinetobacter sp. Indeed, these organisms may survive freezing for considerable periods of time, as witnessed by the isolation of a Carnobacterium sp. preserved in a permafrost ice wedge for 25 000 years. Additional data on the abilities of carnobacteria to grow at low temperatures and to survive frozen storage is available for food products. Also, a cold-active b-galactosidase from C. maltaromaticum and a cold-adapted alanine dehydrogenase from a Carnobacterium sp. related to C. alterfunditum have been reported. Some carnobacterial isolates originate from natural high-pressure habitats, and additional data on resistance to pressure have been reported for high-pressure-processed foods. It has not been described how other physical/chemical parameters such as salt content, atmosphere and pH affect survival and growth of these organisms in the natural environment.

With respect to energy-yielding substrates, one species, C. maltaromaticum, expresses chitinase activity. This may facilitate adherence to and survival on zooplankton as suggested for enterococci, and also explain the isolation of this species from the midgut of the larval stage of a species of moth.

Interestingly, the arginine deiminase pathway is expressed by the most frequently encountered species, C. divergens, C. gallinarum, C. maltaromaticum and C. mobile but not by C. inhibens or C. viridans. Arginine is not a substrate that results in growth of C. alterfunditum and C. funditum, and information is not available for C. pleistocenium. This amino acid may represent an additional energy source for growth and survival when carbohydrates are scarce, and it may offer protection against acid stress, as described for Enterococcus faecalis and related species. Finally, carnobacteria are able to catabolize a range of carbohydrates, although there are considerable interspecies and intraspecies heterogeneities.

Examples of sources of such carbohydrates include animals (e.g. chitin and, to some extent, lactose, although the targets of the lactose hydrolytic activity shown by carnobacteria may instead be byproducts of plant sugar polymers and saccharides adsorbed to humic acid substances in the soil), plants (e.g. salicin and sucrose), fungi (e.g. chitin and trehalose), prokaryotes (N-acetylglucosamine), and living organisms in general (ribose). The importance of these abilities for growth and survival in the environment deserves further study. The genome sizes of C. alterfunditum, C. divergens and C. pleistoconium strains and a Carnobacterium sp. AT7 deep sea isolate have been estimated to be 2.9, 3.2, 3.2 and 2.4Mb, respectively, and for the AT7 isolate, the data are reported in a database described by Liolios (2006). These sizes are relatively large in comparison to many other LAB, suggesting that carnobacterial genomes may encode a range of genes that makes them well adapted to deal with environmental challenges.

Even if carnobacteria are well adapted to temperate or polar aqueous environments, this does not always provide improved ability to survive as compared to other bacteria. Thus, the actual abilities of strains of C. divergens and C. maltaromaticum isolated from a Sphagnum pond to survive in water from this source were not improved as compared to related gram-positive bacteria originating from other sources. At present, therefore, the precise mechanisms by which Carnobacterium spp. persist in the natural environment and their underlying genetics are not known. Finally, it should be noted that the environments from which carnobacteria can be isolated are not always as extreme as they appear at first sight. Thus, Carnobacterium spp. isolated from Lake Vanda, Antarctica were found at a depth of 61 m, where the temperature was c. 15-20 1C.

Dairy, Fish and Meat Products

High concentrations of bacteria (4106-107 CFUg_1) in food are typically required before their activity is sufficient to influence the sensory properties of a product. For this to happen, occurrence and growth kinetics are the key parameters, and databases, including ComBase, are available to determine the effect of food storage conditions and product characteristics on growth of specific bacteria. However, information on carnobacteria has not yet been included in such databases.

Carnobacterium maltaromaticum and another Carnobacterium sp. have been isolated from milk, and they, in addition to C. divergens, have been detected in soft cheeses, including mold-ripened brie, mozzarella, Camembert and other types. The high concentration of C. divergens in the curd of mozzarella, exposed to 10-37 1C during processing, is in agreement with the maximum growth temperature (40 1C) of this species.

The occurrence of Carnobacterium in dairy products (and other foods) is most likely underreported. This is due to the common use of acetate containing media, particularly MRS agar or Rogosa agar, for enumeration of LAB. Growth of Carnobacterium is inhibited by acetate, and both MRS and Rogosa agar media significantly underestimate concentrations in food.

Carnobacterium divergens and C. maltaromaticum are present in seafood and are able to grow to high concentrations in different fresh and lightly preserved products. Studies of naturally contaminated products suggest which storage conditions and product characteristics select for carnobacteria as compared to the other bacteria present in seafood. For chilled fresh seafood, we have found no reports where C.

divergens and C. maltaromaticum dominated the microbial communities in aerobically stored products, but this has been reported for modified atmosphere-packed (MAP) coalfish, cod, pollack, rainbow trout, salmon, shrimp, swordfish and tuna.

After frozen storage (_20 to _30 1C for 5-8 weeks), C. divergens and C. maltaromaticum seem to be particularly prominent in chilled MAP fish, as has been reported for cod, garfish, salmon, and tuna. In addition to freezing, these carnobacteria are relatively resistant to high-pressure processing and are found in high concentrations in vacuum-packed and chilled squid mantle and cold-smoked salmon previously treated with 200-400MPa for 15-20 min. In vacuum-packed coldsmoked or sugar-salted ('gravad') seafood with 3-7% NaCl in the water phase and a pH of 5.8-6.5, high concentrations of C. divergens and C. maltaromaticum are particularly common, as reported for halibut, rainbow trout, salmon, surubim, and tuna.

High concentrations of C. maltaromaticum are also reported in salted lumpfish roe, and it has been isolated from frozen, smoked mussels. Finally, for cooked seafood, high concentrations of C. maltaromaticum have been detected in MAP shrimp after storage at 2-8 1C. Both C. divergens and C. mobile were isolated from cooked and brined MAP shrimps (with NaCl, benzoic acid, citric acid and sorbic acid) after storage at 2-8 1C. Clearly, carnobacteria are common in chilled fresh and lightly preserved seafood, but at higher storage temperatures (15-25 1C), other species, including Enterococcus spp., more frequently dominate the spoilage microbial community of seafood.

Carnobacterium divergens and C. maltaromaticum are able to grow in meat products at temperatures as low as 2 to _1.5 1C, and they are frequently predominant members (up to 50% C. divergens and up to 26% C. maltaromaticum of the gram-positive or LAB isolates obtained) of the microbial community of raw meat (beef, pork, lamb, and poultry).

The two species are found irrespective of whether products have been stored aerobically, vacuum packaged, or subjected to modified atmospheres, including gas compositions of CO_2/N_2 (%) ranging from 10 : 90 to 80 : 20. One study demonstrated the presence of C. divergens in beef stored in air but not in MAP beef with increased concentrations of O_2 (20-40%) in addition to CO_2 (40%). The growth of C. funditum is impaired by oxygen, and it will be of interest to study further whether addition of O_2 to the gas composition of modified atmospheres consistently inhibits growth of carnobacteria, as has been observed for some other bacteria.

Further studies are needed in order to determine whether differences in the presence of carnobacteria in meat are due to variations in storage conditions or variations in contamination levels at the processing plants. The source of carnobacteria in meat products is most probably the processing plant, as these organisms have not been isolated from the gastrointestinal system or skin of chicken, cattle, pigs or sheep, except for one unpublished study. Thus, the source of contamination of broiler carcasses by C. divergens and C. maltaromaticum was shown to be the air in the processing plant and not incoming broiler chickens. In fact, two studies confirmed that C. divergens and C. maltaromaticum present in the raw material were eliminated or reduced in number by cooking of a processed meat product, ham. Carnobacterium divergens and C. maltaromaticum have, however, been detected in a variety of processed meat products, including the cured pork product bacon, a Danish processed pork product ('rullep_lse'), various Spanish processed meat products, cooked poultry meat, pressure-treated (408-888MPa) chicken, and irradiated pork and chicken. On a few occasions, C. maltaromaticum has even been isolated from fermented sausages; as noted by Hammes & Hertel (2003), this contrasts with the usual nonaciduric habitats of carnobacteria. Other Carnobacterium spp. isolated from processed meat products include C. gallinarium (irradiated chicken), C. mobile (cooked turkey) and C. viridans (vacuum-packed Bologna sausage). Although these organisms are frequently isolated from processed meat products, it has been suggested that they are rarely present in high numbers, and that terminal spoilage of cooked, cured meats is primarily caused by aciduric LAB.

Finally, a Carnobacterium sp. has also been isolated from egg contents, and it was shown that this isolate had a similar ability to penetrate the eggshell and contaminate the whole egg as various other gram-positive and gram-negative bacteria.

Transmission routes for carnobacteria from the natural environment into food-manufacturing plants and further on to dairy, fish and meat products are not known to any extent. Knowledge on this topic is essential to evaluate if species and intraspecific clusters that differ in spoilage ability also have different colonization abilities. Such knowledge would also illuminate the feasibility of using the production of metabolites, especially tyramine, by C. divergens and C. maltaromaticum as an index of microbial spoilage of specific fish and meat products.

FUNCTIONAL PROPERTIES OF CARNOBACTERIA

Carnobacteria with the ability to produce antimicrobial peptides, bacteriocins, are commonly encountered in foods. The characterized carnobacterial bacteriocins belong to class I and class II [e.g. Drider et al. (2006) for bacteriocin nomenclature]. So far, only one class I bacteriocin (lantibiotic), UI149, has been reported to be produced by Carnobacterium. In contrast, ten amino acidsequenced bacteriocins belong to class II, and most of these more specifically to class IIa, which comprises small pediocin-like peptides. The inhibition spectrum of carnobacterial class IIa bacteriocins includes Listeria, and antimicrobial activity is exerted by pore formation, dissipation of membrane potential, and leakage of internal low molecular weight substances. Class IIa bacteriocins are ribosomally synthesized as inactive prepeptides that are modified by posttranslational cleavage of the N-terminal peptide leader at a doubleglycine site in order to release mature and active cationic peptides. Carnobacterial class IIa bacteriocins have similar amino acid sequences, with a YGNGV(X)C(X)4C motif (X denotes any amino acid) near the N-terminus of the mature peptide. Two cysteine residues form a disulfide bond in the N-terminal region, and there is an amphipathic a-helix near the C-terminus. The N-terminal region is relatively hydrophilic and conserved, whereas the C-terminus is hydrophobic and diverse. To establish the structure-activity relationships of carnobacterial bacteriocins, the structures of carnobacteriocin B2 and divercin V41 were modified. Thus, amino acid substitutions closer to the N-terminus in carnobacteriocin B2 drastically reduced or eliminated antimicrobial activity, whereas this was not so for substitutions close to the C-terminal part. Divercin V41 contains a second disulfide bond located in the C-terminal region.

When the C-terminal region of divercin V41 was separated from the N-terminus by endoproteinase Asp-N, only the C-terminal fragment was active. After trypsin cleavage next to lysine at position 42 or disulfide reduction, the C-terminus lost its inhibitory activity. These results suggested that both hydrophobicity and folding imposed by this second disulfide bond were essential for antilisterial activity of the C-terminal hydrophobic peptide. Chemical oxidation of tryptophan residues by N-bromosuccinimide showed that these residues were crucial for inhibitory activity, as modification of any one of them rendered divercin V41 inactive. The three-dimensional structure of carnobacteriocin B2, its precursor and the corresponding immunity protein have been solved by nuclear magnetic resonance. These are, at present, the only reported carnobacterial protein structures.

Carnobacterial class II bacteriocins that contain a doubleglycine-type leader peptide are transported by a dedicated ATP-binding cassette (ABC) transport system. In contrast, divergicin A does not require a secretion protein, as the transport depend on the general cellular secretion (sec) pathway. The genes involved in carnobacterial bacteriocin production are generally clustered in operons.

In the simplest case, corresponding to the sec-dependent divergicin A, the bacteriocin operon is composed of only the structural gene followed downstream by the gene encoding an immunity protein that protects the cell from is own bacteriocin. Production of class IIa bacteriocins requires four genes as a minimum, including genes encoding bacteriocin, immunity protein, ABC of transport protein and its membrane-bound accessory protein. Genes for bacteriocin production may be encoded on the chromosome or on plasmids. Carnobacterium maltaromaticum LV17 produces at least three class II bacteriocins.

Carnobacteriocins A and B2 are encoded on different but compatible plasmids, pCP49 (72 kb) and pCP40 (61 kb), respectively. The carnobacteriocin BM1 structural gene and its immunity gene are localized on the chromosome. Activation and export of carnobacteriocin BM1 depend on genes located on plasmid pCP40 encoding carnobacteriocin B2. For carnobacteriocins BM1 and B2, a peptide-pheromone dependent quorum-sensing mode caused by the bacteriocin itself or an autoinducer peptide is involved in the regulation of bacteriocin production by two-and three-component signal transduction systems.

The components of this regulatory system consist of an induction factor, a histidine protein kinase, and a response regulator. Four carnobacterial bacteriocin operons including genes for immunity proteins and regulatory proteins involved in bacteriocin expression and secretion have been sequenced. External parameters also affect bacteriocin production.

Thus, increasing concentrations of NaCl (2-7%) reduced production of A9b/B2 bacteriocin, increasing the temperature from below 19 to 25 1C inhibited production of piscicolin 126, and reducing the pH from 6.5 to 5.5 inhibited production of carnobacteriocins BM1 and B2. Acetate (A9b bacteriocin) or the presence of a bacteriocin-sensitive strain belonging to the same genus induced bacteriocin production. It is clear that, in order to apply carnobacterial bacteriocins for the biopreservation of foods, detailed knowledge of the factors that influence production of the bacteriocin is necessary.

Finally, it should be noted that the bacteriocinogenic activity may be lost, as shown for a C. divergens divercin V41-producing strain that retained only partial activity after being subjected to spray-drying. Interest in applying carnobacterial bacteriocins in foods and feeds has been directed towards inhibiting Listeria monocytogenes and spoilage microorganisms, to extend the shelf-life of lightly preserved seafood. These attempts have generally, but not always [e.g. regarding prevention of spoilage], met with success, although diversity in sensitivity of the target organism has been observed. However, the occurrence of resistant L. monocytogenes target organisms has led to the suggestion that bacteriocin-negative LAB may be more suitable for practical use as bioprotective agents against L. monocytogenes in ready-to-eat foods. Indeed, L. monocytogenes is inhibited by carnobacterial cultures that do not produce bacteriocins, and this is partly due to glucose depletion. One study also reported a successful application of cultures with no demonstrated bacteriocinogenic activity for extension of the shelflife of vacuum-packed cold-smoked salmon. This effect was not, however, observed for a C. divergens strain that was unable to produce the class IIa divercin V41.

Resistance of L. monocytogenes to the class IIa divergicin M35 was probably due to modification of the cell wall fatty acid composition. Listeria monocytogenes strains resistant to the class IIa divercin V41 also showed substantial differences in protein expressions as compared with the wild type strain. A s54-dependent PTS permease of the mannose family, which belongs to the phosphotransferase system (PTS), is responsible for sensitivity of L. monocytogenes to class IIa bacteriocins.

These results suggested that EIIt Man encoded by the mptACD operon might be a target molecule for class IIa bacteriocins. Recently, two genes coding for a glycerophosphoryl diester phosphodiesterase (GlpQ) and a protein with a putative phosphoesterase function (Pde) were identified as also being involved in the class IIa sensitivity of En. faecalis. Finally, it is important to note that the susceptibility of the target strain is affected by various environmental conditions such as NaCl and pH.

Another cause of concern when using carnobacteria for biopreservation is that C. divergens and C. maltaromaticum both produce tyramine, as discussed further below. Therefore, it has been suggested that a C. divergens strain in which the tyrosine decarboxylase gene is inactivated by mutagenesis could be used as a protective culture to prevent growth of L. monocytogenes in cold-smoked salmon. Currently, no carnobacterial culture, bacteriocin producing or not, is commercially applied for protection against the growth of L. monocytogenes or other bacterial pathogens or spoilage organisms in food.

Sensory Characteristics and Safety of Foods

The catabolic activities of carnobacteria may result in sensory spoilage of inoculated fish and meat products. Whether this is so for cheese products is not clear. In naturally contaminated products, it seems other members of the bacterial community are typically more important with regard to sensory effects, including spoilage. It is of interest that spoilage was enhanced if moderate-spoilage strains of C. maltaromaticum were inoculated with nonspoilage Vibrio sp. strains or the moderate-spoilage organism Brochothrix thermosphacta into cold-smoked salmon that was subsequently vacuum-packaged. However, this was not so for combinations of C. maltaromaticum and Photobacterium phosphoreum in this product. In addition, a spoilage synergy effect was observed for combinations of B. thermosphacta and C. divergens, C. maltaromaticum or C. mobile in MAP shrimp.

We will first focus on catabolic reactions with carbohydrates and/or organic acids as substrates and with pyruvic acid as an intermediate metabolite. Respiration might occur in the presence of hematin, as shown for C. maltaromaticum, and, indeed, this species consumes substantial proportions of oxygen during exponential growth under aerobic conditions. Carnobacterium spp. are, however, considered to be homofermentative organisms that produce lactic acid from glucose.

The presence of the glycolytic pathway in C. divergens has been demonstrated. It can be debated whether carnobacteria should instead be considered facultative or atypical heterofermentative organisms, as C. divergens and C. maltaromaticum are able to utilize ribose and gluconic acid as substrates for growth, and may produce acetic acid, formic acid, and CO_2 as end-products of some secondary decarboxylation/dissimilation reactions of pyruvic acid. Indeed, carnobacteria were initially described as heterofermenters. Acetic acid production by C. divergens and C. maltaromaticum can be substantial during growth in laboratory media under aerobic conditions or in MAP shrimp, and quantitatively it can exceed lactic acid production. Production of acetic acid by C. maltaromaticum is also increased relative to lactic acid if glucose is substituted by ribose. Furthermore, C. maltaromaticum can produce large amounts of ethanol from glucose and ribose during growth in a shrimp extract under anaerobic conditions.

Acetoin can be generated by C. maltaromaticum from pyruvic acid, and this reaction is also found for C. divergens and C. gallinarum but not for C. alterfunditum, C. funditum, C. inhibens and C. viridance, according to reactions in the Voges-Proskauer test. Carnobacterium mobile gives variable reactions, and information is not available for C. pleistocenium. The factors affecting acetoin production are not well known, but production is increased by resting cells of C. maltaromaticum in the presence of hematin. In addition, two out of four strains of C. divergens and C. maltaromaticum isolated from mozzarella cheese were reported to be able to metabolize citric acid, but the potential sensory role of this reaction, e.g. by production of acetoin and diacetyl, was not examined.

Production of diacetyl and 2,3-pentanedione by C. maltaromaticum during growth in cold-smoked salmon resulted in a butter-like odor but not in spoilage. In conclusion, even, if carbohydrate catabolism by carnobacteria appears to result in a diverse number of metabolites, these have generally a limited effect on the sensory attributes of foods. H_2O_2 may be produced by C. divergens, and formation of this compound by C. viridans has been associated with spoilage in the form of green discoloration of cured Bologna ham.

Whether carnobacteria possess proteolytic activities of potential importance for taste in products such as cheese is not known, and this deserves further investigation. In contrast, metabolites resulting from the degradation of amino acids certainly cause sensory effects in foods. Generation of branched alcohols and aldehydes (2-methyl-1-butanal, 2-methyl-1-butanol, 3-methyl-1-butanal, 3-methyl-1-butanol, 2-methylpropanal, and 2-methylpropanol) by transamination, decarboxylation and reduction of the amino acids valine, leucine and isoleucine appears to be particularly important. Production of some of these compounds, such as 3-methyl-1-butanal, is strain or species dependent. Production by a C. maltaromaticum strain of 3-methylbutanal, 3-methylbutanol and 3-methylbutanoic acid from leucine was, in general, increased at pH values of 6.5 or higher and in the presence of increased concentrations of a-ketoisocaproic acid and glucose. This strain affected the odor and reduced the leucine content of a sausage mince, but a clear causal relationship was not demonstrated. Production by C. maltaromaticum of alcohols and aldehydes from valine, leucine and/or isoleucine resulted in a malty, green aroma in skimmed milk and shrimp, and has also caused spoilage of cured ham. The association between the presence of these compounds and spoilage is, however, not always straightforward, as production of 3-methyl-1-butanal and/or 3-methyl-1-butanol in shrimp by certain C. maltaromaticum strains did not result in malty off-flavours.

Production of NH_4 from arginine as a result of its catabolism catalyzed by the arginine deaminase pathway may, in theory, cause spoilage of shrimp or squid that contain high levels of free arginine. Carnobacterium maltaromaticum and C. divergens but not C. mobile were able to produce NH_4 in MAP shrimp, but this was not the cause of spoilage of this product. Production of indole from the amino acid tryptophan is also a potential cause of spoilage, although C. divergens, C. maltaromaticum and C. mobile are all unable to carry out this reaction in standard laboratory media. It has, however, been observed that C. divergens and strains belonging to a major phenotypic cluster of C. maltaromaticum were able to use tryptophan as a substrate during growth in MAP shrimp. Whether this resulted in generation of indole was not examined.

Production of tyramine from tyrosine is the only known metabolic reaction by Carnobacterium spp. that constitutes a cause of concern regarding food safety. Not all carnobacterial species possess this ability, as C. mobile does not produce tyramine during growth in shrimp, and variation exists among different strains and phenotypic clusters of C. divergens and C. maltaromaticum for amounts of tyramine produced. Tyramine production by one C. divergens strain was at its maximum during the stationary growth phase and at a low initial pH in the presence of 0.6% glucose, whereas NaCl (10%) was inhibitory. Regardless of strain variation and the effects of environmental parameters, tyramine production by C. divergens and/or C. maltaromaticum has been reported in a range of foods, including meat (up to 28 mg kg_1), a meat-fat mixture (up to 121 mg kg_1), cold-smoked salmon (up to c. 370 mg kg_1), frozen and thawed salmon (up to 40-60 mg kg_1), and shrimp (up to 20-60 mg kg_1).

These levels have no adverse effects on most consumers, but for sensitive individuals, e.g. with reduced monoamine oxidase activity due to medication or hereditary deficiency, very little tyramine can cause migraine headaches, and an intake of no more than 5mg of tyramine per meal has been recommended. Typical consumption of fish and meat products is 50-150 g per meal. As described above, C. divergens and/or C. maltaromaticum are able to form c. 20-370 mg tyramine kg_1 in these products, corresponding to c. 1-55 mg of tyramine per meal. Consequently, tyramine formation by carnobacteria in specific foods can represent a hazard for sensitive individuals who might suffer migraine headaches. This risk for sensitive individuals can be minimized by restricting their consumption of fish and meat to products that are newly processed, i.e. that are not close to the declared shelf-life expiry day.

Growth of Carnobacterium spp. in food products may result in accumulation of a range of volatile alcohols, ketones, hydrocarbons, and other compounds. The metabolic reactions leading to these products have not been studied in detail for Carnobacterium, in contrast to the situation for other LAB, but may be a result of NAD1-generating reactions or nonenzymatic reactions. Several ketones have characteristic odors, but whether they contribute to spoilage off-flavours as a result of carnobacterial metabolic activity is not well understood. With regard to lipids, C. maltaromaticum has been reported to hydrolyze tributyrin, a triglyceride with butyrate as fatty acid, but it is not known whether this lipase activity contributes to flavor changes of dairy, fish and meat products. Carnobacterium divergens and C.maltaromaticum were not able to limit oxidation of linoleic acid during growth. This indicates that these species may not prevent quality deterioration of meat products by lipid oxidation. Finally, C. maltaromaticum has been shown to cause a softer texture of salmon fillets when inoculated in high numbers.

It is worth noting that interspecies and intraspecies differences exist regarding carnobacterial spoilage capacity. Laursen et al. (2006) showed that C. mobile and a minor phenotypic cluster of C. maltaromaticum did not spoil MAP shrimp, in contrast to what was seen with C. divergens and the major phenotypic cluster of C. maltaromaticum. It would be of interest to examine whether similar heterogeneities exist for Carnobacterium spp. growing in other dairy, fish and meat products. As environmental parameters readily affect the metabolism of carbohydrates and amino acids, it is not surprising that product-specific and storage-specific conditions also play important roles. The ability of two C. maltaromaticum strains to relatively rapidly spoil meat during growth under aerobic conditions at 7 1C but not or only after a long storage period in vacuum packs at 2 1C serves as an example.

Pathogenic Organisms and/or Probiotic Cultures

Two human clinical cases caused by opportunistic infection with C. maltaromaticum and a Carnobacterium sp. have been described. Two clinical isolates of C. divergens have also been obtained. Carnobacteria are not known members of the human gastrointestinal microbial community, unlike several other LAB. The exceptions are an unpublished study reporting an uncultured Carnobacterium sp. clone from cow rumen and two studies demonstrating the presence of carnobacteria in pig and horse effluent-impacted environments. Nevertheless, it is safe to conclude that the presence of Carnobacterium spp. in food does not present a risk factor for human illness, except for the production of the biogenic amine, tyramine, as discussed previously. Neither do Carnobacterium spp. appear to present a risk for nocosomial infections in hospitals and similar institutions, although they have, in one instance, been isolated from contaminated blood plasma.

The presence of virulence factors in carnobacteria is not well documented. Thus C. maltaromaticum strains isolated from diseased fish lacked hemolytic and phospholipolytic activities. Carnobacterium viridans shows, however, b-hemolytic activity on sheep blood agar. Although several isolates of carnobacteria produce bacteriocins, none of these compounds has been reported to exert a cytolytic activity as shown for the En. faecalis class I-related bacteriocin cytolysin. Regarding chemotherapeutic agents, fish pathogenic strains of C. maltaromaticum were resistant to several of the agents widely used in aquaculture, such as oxytetracycline, quinolones, nitrofurans and potentiated sulfonamides, but sensitive to erythromycin. This species is not resistant to lysozyme from salmonid eggs, which supports the idea that it is not vertically transmitted, at least in this fish species. Finally, it should be noted that two clinical isolates of C. divergens have been reported to possess a gene encoding a new class of penicillinase. It will be of interest to further explore the distribution of this enzyme among carnobacterial species as well as its functionality.

It has been documented that some strains of C. maltaromaticum are pathogenic for several fish species, including Australian salmonids, carp, rainbow trout, striped bass and channel catfish, and salmon. Pathologic effects vary, and include, for example, septicemia, peritonitis, exophthalmia, accumulation of ascitic fluid, and hemorrhages. In most (but not all) instances, the virulence appears, however, to be low and only causes problems in fish undergoing severe stress, e.g. due to spawning. It is, therefore, not surprising that C. maltaromaticum and C. maltaromaticum-like strains are also found in the intestine or gills of healthy fish, including Arctic charr, Atlantic cod, Atlantic salmon, brown bullhead, trout, and various freshwater fish.

The presence of other carnobacterial species in healthy fish has also been reported, including C. divergens, Atlantic salmon, Atlantic cod and wolffish, trout, and freshwater fish, C. alterfunditum-like [rainbow trout], C. funditum-like [Arctic charr and Atlantic cod], C. gallinarum [Atlantic cod], C. inhibens [Atlantic salmon], C. mobilelike [Arctic charr and Atlantic cod], and Carnobacterium spp. [Arctic charr and carp]. Clearly, further research is necessary to clarify under what circumstances Carnobacterium spp. may be pathogenic for fish and whether the infective capability is species and clone specific. The reported pathogenicity of C. maltaromaticum has not hindered research into the possibility of using other carnobacteria as probiotic cultures in aquaculture, including Carnobacterium sp., C. alterfunditum, C. divergens, and C. inhibens. Isolates of these species, in addition to C. maltaromaticum, exhibit inhibitory activity towards bacterial fish pathogens. Carnobacterium divergens and C. maltaromaticum enhance the cellular and humoral immune responses and cytokine expression ratios of rainbow trout. Use of carnobacteria as probiotics leads to increased survival of the fish in some instances [larvae of cod fry and Atlantic salmon fry, rainbow trout, and salmon], but not in others [larvae of cod fry, and rainbow trout]. One study showed that in vitro exposure to C. divergens did not reverse the effects of bacterial pathogens, although these were alleviated. Additional research is necessary to validate the usefulness of carnobacteria as probiotic cultures.

Carnobacterium maltaromaticum has also been reported to be pathogenic for the fruit fly, Drosophila melanogaster, upon injection into the thorax. This specific case of pathogenesis is probably best understood as a result of opportunistic infection, although C. maltaromaticum (but not C. divergens, C. gallinarum, C. inhibens, C. mobile or C. viridans) exerts chitinolytic acitivity, a feature that can be perceived as targeting the chitin-containing exoskeleton of insects. Indeed, insects may serve as a host for this species.

Genomics

The complete chromosomes of many LAB species have now been sequenced. Currently, 19 complete genome sequences of streptococci and 18 complete genome sequences of the nonpathogenic LAB representing 14 species from the order Lactobacillales are available. However, no genome sequence or physical genetic map is available for Carnobacterium. The LAB have relatively small genomes for nonobligatory bacterial parasites or symbionts, ranging from c. 1.6 to c. 3Mb. For C. divergens and C. pleistocenium, the genome size was estimated to 3.2Mb, and for C. alterfunditum pf4T, it was estimated to be 2.9Mb. At the time of writing (March 2007), there is only one Carnobacterium genome sequencing project. Carnobacterium sp. AT7, a piezophilic strain isolated from the Aleutian trench at a depth of 2500m, is being sequenced for the Moore Foundation Marine Microbial Genome Sequencing Project with a grant to the J. Craig Venter Institute. The data already available indicate that the Carnobacterium sp. AT7 genome contains 2.4Mb and encodes 2388 proteins. Carnobacterium sp. AT7 is closely related to C. alterfunditum and C. pleistocenium. To date, knowledge on the genes and DNA sequences of Carnobacterium is comparatively sparse, concerning mostly bacteriocin-related genes in the species C. divergens and C. maltaromaticum and 16S rRNA and 16S-23S rRNA gene intergenic spacer sequences. Genes involved in some important carnobacterial metabolic traits have been sequenced. The genetic information obtained is, for most sequences, derived from just one strain, and may therefore be strain specific, as shown for a number of L. monocytogenes genes.

Clearly, our knowledge of important phenotypes of strains and species of Carnobacterium would benefit from the availability of a complete genome sequence for a strain representative of C. maltaromaticum, which is the species with most importance for the food and aquaculture industries. The most extensive study on phenotypic variation of C. maltaromaticum revealed that the majority of strains studied belonged to one phenotypic cluster (cluster H). Thus, in our opinion, a suitable candidate for a whole genomic sequence could be either C. maltaromaticum LMG 22901 (isolated from pork meat), LMG 22899 (isolated from cod) or LMG 22898 (isolated from salmon), which all belong to this phenotypic cluster. LMG 22901 does not harbor plasmids, and therefore appears to be a prime candidate for such an endeavor.

7

Climate Change and World Food Supply

In the coming decades, global agriculture faces the prospect of a changing climate (International Panel on Climate Change (IPCC), 1990a, 1992), as well as the known challenge of continuing to feed the world's population, projected to double its present level of five billion by about the year 2060 (International Bank for Reconstruction and Development/World Bank, 1990). The prospective climate change is global warming (with associated changes in hydrological regimes and other climatic variables) induced by the increasing concentration of radiatively active greenhouse gases (IPCC, 1990a, 1992). Climate change could have far-reaching effects on patterns of trade among nations, development, and food security. To help prepare for this uncertain but challenging future, this study examined the potential effects of climate change on crop yields, world food supply, and regions vulnerable to food deficits.

Despite technological advances such as improved crop varieties and irrigation systems, weather and climate are still key factors in agricultural productivity. For example, weak monsoon rains in 1987 caused large shortfalls in crop production in India, Bangladesh, and Pakistan, contributing to reversion to wheat importation by India and Pakistan (World Food Institute, 1988). The 1980s also saw the continuing deterioration of food production in Africa, caused in part by persistent drought and low production potential, and international relief efforts to prevent widespread famine. The effects of climate on agriculture in individual countries cannot be considered in isolation. Agricultural trade has grown dramatically in recent decades and now provides significant increments of national food supplies to major importing nations and substantial income for major exporting nations. These examples emphasize the close links between agriculture and climate, the international nature of food trade and food security, and the need to consider the impacts of climate change in a global context.

Recent research has focused on regional and national assessments of the potential effects of climate change on agriculture. These efforts have, for the most part, treated each region or nation in isolation, without relation to changes in production in other places. At the same time, there has been a growing emphasis on understanding the interactions of climatic, environmental, and social factors in a wider context (Parry, 1990), leading to more integrated assessments of potential impacts in national impact studies completed in the United States, Canada (Smit, 1989), Brazil (Magalhaes (1992) and Indonesia, Malaysia, and Thailand. Regional studies have been conducted in high latitude and semi-arid agricultural areas, and the US Midwest. The results of these and other agricultural impact studies have been summarized in the IPCC Working Group II Report (IPCC, 1990b). Sensitivity studies of world agriculture to potential climate changes have indicated that the effect of moderate climate change on world and domestic economies may be small, as reduced production in some areas is balanced by gains in others. However, there has to date been no integrated (i.e.. combined biophysical and economic) assessment of the potential effects of climate change on world agriculture.

This report describes the study of the potential effects of climate change on world food supply. The research involved estimating the responses of crop yields to greenhouse gas-induced climate change scenarios and then simulating the economic consequences of these potential changes in crop yields. The analysis provides estimates of changes in terms of production and prices of major food crops and the number of people at risk of hunger.

APPROACH IN WORLD FOOD SUPPLY STUDY DESIGN

Agricultural scientists in 18 countries simulated potential changes in grain yields using compatible crop models developed by the US Agency for International Development's International Benchmark Sites Network for Agrotechnology Transfer (IBSNAT 1989). The crops modelled were wheat, rice, maize, and soybeans. Wheat, rice and maize account for approximately 85% of the world cereal exports: soybean accounts for about 67% of trade in protein cake equivalent. The crop models were run for current climate conditions, for arbitrary changes in climate (+2deg. and +4deg.C increase in temperature and +/- 20% precipitation), and for climate conditions predicted by general circulation models (GCMs) for doubled atmospheric CO2 levels. The direct effects of increasing levels of CO2 on crop growth and water use were taken into account. For the GCM climate change scenarios, results from crop model sites were aggregated by current regional production to estimate national crop yield changes, at two levels of farmer adaptation. The national crop yield changes were then extrapolated to provide estimates of yield changes (for the three GCM scenarios) for other countries and crops included in the food trade analysis.

The national crop yield changes derived from the first component of the study were used as inputs into a world food trade model., the Basic Linked System (BLS), developed at the International Institute for Applied Systems Analysis (IIASA). The BLS was run first for a reference scenario projecting the agricultural system to the year 2060 assuming no change in climate, and then with the three GCM climate change scenarios. Other BLS simulations included the effects of two levels of farmer adaptation and scenarios of different future trade liberalization policy, and economic and population growth rates. Outputs from the BLS simulations provided information on food production, food prices and on the number of people at risk of hunger (defined as the population with an income insufficient to either produce or procure their food requirements) for these scenarios projected up to the year 2060.

Throughout the climate change study, a distinction is made between farm-level adaptations tested by the crop models which result in yield changes, and economic adjustments to the yield changes tested by the BLS world food trade model which result in national and regional production changes and price responses. Farm-level adaptations tested in the crop models include: plantingdate shifts, more climatically adapted varieties, irrigation, and fertilizer application. Economic adjustments represented by the BLS include: increased agricultural investment, reallocation of agricultural resources according to economic returns (including crop switching), and reclamation of additional arable land as a response to higher cereal prices. These economic adjustments are assumed not to feed back to the yield levels predicted by the crop modeling study.

Climate change scenarios

Arbitrary climate sensitivity tests were conducted to test crop model responses to a range of temperature (+2deg.C and +4deg.C) and precipitation (+/-20%) changes. While this type of sensitivity analysis is dissociated from the processes that influence climate (temperature and precipitation are physically related in any given region), it does provide better understanding of the factors affecting crop model responses. It can also help to identify climatic thresholds of critical impacts. Sensitivity tests were carried out in 13 of the 18 countries. The sensitivity test results were not utilized in the economic analysis with the BLS world food trade model because of their lack of realism, e.g., temperature change at high latitudes is predicted to be greater than the global mean in winter (IPCC, 1990a), rather than increase by 2deg. or 4deg.C in all regions of the world throughout the year. Farm-level adaptations were not tested in the sensitivity studies.

Scenarios of climate change were developed in order to estimate their effects on crop yields and food trade. A climate change scenario is defined as a physically consistent set of changes in meteorological variables, based on generally accepted projections of concentrations of carbon dioxide (CO2) and other greenhouse gases in the atmosphere (thought to be the likely cause of future climate change). The set of scenarios used is intended to capture a range of possible effects and set limits on the associated uncertainty.

The scenarios for this study were created by changing observed daily data from the current climate (1951-80) according to doubled CO2 simulations of three general circulation models available at the initiation of the study in 1989. The GCMs used are those from the Goddard Institute for Space Studies (GISS), Geophysical Fluid Dynamics Laboratory (GFDL), and United Kingdom Meteorological Office (UKMO). The temperature changes of these GCM scenarios (4.0-5.2deg.C) are at or near the upper end of the range (1.5-4.5deg.C) projected for doubled CO2 warming by the IPCC (IPCC, 1990a, 1992). The GISS and GFDL scenarios, however, are near the mean temperature change (3.8deg.C) of recent doubled CO2 experiments documented for atmospheric GCMs with a seasonal cycle and a mixed-layer ocean (IPCC, 1992). Mean monthly changes in temperature, precipitation, and solar radiation from the appropriate GCM gridbox were applied to observed daily climate records to create climate change scenarios for each site.

While GCMs currently provide the most advanced means of predicting the potential future climatic consequences of increasing amounts of radiatively active trace gases, their ability to simulate current climate varies considerably from region to region. They have been shown to simulate current surface air temperatures reasonably well, but do not reproduce current precipitation as accurately (IPCC, 1990a). Of special importance for agricultural climate change impacts, there is a notable lack of consensus among GCMs in prediction of regional soil moisture changes. Furthermore, GCMs are not yet able to produce reliable projections of changes in climate variability, such as alterations in the frequencies of drought and storms, even though these could affect crop yields significantly.

For the crop modeling part of this study, climate changes from doubled CO_2 GCM simulations are utilized with an associated level of 555 ppm CO_2; the assumed timing for the BLS world food trade projections is that these conditions will occur in 2060. This approach, which mixes equilibrium climate and transient CO_2 projections, is the best that can be done given the current lack of availability of GCM transient climate change simulations for impact studies and the need for a dynamic time course for the economic model. It is not known what rates of future emissions of trace gases will be and when the full magnitude of their effects will be realized.

Because atmospheric concentrations of other greenhouse gases besides CO2 (e.g.. methane (CH4), nitrous oxide (N2O)), and the chlorofluorocarbons (CFCs)) are also increasing, an 'effective CO2 doubling' has been defined as the combined radiative forcing of all greenhouse gases having the same forcing as doubled CO_2. Level of CO2 is important when estimating potential impacts on crops, because crop growth and water use have been shown to benefit from increased levels of CO2 (Cure and Acock, 1986). A CO2 level of 555 ppm was associated with the effective doubled CO2 climate projections for use in the crop modeling simulations. This was based on the GISS GCM transient trace gas scenario A described in Hansen *et al.* (1988), in which the simulated climate has warmed to the effective doubled CO2 level of about 4degC by 2060. This level assumes that non-CO2 trace gases contribute ~15% of the change in radiative forcing from 300 to ~600 ppm.

Crop models and yield simulations

The IBSNAT crop models were utilized by the participating agricultural scientist to estimate how climate change and increasing levels of carbon dioxide may alter yields of world crops at 112 sites in 18 countries. The sites represent both major and minor production areas at low, mid, and high latitudes. The crop models used were CERES-Wheat, CERES-Maize, CERES-Rice, and SOYGRO.

The IBSNAT models are comprised of parameterizations of important physiological processes responsible for plant growth and development, evapotranspiration, and partitioning of photosynthate to produce economic yield. The simplified functions enable prediction of the growth of crops as influenced by the major factors that affect yields, ie. genetics, climate (daily solar radiation, maximum and minimum temperatures, and precipitation), soils, and management practices. This type of dynamic process crop growth model is considered to be a significant advance over traditional regression-based methods (eg. Thompson, 1969) which were used to estimate crop yields from simple climate and management inputs with geographical and temporal specificity. The models include a soil moisture balance submodel so that they can be used to predict both rainfed and irrigated crop yields. The cereal models simulate the effects of nitrogen fertilizer on crop growth, and these were studied in several countries in the context of climatic change. For the most part, however, the results of this study assume optimum nutrient levels.

The IBSNAT models were selected for use in this study because they have been validated over a wide range of environments and are not specific to any particular location or soil type. They are better suited for large-area studies in which cropgrowing and soil conditions differ greatly, than more detailed physiological models that have not been as widely tested. The validation of the crop models over different environments also improves the ability to estimate effects of changes in climate. Because the crop models have been tested over essentially the full range of temperature and precipitation regimes where crops are grown in today's climate, and to the extent that future climate change brings temperature and precipitation regimes within these ranges, the models may be considered useful tools for assessment of potential climate change impacts. Furthermore, because management practices, such as the choice of varieties, the planting date, fertilizer application, and irrigation, may be varied in the models, they permit experiments that simulate adaptation by farmers to climatic change.

Most plants growing in experimental environments with increased levels of atmospheric CO2, exhibit increased rates of net photosynthesis (i.e.. total photosynthesis minus respiration) and reduced stomatal openings. Partial stomatal closure leads to reduced transpiration per unit leaf area and, combined with enhanced photosynthesis, often improves water-use efficiency (the ratio of crop biomass accumulation or yield to the amount of water used in evapotranspiration). Thus, by itself, increased CO2, can increase yield and reduce water use (per unit biomass).

The crop models used in this study account for the beneficial physiological effects of increased atmospheric CO2 concentrations on crop growth and water use. Ratios were calculated between measured daily photosynthesis and evapotranspiration rates for a canopy exposed to high CO2 values, based on published experimental results, and the ratios were applied to the appropriate variables in the crop models on a daily basis. The photosynthesis ratios ppm (555 ppm CO2/ 330 ppm CO2) for soybean, wheat and rice. and maize were 1.21, 1.17, and 1.06. respectively. Changes in stomatal resistance were set at 49.7/34.4 s/m for C3 crops and 87.4/55.8 s/m for C4 crops, based on experimental results by Rogers *et al.* (1983). As simulated in this study, the direct effects of CO2 may bias yield changes in a positive direction, since there is uncertainty regarding whether experimental results will be observed in the open field under conditions likely to be operative when farmers are managing crops. Plants growing in experimental settings are often subject to fewer environmental stresses and less competition from weeds and pests than are likely to be encountered in farmers' fields. Recent field free-air release studies have found overall positive CO2 effects under current climate conditions (Hendry, 1993).

The crop models embody a number of simplifications. For example, weeds, diseases, and insect pests are assumed to be controlled; there are no problem soil conditions (e.g.. salinity or acidity); and there are no extreme weather events such as tornadoes. The models are calibrated to experimental field data which often have yields higher than those currently typical under farming conditions. Thus, the absolute effects of climatic change on yields in farmers' fields may be different from those simulated by the crop models.

The crop models simulate the current range of agricultural technologies available around the world, including the use of high-yielding varieties that are responsive to technological inputs, but by the year 2060 agricultural technology is likely to be very different. The models may he used to test the effects of some potential improvements in agricultural production, such as varieties with higher thermal requirements and installation of irrigation systems, but do not include possible future improvements. (The BLS economic model used in the study does include future trends in yield improvement, but not technological developments induced by negative climate change impacts.) Finally, models for crops such as millet and cassava were not yet sufficiently tested for use in this study. Potential yield changes of such crops, which may respond differently to both climate change and increases in CO2, are needed for better assessment of climate change impacts in tropical and sub-tropical regions.

Crop modelling simulation experiments were performed for baseline climate (1951-80), arbitrary sensitivity tests, and GCM doubled CO2 climate change scenarios with and without the physiological effects of C02. This involved the following tasks:

- for the countries studied, geographical boundaries were defined for the major production regions, agricultural systems (e.g.. rainfed and/or irrigated production, number of crops grown per year) were described, and data on regional and national rainfed and irrigated production of major crops were gathered.
- observed climate data for representative sites within these regions were obtained for the baseline period (1951-80), or for as many years of daily data as were available, and the soil, crop variety, and management inputs necessary to run the crop models at the selected sites were specified.
- The crop models were validated with experimental data from field trials, to the extent possible.
- The crop models were run with baseline data, arbitrary sensitivity tests, and GCM climate change scenarios, with and without the direct effects of CO2, on crop growth. Rainfed and/or irrigated simulations were carried out as appropriate to current growing practices.
- Alterations in farm-level agricultural practices that would lessen any adverse consequences of climate change were identified and evaluated, by simulating irrigated production and other adaptation responses (e.g.. shifts in planting date and substitution of crop varieties).

DERIVING ESTIMATES OF POTENTIAL CROP YIELD CHANGES

The percentages of world production of wheat, rice, maize, and soybean for the countries in which simulations were conducted. Simulations were carried out in regions representing 70-75% of the current world production of wheat and maize. Even though model runs for soybean were conducted in only two countries (Brazil and USA), these together account for 76% of world production. Rice production was less well represented in the model simulations than the other crops, because India, Indonesia and Vietnam have significant production areas not included in the study. Further research is needed in these key countries in order to improve the reliability of the projections of climate change impacts on rice production.

Crop model results for wheat, rice, maize and soybean from the 112 sites in the 18 countries were aggregated by weighting regional yield changes (based on current production) to estimate changes in national yields. The aggregations were either calculated by the participating scientists or developed jointly with them. The scientists in each country selected sites representative of major agricultural regions, described the regional agricultural practices, and provided production data for estimation of regional contributions to the national yield changes. Other production data sources included the United Nations Food and Agriculture Organization (FAO, 1988), the US Department of Agriculture (USDA) Crop Production Statistical Division, and the USDA International Service. The regional yield estimates represent the current mix of rainfed and irrigated production and the current crop varieties, nitrogen management and soils.

Changes in national yields of other crops and commodity groups and for other regions not simulated were estimated based on three criteria:

- similarities to growing conditions for modelling crops,
- results from about 50 previously published and unpublished regional climate change impact studies,
- projected temperature and precipitation changes (and

hence soil moisture availability for crop growth) from the GCM climate change scenarios.

Estimates were made of yield changes with and without the direct effects of CO2. Increments added to the estimated crop yield changes to account for direct CO2 effects were based on average responses to CO2 and climate change scenarios in the crop model simulations. These increments differ from the photosynthesis ratios employed in the crop models because they incorporate the combined responses of the simulated crops to changes in photosynthesis and evapotranspiration, as well as climate. In the crop model simulations, the responses to CO2 did not vary greatly across regions and climate change scenarios.

The primary source of uncertainty in the estimates lies in the sparseness of the crop modelling sites and the fact that they may not adequately represent the variability of agricultural regions within countries, the variability of agricultural systems within similar agroecological zones, or dissimilar agricultural regions.

However, since the site results relate to regions that account for about 70% of world grain production. the conclusions concerning world totals of cereal production contained in this study are believed to be substantiated adequately. Another source of uncertainty lies in the simulation of grain crops only, leading to estimation of yield changes for other commodities such as root crops and fruit based primarily on previous estimates. The previous estimates tended to be less negative than the crop responses modelled in this study, and this introduced a bias in favour of these other crops in the world food trade model.

In each country, the agricultural scientists used the crop models to test possible responses to the worst climate change scenario (this was usually, but not always, the UKMO scenario). These adaptations included change in planting date, change of cultivar, irrigation, fertilizers and change of crop. Irrigation simulations in the crop models assumed automatic irrigation to field capacity when plant available water dropped to 50% and 100% irrigation efficiency. All adaptation possibilities were not simulated at every site and country: choice of adaptations to be tested was made by the participating scientists, based on their knowledge of current agricultural systems.

Limitations of adaptation analysis

The adaptation simulations were not comprehensive because all possible combinations of farmer responses were not tested at every site. Spatial analyses of crop, climatic, and soil resources are needed to test fully the possibilities for crop substitution. Neither the availability of water supplies for irrigation nor the costs of adaptation were considered in this study; these are both critical needs for further research. A related study on the Integrated Impacts of Climate Change on Egypt. which utilized the results of this work, does address future water availability for national agricultural production in that country (Strzepek *et al.*, 1993).

At the local level, there may be social or technical reasons why farmers are reluctant to implement adaptation measures. For example, increased fertilizer application and improved seed stocks may be capital-intensive and not suited to indigenous agricultural strategies. Furthermore, such measures may not necessarily result in sustainable production increases. In the case of irrigation, initial benefits may eventually give way to soil salinization and lower crop yields.

Thus, Adaptation Level 2 represents a fairly optimistic assessment of world agriculture's response to changed climate conditions as characterized by the GCMs tested in this study, possibly requiring substantial changes in current agricultural systems, investment in regional and national agricultural infrastructure, and policy changes. However, changes in regional, national and international agricultural policies relating to farm-level adaptation were beyond the scope of the analysis.

THE WORLD FOOD TRADE MODEL

The world food system is a complex dynamic interaction of producers and consumers, interacting through global markets. Related activities include input production and acquisition, transportation, storage and processing. While there is a trend towards internationalization in the world food system, only about 15% of total world production currently crosses national borders. National governments shape the system by imposing regulations and by investments in agricultural research, infrastructure improvements, and education. The system functions to meet the demand for food, to produce food in increasingly efficient ways, and to trade food within and across national borders. Although the system does not guarantee stability, it has generated long-term real declines in prices of major food staples.

The Basic Linked System consists of linked national agricultural sector models. The BLS was designed at IIASA for food policy studies but it also can be used to evaluate the effect of climate-induced changes in yield on world food supply and agricultural prices. It consists of 16 national (including the European Community (EC)) models with a common structure, four models with country-specific structure, and 14 regional group models. The 20 models in the first two groups cover about 80% of attributes of the world food system such as demand, land and agricultural production. The remaining 20% is covered by 14 regional models for countries which have broadly similar attributes (e.g.. African oil-exporting countries, Latin American high-income exporting countries, Asian low-income countries etc.). The grouping is based on country characteristics such as geographical location, income per capita and the country's position with regard to net food trade.

The BLS is a general equilibrium model system, with representation of all economic sectors, empirically estimated parameters and no unaccounted supply sources or demand sinks. In the BLS, countries are linked through trade, world market prices and financial flows. It is a recursively dynamic system: a first round of exports from all countries is calculated for an assumed set of world prices, and international market clearance is checked for each commodity. World prices are then revised, using an optimizing algorithm, and again transmitted to the national model. Next, these generate new domestic equilibria and adjust net exports. This process is repeated until the world markets for all commodities are cleared. At each stage of the iteration, domestic markets are in equilibrium.

This process yields international prices as influenced by governmental and inter-governmental agreements. The system is solved in annual increments, simultaneously for all countries. Summary indicators of the sensitivity of the world system include world cereal production. world cereal prices and prevalence of population in developing countries at risk of hunger.

The BLS does not incorporate any climate relationships per se. Effects of changes in climate were introduced to the model as changes in the average national or regional yield per commodity. Ten commodities are included in the model: wheat, rice, coarse grains, protein feed. bovine and ovine meat, dairy products, other animal products, other food, non-food agriculture and non-agriculture. Yield change estimates for coarse grains were based on the percentage of maize grown in the country or region; soybean crop model results were used to estimate the protein feed category; the estimates for the non-grain crops were based on the modelling grain crops and previous estimates of climate change impacts as described above. A positive bias toward non-grain crops was introduced by this procedure, since the previous estimates of yield changes of the non-grain crops were less negative than the modelled results from this study.

Economic growth rates

Economic growth rates are a product of several BLS functions. Non-agricultural production utilizes a Cobb-Douglas production function with labour and capital as production factors. Non-agricultural labour input depends primarily on population growth and somewhat on relative prices between agriculture and non-agriculture by means of a sector migration function. Capital accumulation depends on investment and depreciation, which in turn depend on saving and depreciation rates. Depreciation rates and saving rates are estimated from historical data and are kept constant after 1990. There is an exogenous assumption based on historical data for technical progress in the production function. For the lower growth scenario, the savings rate was reduced, resulting in about 10% lower GDP in 2060.

The economic growth rates predicted by the BLS in the reference case follow historical trends. For the period 1980 to 2060, the BLS produces a growth of 1.3%, 1.7%, and 2.4% annually for world, developed, and developing countries, respectively, as compared to an average population growth of 1.1 %, 0.3%, and 1.3%.

In general, the rate of exogenous technical progress starts from historical values and for cereal crops approaches 0.5% per annum by 2060. Representing improvement in agriculture productivity due to technological progress, the annual yield trends used in the BLS for the period 1980-2000 are 1.2%, 1.0%, and 1.7% for global, developed country, and developing countries, respectively. According to FAO data, yields have been growing at an average of around 2% annually during the period 1961-90, both for developed and developing (excluding China) countries (FAO, 1991). Recent increase (1965-85) in annual productivity for less-developed countries is about 1.5%/year. In the 1980s, however, yields grew globally at an average yield increase of only 1.3%, implying a falling trend in yield growth rates.

The falling growth rates utilized in the reference case of the BLS may be justified for several reasons. Historical trends suggest decreasing rates of increase, and yield improvements from biotechnology have yet to be realized. Much of the large yield increases in developed countries in the 1950s and 1960s and in developing countries thereafter has been due to intensification of chemical inputs and mechanization. Apart from economic reasons and environmental concerns which suggest that maximum input levels may have been reached in many developed countries, there are likely bc diminishing rates of return for further input increases. In some developing countries, especially in Africa, increase in input levels and intensification of production are likely to continue for some time, but may also ultimately level off. Furthermore, since Africa has the lowest average cereal yields of all the regional groups combined with a high population growth rate. it will contribute an increasing share of cereal production. thereby reducing average global yield increases.

Availability of arable land for expansion of crop production is based on FAO data. In the BLS standard national models, a piece-wise linear time-trend function is used to impose upper bounds (inequality constraints) on land use. In addition, this time trend function is modified with an elasticity term (usually 0.05 or less) that reacts to changes in shadow prices of land in comparison to 1980 levels. The upper limits imposed by the time trend function utilize the FAO data on potential arable land. The arable land limits are not adjusted due to climate change, even though they may be affected positively in some locations by extension of season length or drying of wet soils, or negatively by sea-level inundation or desertification.

The indicator of number of people at risk from hunger used in the BLS is defined as the population with an income insufficient to either produce or procure their food requirements in developing countries (excluding China). The measure is derived from FAO estimates and methodology for developing market economies (FAO, 1984 and 1987). The FAO estimates were obtained by stipulating that calorie consumption distribution in a country is skewed and can be represented by a beta distribution. The parameters of these distributions were estimated by FAO for each country based on country-specific data and cross-country comparisons. The estimate of the energy requirement of an individual is based on the basal metabolic rate (time in a fasting state and lying at complete rest in a warm environment). Body weight, age and sex have an impact on this requirement. FAO presents two estimates of undernourished people, based on minimum maintenance requirements of 1.2 and 1.4 (the latter judged as more appropriate) basal metabolic rate. The BLS estimate for 1980, based on the 1.4 basal metabolic rate requirements, is 501 million undernourished people in the developing world, excluding China.

The economic adjustments simulated by the BLS are assumed not to alter the basic structure of the production functions. These relationships may be altered in a changing climatic regime and under conditions of elevated C02. For example, yield responses to nitrogen fertilization may be altered due to changing nutrient solubilities in warmer soils. Furthermore, in the analysis of BLS results, consideration is limited to the major cereal food crops, even though shifts in the balance of arable and livestock agriculture are also likely under changed climatic regimes. Livestock production is a significant component of the global food system and is also potentially sensitive to climatic change. The nonagriculture sector is poorly modelled in the BLS, leading to simplifications in the simulation of responses to climatic change.

Finally, recent changes in global geopolitics and related changes in agricultural production are not well represented in the BLS. To account for these changes, prices in previously planned economies were made more responsive compared to earlier versions, 'plan targets' for allocation decisions were replaced, and some constraints were relaxed in the agricultural sector model. Better analysis depends on development of new models for these emerging capitalist economies.

The set of model experiments

The estimates of climate-induced changes in food production potential were used as inputs to the BLS in order to assess possible impacts on future levels of food production, food prices and the number of people al risk from hunger. Impacts were assessed for the year 2060, with population growth, technology trends and economic growth projected to that year. Assessments were first made for a reference scenario assuming no climate change and subsequently with the GCM 2 x CO2 scenarios of climate change. The difference between the two assessments is the estimated climate-induced effect. A further set of assessments examined the efficacy of two levels of farmer adaptation in mitigating climate change impacts and the effect on future production of different rates of economic and population growth, and of liberalizing the world trade system.

The reference scenario projects the agricultural system to the year 2060 with no climate change and with no major changes in the political or economic context of world food trade. It assumes:

- UN medium population estimates (10.2 billion by 2060)

(UN, 1989; International Bank for Rural Development/ World Bank, 1990).

- 50% trade liberalization in agriculture (e.g.. removal of import restrictions) introduced gradually by 2020.
- Moderate economic growth (ranging from 3.0%/year in 1980-2000 to 1.1%/year in 2040-60).
- Technology projected to increase yields over time (1990-2060). Cereal yields of world total, developing countries and developed countries were assumed to increase annually by 0.7%, 0.9%, and 0.6%, respectively.

These are projections of the world system including effects on agricultural yields under the doubled CO_2 scenarios for GISS, GFDL and UKMO GCMs. The food trade simulations for these three scenarios were started in 1990 and assumed a linear change in yields until the doubled CO_2 changes are reached in 2060. Simulations were made both with and without the physiological effects of 555 ppm CO_2 on crop growth and yield for the equilibrium yield estimates. In these scenarios, internal economic adjustments in the model occur such as increased agricultural investment, reallocation of agricultural resources according to economic returns (including crop switching), and reclamation of additional arable land as a response to higher cereal prices. These are based on shifts in supply and demand factors that alter the comparative advantage among countries and regions in the world food trade system. These economic adjustments are assumed not to feed back to the yield levels predicted by the crop modelling study.

The food trade model was first run with yield changes assuming no external farm-level adaptation to climate change and was then re-run with different climate-induced changes in yield assuming the two levels of adaptation described above. Adaptation Level 1 includes those adaptations at the farm level that would not involve major changes in agricultural practices. It thus included changes in planting date, in amounts of irrigation, and in choice of crop varieties that are currently available. Adaptation Level 2 includes, in addition to the former, major changes in agricultural practices, e.g.. shifts of planting date of greater than one month, the availability of new cultivars, expansion of irrigation systems and increased fertilizer application. This level of adaptation would be likely to involve policy changes at the regional, national and international level and would also be likely to involve significant costs. However, policy, cost, and water resource availability were not studied explicitly and assumed not to be barriers to adaptation. Switching from one enterprise to another based on production and demand factors is included in the BLS.

A final set of scenarios assumed changes to the world tariff structure and different rates of growth of economy and population, yielding insight into alternate futures. As with the previous experiments, these were conducted both with and without climate change. These scenarios included:

- Trade liberalization: Full trade liberalization in agriculture introduced gradually by 2020.
- Lower economic growth: (ranging from 2.7%/year in 1980-2000 to 1.0% in 2040-60). This results in global GDP in 2060 10.3% lower than the reference scenario, 11.2% lower in developing countries and 9.8% lower in developed countries.
- Low population growth: UN low population estimates (8.6 billion by 2060)

The analysis of trade liberalization in this study is restricted to removal of distortions between trade prices and domestic prices at the level of the raw materials of the agricultural commodities. Where applicable, trade and production quota are released. Other types of domestic assistance, e.g.. input subsidies, export credit, insurance, etc., are not included in the analysis. For a given world market price of an agricultural commodity, the domestic price under trade liberalization depends upon whether the country is a net exporter or net importer of the commodity, the differential being a margin for international freight and insurance.

EFFECTS ON CROP YIELDS

With the direct effects of CO_2, and precipitation held at current levels, average crop yields weighted by national production show a positive response to +2deg.C warming and a negative response to +4deg.C. Wheat and soybean yields increase 10-15%, and maize and rice yields increase about 8% with a +2deg.C temperature rise. Yields of all four crops turn negative at +4deg.C, indicating a threshold of the compensation of direct CO_2 effects for temperature increases between 2 and 4deg.C, as simulated in the IBSNAT crop models. Rice and soybean are most negatively affected at +4deg.C. These averaged results, however, mask differences among countries. For example, the effects of latitude are such that in Canada, a +2deg.C temperature increase with no precipitation change results in wheat yield increases (with direct effects of CO2 taken into account), while the same changes in Pakistan result in average wheat yield decreases of about 12%. In general, 20% increase in precipitation improved the simulated yields of the crops tested, and 20% decrease lowered yields of all crops.

Crop yields without adaptation

The GCM doubled CO_2, climate change scenarios (the yield changes include results from both rainfed and irrigated simulations, weighted by current percentage of the respective practice). Climate changes without the direct physiological effects of CO_2 cause decreases in simulated wheat yields in all cases, while the direct effects of CO_2 mitigate the negative effects primarily in mid-and high-latitudes.

The magnitudes of the estimated yield changes vary by crop. Global wheat yield changes weighted by national production are positive with the direct CO_2 effects, while maize yield is most negatively affected, reflecting its greater production in low-latitude areas where simulated yield decreases are greater. Maize production declines most with direct CO_2 effects, probably due to its lower response to the physiological effects of CO_2 on crop growth. Simulated soybean yields are most reduced without the direct effects of CO2, but are least affected in the less severe GISS and GFDL climate change scenarios when direct CO_2 effects are simulated. Soybean responds positively to increased CO_2, but is the crop most affected by the high temperatures of the UKMO scenario.

The differences among countries in simulated crop yield

responses to climate change without the direct effects of CO2 are primarily related to differences in current growing conditions. Higher temperatures tend to shorten the growing period at all locations tested. At low latitudes, however, crops are currently grown at higher temperatures, produce lower yields, and are nearer the limits of temperature tolerances for heat and water stress. Warming at low latitudes thus results in accelerated growing periods for crops, more severe heat and water stress, and greater yield decreases than at higher latitudes. In many mid-and high-latitude areas, where current temperature regimes are cooler, increased temperatures, while still shortening grain-filling periods, thus exerting a negative influence on yields, do not significantly increase stress levels. At some sites near the high-latitude boundaries of current agricultural production, increased temperatures can benefit crops otherwise limited by cold temperatures and short growing seasons, although the extent of soil suitable for expanded agricultural production in these regions was not studied explicitly. Potential for expansion of cultivated land is embedded in the BLS world food trade model and is reflected in shifts in production calculated by that model.

Simulated yield increases in the mid-and high-latitudes are caused primarily by:

- Positive physiological effects of CO2. At sites with cooler initial temperature regimes, increased photosynthesis more than compensated for the shortening of the growing period caused by warming.
- lengthened growing season and amelioration of cold temperature effects on growth. At some sites near the high-latitude boundaries of current agricultural production increased temperatures extended the frost-free growing season and provided regimes more conclusive to greater crop productivity.

The primary causes of decreases in simulated yields are:

- Shortening of the growing period. Higher temperatures during the growing season speed annual crops through their development (especially grain-filling stage), allowing less grain to be produced. This occurred at all sites except those with the coolest growing-season temperatures in Canada and the former USSR.

- Decrease in water availability. This is due to a combination of increases in evapotranspiration rates in the warmer climate, enhanced losses of soil moisture and, in some cases, a projected decrease in precipitation in the climate change scenarios.
- Poor vernalization. Vernalization is the requirement of some temperate cereal crops, e.g.. winter wheat, for a period of low winter temperatures to initiate or accelerate the flowering process. Low vernalization results in low flower bud initiation and ultimately reduced yields. Decreases in winter wheat yields at some sites in Canada and the former USSR were caused by lack of vernalization.

The estimated potential changes in average national grain crop yields for the GISS, GFDL, and UKMO doubled CO2 climate change scenarios allowing for the direct effects of CO2 on plant growth.

The maps are created from the nationally averaged yield changes for wheat, rice, coarse grains, and protein feed estimated for the BLS simulations for each country or group of countries in the world food trade model; regional variations within countries are not reflected. Latitudinal differences are apparent in all the scenarios. With direct CO2 effects, high latitude changes are less negative or even positive in some cases, while lower latitude regions suffer more detrimental effects of climate change on agricultural yields.

The GISS and GFDL climate change scenarios produced yield changes ranging from +30 to-30%. Effects under the GISS scenario are, in general, more adverse than under the GFDL scenario to crop yields in parts of Asia and South America, while effects under the GFDL scenario result in more negative yields in the USA and Africa and less positive results in the former USSR. The UKMO climate change scenario, which has the greatest warming (5.25deg.C global surface air temperature increase), causes average national crop yields to decline almost everywhere (up to-50% in Pakistan).

CROP YIELDS WITH ADAPTATION

The adaptation studies conducted by the scientists participating in the project suggest that ease of adaptation to climate change is likely to vary with crop, site, and adaptation technique. For example, at present, many Mexican producers can only afford to use small doses of nitrogen fertilizer at planting; if more fertilizer becomes available to more farmers some of the yield reductions under the climate change scenarios might be offset. However, given the current economic and environmental constraints in countries such as Mexico, a future with unlimited water and nutrients is unlikely (Liverman *et al.*, (1992). In contrast. switching from spring to winter wheat at the modelling sites in the former USSR produces a favorable response (Menzhulin *et al.*, (1992), suggesting that agricultural productivity may be enhanced there with the relatively easy shift to winter wheat varieties.

Yield estimates for the two levels of adaptation developed for the BLS simulations for the UKMO scenario. The averages for countries and groups of countries, and regional variations within countries are not reflected. Direct CO2 effects on crop growth and water use are taken into account. Adaptation Level 1, simulating minor changes to existing agricultural systems, compensated for the climate change scenarios incompletely, particularly in the developing countries. For the GISS and GFDL scenarios, adaptation implying major changes to current agricultural systems (Adaptation Level 2) compensated almost fully for the negative climate change impacts. With the high level of global warming as projected by the UKMO climate change scenario, neither Level 1 nor Level 2 Adaptation fully overcomes the negative climate change effects on crop yields in most countries, even when the direct CO2 effects are taken into account.

EFFECTS ON FOOD PRODUCTION, FOOD PRICES AND HUNGER

Assuming no effects of climate change on crop yields and current trends in economic and population growth rates, world cereal production5 is estimated at 3286 million metric tons (mmt) in 2060 (cf. 1795 mmt in 1990). Per capita cereal production in developed countries increases from 690 kg/cap in 1980 to 984 kg/cap in 2060. In developing countries (excluding China) cereal production increases from 179 to 282 kg/cap. Aggregated world per capita cereal production grows from 327 kg/cap in 1980 to 319 kg/cap in 2060. The declining aggregate trend for the future is caused by the relatively large difference in per capita cereal production in the developed and developing countries and the demographic changes assumed by the model.

Cereal prices are estimated at an index of 121 (1970 = 100) for the year 2060, reversing the trend of falling real cereal prices over the last 100 years. This occurs because the BLS standard reference scenario has two phases of price development. During 1980 to 2020, while trade barriers and protection are still in place but are being reduced, there are increases in relative prices; price decreases follow when trade barriers are removed. The number of hungry people is estimated at about 640 million or about 6% of total population in 2060 (cf. 530m in 1990, about 10% of total current population).

Effects of climate change

The BLS includes the ability to simulate adjustments that the world food system might make to changes of yield (e.g.. reallocation of agricultural land use, change in fertilizer use, and application of irrigation water). Simulations of the effects of climate change without such internal adjustments are of theoretical interest only as these would unrealistically imply no economic or behavioural response of producers and consumers. However, as a measure of distortion of the economic system these hypothetical impacts help to define the adjustments taking place in the system over time. Under these conditions the effects of climate change and increased atmospheric CO2 on crop yields derived from the GCM scenarios imply a 5% to almost 20% reduction in total cereal production. These estimates are changes to production levels projected for 2060 without climate change.

Adjustments within the economic system tend to counteract negative yield impacts as agricultural production shifts to regions of more favourable comparative advantage. The BLS offsets 65-80% of the potential impact on yield in scenarios for impacts below 10% of global cereal production (the GISS and GFDL climate change scenarios). The offset decreases to 60% under a scenario of greater yield reduction (e.g.., UKMO).

Farm-level adaptation

Changes in cereal production, cereal prices, and people at risk of hunger estimated for the GCM doubled CO2 climate change scenarios (with the direct CO2 effects taken into account). These estimations are based upon dynamic simulations by the BLS that allow the world food system to respond to climate-induced supply shortfalls of cereals and consequently higher commodity prices through increases in production factors (cultivated land, labour, and capital) and inputs such as fertilizer. The testing of climate change impacts without farm-level adaptation is unrealistic, but is done for the purpose of establishing a baseline with which to compare the effects of farmer response. We can safely assume that at least some farm-level adaptations will be adopted, especially techniques similar to those tested in Adaptation Level 1 that do not imply major changes to current agricultural systems.

Under the GISS scenario (which provides lower temperature increases) cereal production is estimated to decrease by just over 1%, while under the UKMO scenario (with the highest temperature increases) global production is estimated to decrease by more than 7%. The largest negative changes occur in developing regions, which average-9% to-11%, though the extent of decreased production varies greatly by country depending on the projected climate. By contrast, in developed countries production is estimated to increase under all but the UKMO scenario (+11% to-3%). Thus, disparities in crop production between developed and developing countries are estimated to increase.

Price increases resulting from climate-induced decreases in yield are estimated to range between 25% and 150%. In the case of the GISS scenario, the 5.3% reduction in yields of the unadjusted scenario causes a disequilibrium that is resolved via market mechanisms in the adjusted case. This results in a-1.2% consumer response and about a +4% (relative) producer response and leads to 24% higher relative prices for cereals. While this price response seems to be high, cereal prices only account for a modest fraction, perhaps one third or less, of retail food prices. Hence, a 24% increase in world cereal prices does not imply a 24% increase in food prices.

These increases in price are likely to affect the number of people with insufficient resources to purchase adequate amounts of food. The estimated number of hungry people increases approximately 1% for each 2-2.5% increase in prices (depending on climate change scenario). People at risk of hunger increase by 10% to almost 60% in the climate change scenarios tested, resulting in an estimated increase of between 60 and 350 million people in this condition (above the reference case of 640 million) by 2060.

Different levels of farmer adaptation

Globally, both minor and major levels of adaptation help restore world production levels, compared to the climate change scenarios with no adaptation. Averaged global cereal production decreases by up to about 160 mmt (0% to-5%) from the reference case of 3286 mmt with Level 1 adaptations. These involve shifts in farm activities that are not very disruptive to regional agricultural systems. With adaptations implying major changes, global cereal production responses range from an additional 30 mmt to slight increase to a slight decrease of about 80 mmt (+1% to-2.5%).

Level 1 adaptation largely offsets the negative climate change yield effects in developed countries, improving their comparative advantage in world markets. In these regions cereal production increases by 4% to 14% over the reference case. However, developing countries are estimated to benefit little from this level of adaptation (-9% to-12% change in cereal production). More extensive adaptation (Level 2) virtually eliminates global negative cereal yield impacts derived under the GISS and GFDL climate scenarios and reduces impacts under the UKMO scenario to one third.

The effects of climate change, and climate change with both levels of adaptation, on cereal prices in 2060. As a consequence of climate change, world cereal prices are estimated to increase by about 25% to almost 150%. Under Adaptation Level 1, price increases range from 10% to 100%; under Adaptation Level 2, cereal price responses range from a decline of about 5% to an increase of 35%.

As a consequence of climate change and Adaptation Level 1, the number of people at risk from hunger increases by about 40 million to 300 million (6% to 50%) from the reference case of 641 million. With more significant farmer adaptation (Level 2), the number of people at risk from hunger is altered by between-12 million for the GISS scenario and 120 million for the UKMO scenario (-2% and +20%). These results indicate that, except for the GISS scenario under Adaptation Level 2, the simulated farm-level adaptations did not entirely mitigate the negative effects of climate change on potential risk of hunger, even when economic adjustments, i.e.. the production and price responses of the world food system, are taken into account.

Lower economic growth rates, and population growth rates

For each of these alternate future assumptions, a new reference scenario was established with the BLS, and then tested with the GCM climate change scenarios.

Assuming full agricultural trade liberalization and no climate change by 2020 provides for more efficient resource use. This leads to a 3.2% higher value added in agriculture globally and 5.2% higher agricultural GDP in developing countries (excluding China) by 2060 compared to the original reference scenario. This policy change results in almost 20% fewer people at risk from hunger. Global cereal production increases by 70 mmt, with most of the production increases occurring in developing countries.

Climate change impacts were then simulated under these new reference conditions. Under the same trade liberalization policies, global impacts due to climate change are slightly reduced, with enhanced gains in production accruing to developed countries. Losses in production are greater in developing countries. **Price increases are reduced slightly from what would occur without full trade liberalization, and the** number of people at risk from hunger is reduced by about 100 million.

Estimates were also made of impacts under a lower economic growth scenario (10% lower than reference). Lower economic growth results in a tighter supply situation, higher prices, and more people below the hunger threshold.

The effect of climate change on these trends is generally to reduce production, increase prices, and increase the number of people at risk from hunger. Developed countries increase cereal production in the GISS and GFDL scenarios even with the projected lower economic growth rates, but developing countries decrease production under all climate change scenarios.

Lower population growth has a significant effect on cereal production, food prices, and number of hungry people. Simulations based on rates of population growth according to UN Low Estimates result in a world population about 17% lower in year 2060 when compared to UN Mid Estimates as used in the reference run. The corresponding reduction in the developing countries (excluding China) would be about 19.5%, from 7.3 billion to 5.9 billion. The combination of higher GDP/capita (about 10%) and lower world population produces an estimated 40% fewer people in hunger in the year 2060 compared to the reference scenario.

Even under the most adverse of the three climate scenarios (UKMO) the estimated number of hungry is some 10% lower than the estimated reference scenario without any climate change. Increases in world prices in agricultural products, in particular of cereals, under the climate change scenarios employing the low population projection are around 75% of those using the UN Mid Estimate.

Climate change induced by increasing greenhouse gases is likely to affect crop yields differently from region to region across the globe. Under the climate change scenarios adopted in this study, the effects on crop yields in mid-and high-latitude regions appear to be less adverse than those in low-latitude regions. However, the more favourable effects on yield in temperate regions depend to a large extent on full realization of the potentially beneficial direct effects of CO2 on crop growth. Decreases in potential crop yields are likely to be caused by shortening of the crop growing period, decrease in water availability due to higher rates of evapotranspiration, and poor vernalization of temperate cereal crops. When adaptations at the farm level were tested (e.g.. change in planting date, switch of crop variety, changes in fertilizer application and irrigation), compensation for the detrimental effects of climate change was more successful in developed countries.

When the economic implications of these changes in crop yields are explored in a world food trade model, the relative ability of the world food system to absorb impacts decreases with the magnitude of the impact. Regional differences in effects remain noticeable: developed countries are expected to be less affected by climate change than developing economies. Dynamic economic adjustments can compensate for lower-impact scenarios such as the GISS and GFDL climate scenarios but not higher-impact ones such as the UKMO scenario. Prices of agricultural products are related to the magnitude of the climate change impact, and incidence of food poverty increases even in the least negative climate change scenario tested.

When the effects of lower future population and economic growth rates and trade liberalization were tested in the food trade model, reduced population growth rates would have the largest effect on minimizing the impact of climate change. Lower economic growth results in tighter food supplies, and consequently would result in higher rates of food poverty. Full trade liberalization in agriculture, on the other hand, provides for more efficient resource use and would reduce the number of people at risk from hunger by about 100 million (from the reference case of c. 640 million in 2060). However, all of the scenarios of future climate adopted in this study increase the estimates of the number of people at risk from hunger.

It should be emphasized that the results reported here are not a forecast of the future. There are very large uncertainties that preclude this: particularly the lack of information on possible climate change at the regional level, the effects of technological change on agricultural productivity, trends in demand (including population growth), and the wide array of possible adaptations. The adoption of efficient adaptation techniques is far from certain. In developing countries there may be social or technical constraints, and adaptive measures may not necessarily result in sustainable production over long timeframes. The availability of water supplies for irrigation and the costs of adaptation are both critical needs for further research.

Future trace gas emission rates, as well as when the full magnitude of their effects will be realized, are not certain, and only a limited range of GCM climate change scenarios, representing the upper end of the projected warming, was tested. However, it can be argued that the use of scenarios from the higher GCM projections provides perspective on the downside risk of global warming projections. Because of these uncertainties, the study should be considered as an exploratory assessment of the sensitivity of the world food system to a limited number of what is, in effect, a much wider array of possible futures.

Determining how countries, particularly developing countries can and will respond to reduced yields and increased costs of food is a critical research need arising from this study. Will such countries he able to import large amounts of food? From a political and social standpoint, these results show a decrease in food security in developing countries. The study suggests that the worst situation arises from a scenario of severe climate change, low economic growth, and little farm-level adaptation. In order to minimize possible adverse consequences-production losses, food price increases, and people at risk of hunger-the way forward is to encourage the agricultural sector to continue to develop crop breeding and management programmes for heat and drought conditions (these will be immediately useful in improving productivity in marginal environments today), in combination with measures taken to slow the growth of the human population of the world. The latter step would also be consistent with efforts to slow emissions of greenhouse gases. the source of the problem, and thus the rate and eventual magnitude of global climate change.

Bibliography

Allen, P.: *Food For the Future: Conditions and Contradictions of Sustainability*, New York: John Wiley and Sons, 1993.

Anderson, Kenneth: *International Dictionary of Food & Nutrition*. New York: Wiley, 1993.

Arnott, M.L.: *Gastronomy: The Anthropology of Food and Food Habits*, The Hague: Mouton, 1975.

Asiedu, J.J.: *Processing Tropical Crops*, MacMillan Press Ltd, London, 1989.

Barlow K: *Ecology of Food and Nutrition*, Oceania, New Guinea, 1984.

Cantrell, P.: *The Food and Agriculture Workbook*. Old Snowmass, Colorado: Rocky Mountain Institute, 1991.

Fellows, P. and Hidellage, V.: *Making Safe Food,* IT Publications, London, 1992.

Griffiths, D. C. : *Climate Change: The IPCC Impacts Assessment*. Canberra: Australian Government Publishing Service, 1994.

Hendry, G. R. *FACE: Free-Air CO2 Enrichment for Plant Research in the Field*. Boca Raton: Smoley, C. K. CRC Press, 1993.

Hobbs, B. and Roberts, D.: *Food Poisoning and Food Hygiene,* Edward Arnold Ltd, London, 1987.

Hollander, H.: *The Lehigh Valley Food System: Opportunities for Economic Growth*, Emmaus, Pennsylvania, 1983.

Iglesias, A. : *Implications of Climate Change for International Agriculture: Crop Modeling Study*. Washington, DC: US Environmental Protection Agency, 1993.

Ihekoronye, A.I., and Ngoddy, P.O., : *Integrated Food Science and Technology for the Tropics*, Macmillan Press Ltd., London, 1985.

Jay, J.M.: *Modern Food Microbiology,* D van Nostrand, New York, 1978.

Kane, S., Reilly, J. and Tobey. J. : *Climate Change: Economic Implications for World Agriculture*. US Department of Agriculture. Economic Research Service. 1991.

Kiniry, J. R. *CERES-Maize. A Simulation Model of Maize Growth and Development*. College Station. Texas A&M Press, 1986.

Konijn, N. T. : *The Impact of Climatic Variations on Agriculture, Volume 2, Assessments in Semi-Arid Areas*. Dordrecht, Netherlands: Kluwer, 1988.

Magalhaes, A. R. : *Impacts of Climatic Variations and Sustainable Development in Semi-arid Regions*. Proceedings of International Conference. ICID. Fortaleza, Brazil, 1992.

Messing, P.: *TheYork State Food System: Growing Closer to Home,* Emmaus, Pennsylvania: The Cornucopia Project of Rodale Press, 1981.

Panich, S., : *The Potential Socio-Economic Effects of Climate Change in South-East Asia*. Nairobi: UN Environmental Programme, 1992.

Parry, M. L. *Climate Change and World Agriculture*. London: Earthscan, 1990.

Pollock NJ: *The Concept of Food in Pacific Society: A Fijian Example*, Oceania, Fiji, 1985.

Sandhu, R., *Fruit Processing*, IT Publications, London, 1993.

Sprenger, R.A.: *The Food Hygiene Handbook,* Highfield Publications, Doncaster, 1996.

Tindall, H.D.: *Vegetables in the Tropics*, MacMillan Press Ltd., London, 1983.

Tudge, C. : *Future Food: Politics, Philosophy and Recipes for the 21st Century*. New York: Harmony Books, 1980.

Zaccarelli, Herman E.: *Food Service Management by Checklist: A Handbook of Control Techniques*. New York: Wiley, 1991.

Index

A

Adaptation options, 8, 12.
Agricultural Development, 25, 79, 85, 136, 146, 150, 171, 186, 194, 195.
Approach, 7, 8, 32, 60, 63, 68, 109, 139, 152, 160, 190, 193, 199, 211, 225, 228, 230, 233, 257, 259.

C

Climate Change, 15, 16, 17, 29, 41, 43, 47, 48, 57, 73, 74, 89, 92, 93, 108, 111, 120, 131, 162, 176, 181, 184, 196, 199, 201, 205, 207, 210, 255, 266.
Climate Forecasts, 137, 139, 140, 141, 142, 143, 144, 145, 146, 147, 151.
Climate Impact Assessment, 94, 97, 98.
Climate Prediction, 113, 136, 138, 140, 141, 145.
Climate Risk Problem, 138.
Company, 228, 229, 230, 231, 232.
Crop Modelling, 136, 139, 263, 265, 272.
Crop Pathogens, 65.
Crop Pests, 62, 63, 69, 71, 93, 107, 159.
Crop Yields, 7, 10, 29, 43, 44, 45, 46, 53, 61, 62, 69, 72, 89, 90, 91, 93, 94, 106, 109, 110, 121, 123, 124, 132, 136, 140, 141, 143, 177, 200, 221, 255, 256, 258, 259, 260, 261, 266, 273, 274, 276, 277, 278, 282, 283.

D

Distributions, 11, 71, 113, 236, 270.

E

Environmental Impact, 108, 132.
Environmental Protection, 215.

F

Food Production, 1, 6, 7, 8, 12, 24, 40, 43, 46, 49, 53, 57, 58, 79, 80, 81, 86, 88, 93, 94, 95, 110, 111, 112, 135, 137, 144, 152, 153, 157, 158, 160, 161, 165, 167, 168, 176, 177, 178, 181, 186, 196, 198, 200, 203, 205, 207, 209, 210, 211, 212, 213, 214, 215, 255, 257, 271, 277.
Food Systems, 2, 3, 4, 5, 7, 8, 9, 12, 14, 15, 57, 59.
Fresh Produce, 231, 233, 237.

G

Global Climate Change, 162, 208, 284.
Global Environment, 12.
Global Food Security, 43, 53, 86, 94, 95.
Global Markets, 180.
Global Water Crisis, 27.
Grain Production, 38, 80, 81, 95, 125, 207, 265.
Greenhouse Gas Emissions, 77, 131, 132, 200, 205, 210.

H

Heath Promotion, 72.

I

Investments, 27, 30, 46, 61, 71, 195, 196, 197, 198, 199, 208, 218, 219, 284.

M

Management, 10, 11, 13, 14, 40, 44, 45, 48, 76, 82, 85, 91, 96, 99, 102, 103, 104, 107, 108, 116, 120, 137, 147, 148, 149, 150, 151, 153, 158, 160, 161, 162, 163, 164, 165, 169, 172, 173, 174, 175, 183, 184, 207, 215, 218, 226, 235, 236, 237, 238, 241, 244, 246, 248, 256, 283, 284.

N

Natural Environment, 40, 238, 239, 243.

O

Ocean Warming, 189, 191, 194.
Ownership, 25, 101.

P

Policy, 3, 6, 8, 12, 15, 40, 43, 46, 51, 55, 57, 59, 76, 77, 93, 96, 98, 102, 125, 136, 143, 144, 147, 159, 160, 163, 169, 170, 172, 173, 182, 195, 198, 202, 213, 257, 266, 267, 273, 281.

R

Research, 3, 7, 8, 9, 17, 19, 37, 38, 49, 54, 58, 59, 60, 72, 84, 85, 96, 97, 98, 102, 109, 110, 123, 127, 136, 139, 140, 145, 146, 147, 148, 151, 158, 160, 163, 167, 172, 173, 174, 175, 183, 184, 188, 191, 194, 198, 204, 206, 209, 214, 231, 233, 252, 253, 256, 264, 266, 267, 284.
Risk Management, 148, 151, 152, 234.

S

Subsistence Agriculture, 33, 99, 109.

T

Technology, 35, 39, 83, 90, 91, 92, 94, 96, 99, 137, 140, 147, 148, 149, 150, 160, 172, 173, 175, 176, 177, 179, 182, 183, 203, 205, 236, 262, 271, 272.

W

World Food Summit, 33, 152.
World Food Supply, 44, 53, 55, 255, 256, 257, 267.

❑❑❑